D1579221

SLIM JIM BAXTER

SLIM JIM BAXTER

The Definitive Biography

Ken Gallacher

This paperback edition published in Great Britain in 2003 by
Virgin Books
Thames Wharf Studios
Rainville Road
London W6 9HA

This edition produced exclusively for *The Sunday Mail* 2010

First published in 2002 by Virgin Books Ltd

Copyright © The Estate of Ken Gallacher 2002

A catalogue record for this book is available
from the British Library.

ISBN 978 0 7535 1946 2

Typeset by Phoenix Photosetting, Chatham, Kent

The Random House Group Limited supports The Forest Stewardship
Council (FSC®), the leading international forest certification organisation.
Our books carrying the FSC label are printed on FSC® certified paper.
FSC is the only forest certification scheme endorsed by the leading
environmental organisations, including Greenpeace. Our
paper procurement policy can be found at
www.randomhouse.co.uk/environment

Printed and bound in Great Britain by Clays Ltd, St Ives PLC

CONTENTS

ACKNOWLEDGEMENTS

I would like to thank all the former players, both team mates and opponents, as well as the managers and coaches who were willing to share their recollections with me of Jim Baxter, the footballer and the man. I am particularly grateful to Alex Willoughby who keeps in touch with so many ex-Ibrox players and the information provided by him allowed me to make contact with them.

The support and encouragement I received from Jim's sons, Allan and Steven, meant a great deal to me and, acting on their advice, a donation from the proceeds of the book will go to the Liver Transplant Unit at the Royal Infirmary of Edinburgh.

Two former sports' editors of mine, Charlie Smith and Ian Scott, brought some meaningful insights to the book as it took shape and I appreciate their input.

Mention, too, must be made of Derek Clarkson who provided several of the photographs, some of which are appearing for the first time.

Finally, my one regret is that I failed to track down Eddie McCreadie who played in the 1967 Scotland team at Wembley. I did trace him as far as Memphis but there, sadly, the trail petered out.

1 A CITY UNITED IN GRIEF

His mother and father to whom he had been so close made the long, sad journey down from Fife to join the other members of his family in the Cathedral. The cortege then made its way from Castle Street through the city streets that were lined with people paying their last respects as the cars moved slowly past them and on to Ibrox where a wreath was laid. Then the procession travelled to Linn Crematorium where another 400 mourners, Rangers and Celtic supporters alike, were united in grief at the final service. Poor Alex Willoughby, who had been such a support to his old team-mate, broke down and was consoled by Craig Watson. Finally, at the Crematorium, in a typical Baxter flourish, a tape of Frank Sinatra, one of his idols, was played.

It was entirely fitting that the cortege should have paused at Ibrox, at the stadium where he had known most success. After all, despite his friendships with Celtic players, Baxter would always insist: 'I shall be a Ranger until the day I die – that was the best club I ever played for.'

The day following Jim Baxter's death a Scottish Cup semi-final took place at the new-look Hampden Park, now known more formally as the National Stadium, where Celtic were meeting Dundee United. At the Celtic end of the ground a banner had been draped from the stand by the Parkhead fans as they remembered, with respect, their old tormentor. It read 'Slim Jim. Simply The Best' as the supporters even went out of their way to acknowledge the unofficial Ibrox anthem. It was a straightforward, sincere and moving message and one that Baxter – who, of course, had had little time for the sectarian divides in his adopted city of Glasgow – would have appreciated. The tribute at the semi-final, which Celtic won 3–1 on their way to a domestic 'treble', was a public recognition of his standing on that issue and an indication that his Old Firm rivals respected and honoured his views.

It was also a genuine salute to one of the greatest footballers the country had produced. He was, after all, a man whose skills crossed all boundaries and whose talents were savoured by soccer connoisseurs around the world. He may never have lost that distinctive singsong Fife accent even though he had been away from the coalfields which spawned him for more than forty years, but the language he spoke on the football field needed no translation.

His tragic death at the age of 61 came after years of illness and followed a shorter spell of less than three months' suffering after he had been warned by doctors that he had only a little time left to live. As a footballer his career had been one of near-constant controversy, and that was something that dogged him even when he had long stopped playing and had had an earlier brush with death seven years before.

It was as if the arguments that so often raged around him

throughout his life had been added at birth as a counterweight to the sublime skills that set him apart from almost every footballer of his generation. So many of his friends talked about the 'imp' that always lay hidden in him, the mischief that when let loose carried him into all kinds of trouble. It was forever there, lurking just beneath the surface, sometimes bringing with it laughter as he teased opponents on the field.

Or, at worst, anger as he swept his way arrogantly through the nightlife of Glasgow, its casinos and its clubs and its cocktail bars. And that behaviour was to continue in the other cities where he plied his trade, Sunderland and Nottingham. If these last two seem unlikely venues for a serious 'night life' you could always be assured that Jim Baxter would find drinking dens and gambling clubs wherever he went. On occasions, of course, he would also find trouble.

For the most part, however, when he died in April 2001, he was remembered for the soccer romanticism he championed in the years he spent with Rangers and with Scotland. There was much talk of Wembley and the two games he played there against England when he finished on the winning side each time, in 1963, when he scored Scotland's two goals, and in 1967, when he took on the role of ringmaster as he ran the show as no one else could have done, when the world champions England lost for the first time since taking the Jules Rimet trophy less than a year earlier. Of the two games he talked most fondly of the first, but it was the second that granted him immortality in the eyes of the Tartan Army. That day Baxter had not only given them a momentous win to celebrate, he had also demonstrated that the credo he followed, one which insisted that entertaining play meant as much as victory, that individual brilliance was more meaningful than the drab uniformity that slavish tactics brought to the game, remained as valid then as it had been before Sir Alf Ramsey and his method men had taken the joy from football.

It was Pele who talked about the 'beautiful game' and Baxter was always a disciple of that simple philosophy. It has been said that the Scot, with his talent and his sense of theatre, should have been born a Brazilian. But those who express that view do not understand that the Scots still cling to the belief, however out of date it may seem in these corporate days, that football is there to be enjoyed. Baxter was the very embodiment of that belief and he knew that and revelled in the role.

Unfortunately there was another peculiarly Scottish trait that ate away at him over the years: the capacity to self-destruct, which has damaged so many of the nation's sporting giants. There was the boxer Benny Lynch, who became a world champion and could beat most of his opponents in the ring, but who never did learn to beat the bottle.

Then there was Hughie Gallacher, the centre forward of the 'Wembley Wizards', the Scottish team which defeated England 5–1 in the Home International Championship in 1928, but whose life ended in suicide. And there was the Hearts and Hibs inside forward Willie Hamilton, a contemporary of Baxter's and the player the legendary manager Jock Stein reckoned was the most gifted he had ever worked with and whose career petered out long before it should have done and who died young after a long and unsuccessful fight against alcohol.

There were others too, less spectacular but no less tragic, who destroyed their lives in one way or another. Jim Baxter was one of them. The fall was not as swift as that of Lynch or Hamilton nor as desperately sad as that of Gallacher but, in any final analysis, it is clear that he was the architect of his own downfall and he was never one to shirk that truth while he was alive. He knew that he had made mistakes. He knew that there were areas of his life that could have been immeasurably better if the proper career choices had been made or if he had somehow kept that 'imp' in the bottle and avoided the troubles he so often brought upon himself.

Sometimes in his latter years he would wonder if it might have been better for him to have had a hard taskmaster as a manager, but then he would rationalise: 'I don't know if that would have worked for me. When I joined Rangers Scot Symon was a good manager but there have been times when I wish some manager would have taken a grip of me and forced me to train properly and fulfil my potential as a player. Yet when I do think that, there is always a wee voice comes into my mind saying that if I had been disciplined then I might not have been the player I was. It was taking the risks, making those gambles on the field that made me different, I think.'

There is no doubt that Baxter was always different, it was almost as if he searched for that yet, from all accounts, it was something that came naturally to him. There was an extraordinary insouciance that was, perhaps, developed into a personal statement over the years, but it was a piece of his personality that was there from the beginning and that never left him. While other players suffered from nerves before a game Baxter sat in the dressing room as if he had not a care in the world. His old friend Billy McNeill remembers an international for Scotland. 'Everyone was getting excited. Dressing rooms can be funny places before major matches because every player has his own little bits before going out on to the field. In the middle of all that was going on, Jimmy was sitting there reading a newspaper!

'This was maybe only ten minutes before we were due to go out for the warm-up before the kick off. People are going crazy round about him and he was totally unconcerned.'

This was just situation normal for Baxter even in the most torrid atmosphere of all – that preceding an Old Firm game, the most demanding 'derby' game in British football.

Players who have reached the top levels of the game have been intimidated by the passion that sweeps through Glasgow before Rangers and Celtic meet whether the game is at Ibrox or Parkhead or Hampden. I recall the former Rangers manager Walter Smith telling me how Terry Butcher, then England's captain and a highly experienced player who had returned from playing in the World Cup in Mexico with England, was consumed by nerves on his Old Firm debut. He was not alone in that and Willie Henderson admits: 'No matter how many times you played against Celtic you always felt these butterflies.

'It's like no other game I ever played in. Even at Hampden or Wembley, before matches against England, you didn't get the same feeling you got when you were getting ready for an Old Firm match. You used to get guys being physically sick beforehand. Davie Provan, our full back at that time, played in dozens of these games and yet he was always sick in the dressing room right before the kick off. And Baxter, he would be sitting there as if it was just another game. I think that every player felt the tension on these occasions – I know that I did – yet Jimmy was always calm. He loved these games, of course. But even allowing for that, he was on his own when it came to handling pressure. It just never got to him. Mind you, the rules that applied to the rest of us went out of the window where he was concerned.'

Sir Alex Ferguson was another who was startled by Baxter's apparent indifference before games. He says: 'There was one time when I was still playing for Dunfermline and we went to Ibrox for a league game and I was injured at the time. There was no way that I was going to be playing and so I was out at the front door giving tickets to my family and mates about twenty minutes or so before kick off.

'I turned round and there was Baxter just behind me doing the same thing. He was standing there, still with his suit on, and absolutely unconcerned, to such an extent that I thought he was out of the team, that he was not going to be playing against us.

'So I went in to tell our manager Willie Cunningham that Baxter was not going to be playing – but he was. It was just his way of doing things. I don't think he had a single nerve in his body.'

Most of that attitude stemmed from his all-consuming self-belief, an inner knowledge that no matter what company he was in on the field he was going to be as good as anyone.

His skills came to him naturally, he often said that he had not practised in the manner that other players had done. He had not run in and out of a line of milk bottles with a tennis ball at his feet as the Celtic winger Jimmy Johnstone had done when he was perfecting his dribbling technique. He had not gone off on his own to play keepy-uppy – he kept that trick for the real thing, for the main event at Wembley for instance – and when he would sometimes take time out at Ibrox deliberately to hit ball after ball against the training pitch crossbar and wait for them returning to that incomparable left foot, it was not a case of practice making perfect, it was just a minor piece of showboating to impress the younger players. He *knew* he could do that and most other things he wanted to do with a ball and so the talent he was born with did not need honing during his brief period at soccer's summit.

When he played in World or European select teams, as he did on several occasions, he was never overawed at the august company he might find himself in. Willie Henderson recalls playing with him in a tribute match for Sir Stanley Matthews when his Ibrox team-mate deliberately held up the bus leaving from the hotel as if to tell the stars from around Europe that he was every bit as important as any of them.

His problem was that, while he had as much ability as any of those who played in such games, he did not have the staying power. He peaked when he was still in his mid-twenties and still playing with Rangers and it was all over by the time he returned there in time to mark his thirtieth birthday. There was that one glorious Wembley in 1967 that shone like a beacon through the dark years of his decline but little more to excite the imagination as he sleepwalked his way through the years with Sunderland and Forest.

His sojourn in the Midlands came just before the failed attempt to resurrect his career with Rangers when the then manager Davie White tempted him to make that journey back home. He did not need too much persuading for, just as he doubtless saw Wembley as his spiritual home, he knew deep down that Ibrox was his true football home – the stadium where he had developed into a world-class footballer – and that Rangers was the club where he had known more success and happiness than at any other time in his life. Certainly he had a major disagreement with the Glasgow giants before storming off to Roker Park when the directors refused to meet his wage demands, which were minuscule by today's ludicrously inflated standards and modest even by the salary structures of the time.

It says a great deal about the entrenched beliefs of the Ibrox board in those far-off days in the 1960s that Sunderland, a club destined to struggle in the English First Division and one with neither the style nor the substance of Rangers, could afford to give Baxter what he wanted while they refused to come even close to the money he was looking for. The rancorous departure from Rangers was the first of the poor career choices made by Baxter, and it was compounded when he left the North-East and joined Nottingham Forest. By then, though, there were few 'choices' remaining for the out-of-condition, out-of-control Scot and inside eighteen months things became even worse when he exhausted the patience of his second English club and was handed a humiliating free transfer.

It is all the more amazing that his impact on the national psyche was so immense when his time in football was so short. When people have looked at just how brief his good times were there is a sense of regret and, often, frustration that he did not do more.

Harold Davis, the old 'Iron Man' of Ibrox, is one man who remains angered at how Baxter frittered away his talents. It is easy to understand his feelings when you look at his own background. Davis was wounded while serving in the Korean War and the injuries were so severe that the Army doctors did not know if he would ever be able to pick up the reins of a proper life when he was invalided out of the forces. Not only did he fight his way back to health but he also carved out a football career with East Fife, Rangers and then Partick Thistle. He did so by sheer force of will and on the field it was his power and strength that complemented the talents of the other Rangers wing half.

He was, of course, a precocious young man who had been signed from Raith Rovers for the sum of £17,500. It must have been galling for Davis, who could not aspire to the genius now set alongside him, to see it being wasted. Even now he insists: 'Jim had a superb gift but he seemed determined to waste the talents he had been born with.

'That used to annoy me because while he was, without any doubt, a football genius, he was only a genius every third or fourth week when it came up his back to really play. It was as if Rembrandt had painted one or two masterpieces and then given up painting because it was all too much trouble for him. There was a flaw in Jim's character I suppose which saw him going off the straight and narrow too often. It saddened me that he gave the public and the rest of us maybe just fifty per cent of what he had. He should have treasured that talent instead of just wasting so much of it.

'But for all that he was one of the most skilled players ever to appear in Scotland, and while I suppose I always felt, even dreaded, that it would all end in tears, I still have this great sadness about what happened to him. What happened to his career and what happened to him at the end of his life. Everything was just too short.'

Short as it was, Baxter had crammed more living into his 61 years than most people would be able to fit into a longer period on this earth. Much of it, so many of the excesses he took on board in his pursuit of enjoyment, the drinking and the late nights, damaged him severely but, out there on the football field, in the middle of 'the arena' as he referred to the pitch when talking to his 1967 Wembley colleague Jim McCalliog, he came magically, poetically to life in a fashion others can only dream about.

That is why his death and his subsequent funeral, some days

later, silenced his adopted city. The people of Glasgow, and all around Scotland for that matter, knew that something had vanished from their lives, that a great original Scot had gone forever.

Those spokespersons for the 'unco guid', who had complained about Baxter being allowed a liver transplant seven years earlier, were surely made to realise by the extent of the public mourning that a national treasure had been saved and given the gift of life by the doctors at Edinburgh Royal Infirmary in 1994. Their carping criticisms seemed even more small-minded than they had appeared at the time as people from all walks of life came forward to say what Jim Baxter had meant to them.

So many of them simply wanted to share their memories of him with the world at large or to say how much pleasure he had provided or how he had added some stardust to their workaday lives.

In the days following his death the gates of Ibrox were festooned with scarves – significantly there were the green and white of Celtic's colours mingling with the royal blue of Rangers – and a sea of flowers appeared there as the ordinary fans honoured their fallen hero, one of the greatest players – if not *the* greatest – who ever played for Rangers and for Scotland.

On 20 April the funeral service was held at Glasgow Cathedral. One thousand mourners, all the great and the good from Scottish public life, were inside the Church, something that would have afforded Baxter, that lifelong rebel and a constant thorn in the side of the country's football establishment, a wry smile. Outside, another thousand or more, his own people if you like, stood in the street listening to a broadcast relay of the service as it took place. The Chancellor of the Exchequer, Gordon Brown, who had admitted to being in tears when Raith Rovers sold the young wing half to Rangers, was there to give the reading from the bible while novelist Willie McIlvanney and Baxter's team-mate and friend Ralph Brand spoke. McIlvanney explained later how the ever-irreverent Baxter had requested that he speak because he reckoned that the writer wouldn't let him down.

In the moving eulogy McIlvanney, referring to the short space of time that Baxter enjoyed at the top, declared: 'Brevity doesn't deny greatness. John Keats died in his twenties. People like to bring up the old idea of an idol with feet of clay in relation to Jim. That was never him. In his case, the feet were made of gold – with the left one presumably inlaid with diamonds as well. It was the rest of him that was made of all too fallible clay. But that's all right. Isn't that what we're all made of anyway?

'He remarked to me once that he had offended a right lot of people on the way [through life]. I hope they bear no grudges now. If they do, I would say this: As far as I'm concerned, if you didn't like Jim Baxter, it was just that you didn't know him well enough.

'He lived on his own terms, and the biggest risks he took were with himself. That's not such a bad epitaph.'

The pallbearers were all former Rangers players and had been chosen by Baxter beforehand as he made his plans for that last day. They were Craig Watson, who was ill at the time and who was to die within a few months of his old friend, Alex Willoughby, Willie Henderson, Ralph Brand, John Greig and Sandy Jardine. The piper, who had been organised by Willoughby, came from Baxter's own National Service regiment the Black Watch and he played 'A Scottish Soldier', again at the dead star's request.

His mother and father to whom he had been so close made the long, sad journey down from Fife to join the other members of his family in the Cathedral. The cortege then made its way from Castle Street through the city streets that were lined with people paying their last respects as the cars moved slowly past them and on to Ibrox where a wreath was laid. Then the procession travelled to Linn Crematorium where another 400 mourners, Rangers and Celtic supporters alike, were united in grief at the final service. Poor Alex Willoughby, who had been such a support to his old team-mate, broke down and was consoled by Craig Watson. Finally, at the Crematorium, in a typical Baxter flourish, a tape of Frank Sinatra, one of his idols, was played.

It was entirely fitting that the cortege should have paused at Ibrox, at the stadium where he had known most success. After all, despite his friendships with Celtic players, Baxter would always insist: 'I shall be a Ranger until the day I die – that was the best club I ever played for.'

And Pat Crerand would always echo that, saying: 'Jimmy was never bigoted in the slightest, but he was always a Rangers man. He loved that club, but he never allowed that to affect his friendships with myself and other Celtic players, and I know that Celtic supporters loved him because they could recognise his greatness.'

As he had confided to Willie McIlvanney, there had been a lot of people he had offended during his lifetime but, at the end, there were more people around who remembered the thoughtfulness that Jim Baxter could so often demonstrate and the kind words he could dispense when he felt these to be appropriate. He went out of his way to encourage young players and he did not like to see injustice.

Even when faced with troubles of his own he could take time out to tell Sir Alex Ferguson he felt that the Manchester United supremo had been shabbily treated by Rangers during his spell as a player with the club and, shortly before he died, when the Old Trafford manager phoned to speak to him, he found Baxter congratulating him on how well he had done as a manager down south, rather than talk to him about his own illness.

And when he looked back over his life with his close friends, after that fatal cancer had been discovered, they found that he would not blame anyone else for the various problems that had blighted his career and his health.

He knew what had gone wrong and he knew who was to

blame, and the man who took him to Sunderland, Ian McColl, felt that there were times when they met in the years following the debacle at Roker Park that Baxter was very conscious of the fact that he should have done more there and that he was genuinely sorry that he had let down the manager who had taken him south.

There is no doubt that he had genuine regrets about the direction his life took at various times, but he was always ready to face up to the responsibility and to take all of the blame for the mistakes on to his own shoulders. However, we are left to wonder how things might have been if the Board of Directors of Rangers Football Club had realised the talent they had at their disposal and had moved out of Victoriana and handed their young left half the contract he wanted. If these men had had the modern-day vision that was introduced to Ibrox first by Graeme Souness on his arrival as manager in 1986 and then continued by the current chairman David Murray – both men Baxter admired, incidentally – then he would probably never have left the club.

It is difficult now even to attempt to come to terms with the fact that the signing-on fee Baxter wanted to stay with Rangers was around half the amount paid as a weekly wage to such present-day Ibrox stars as Tore Andre Flo. And it's even more ironic that when he returned as a player, well past his sell-by date, he was given the equivalent – in the shape of a brand new house – of what he had looked for and that whenever he met up with Davie White, the manager who brought him back, he would insist on introducing him as 'the man who paid me more money than any other manager I ever played for'.

If only the purse strings had been loosened earlier the Jim Baxter story might have had a happier ending. Not that he would thank me for suggesting that, because in public he would never own up to having any real regrets. More than once he famously stated: 'I look on myself as one of the luckiest guys in the world because I came out of the pits and was able to meet so many people and to live, at times, like a millionaire. I may never have been a millionaire but I always wanted to live like one and I've done that.'

That from a man who went from earning a few pounds a week sorting out coal from the stone at the pithead to just a few pounds more playing for the juniors. That from a teenager who believed he had hit the big time when he received a signing on fee of £50 which allowed him to buy his mother a washing machine. From there via a three-year apprenticeship in the senior game at Raith Rovers Baxter moved almost effortlessly to the legendary status that is afforded only the true greats. Forget how short-lived his time was in the spotlight and think instead of the indelible impression he made on the football history of his country, which is what every Scot did on the day he died.

2   ESCAPE FROM THE PITS

Baxter's own swaggering virtuoso performance that day convinced the usually cautious Ibrox manager Scot Symon that his maverick talents could transform the Rangers team. The game was on 29 November 1959 and, subsequently, when he was signed some six months or so later, Symon revealed to him: 'When I watched you that day I knew that I had to sign you. You ran the game, the whole show. You controlled everything and that was in a Raith Rovers jersey and I wondered just what you would be capable of wearing a Rangers jersey.'

That was a question that would soon be answered after the transfer formalities were concluded. What remains a surprise, even allowing for Baxter's extravagant skills, is the determination Symon displayed in his efforts to clinch the transfer on the very eve of a Scottish Cup Final against Kilmarnock.

When Raith Rovers first began to play their new signing from the Fife Junior side Crossgates Primrose there was little to suggest that he was going to become the greatest Scottish player of his generation.

Jim Baxter arrived at Stark's Park with little fanfare. He had served his apprenticeship with the juniors – which was the normal route into senior football at that time. He had been invited to play a trial game for the reserves and had come through that impressively enough to be offered a contract by the club.

Ironically that first game had been against a Rangers reserve side and Baxter had been forced to ask for time off from his shift at Fordel Colliery to allow him to make the kick-off. Back then Saturday morning was part of the working week and in the case of those who worked in the mines the shift did not finish until 1.30 p.m. Baxter had to request that he be released at midday to enable him to get to Kirkcaldy for a trial that was to change the course of his life. Until then the slim fresh-faced youngster had had little ambition to become a professional footballer. Indeed, not too long before he had stopped playing the game altogether. Typically, and his later life would bring repeated acts of a similar nature, he had become fed up when the youth team he was playing for had become 'too organised' for his taste.

He would often recall: 'They started to get themselves blazers and flannels and they wanted to have properly organised training sessions. That was not for me.'

And so Cowdenbeath Royals, as the team was extravagantly titled, became the first victims of Baxter's lifelong fight against authority. Before playing for that team he had played for Hill o' Beath Primary School team and after that – at fourteen years old – for Cowdenbeath High School. He won his first medal in a competition for Fife schools, the Dick Cup. But his talents went unnoticed as far as Scottish Schools internationals were concerned and when he left school he had a brief flirtation with the Royals and then dropped out of organised football for almost a year, simply playing in rough and ready matches with other lads from the miners' rows.

These were games that were never really organised, sometimes with as many as twenty-a-side playing. When there was a shortage of players – which was not too often – they would play across the pitch in six or seven-a-side teams. Anything so long as they were able to kick a ball about and proper organisation, of course, was absent, which suited the young Baxter perfectly. In these surroundings he was allowed to express himself and was learning to avoid the tackles that flew in his direction from older and stronger players. He realised that was essential if he was to survive and, while the structure which had taken over at Cowdenbeath Royals had brought him some disillusion, he had also suffered in training when he had been injured by more senior players in a practice match, and that, too, had helped make up his mind to stop playing for the team.

Again he would sometimes reminisce: 'At that time I didn't miss football the way you might think I would. We used to play on a Sunday. A whole gang from the village would get together and we would play locally for fun. I knew I had skill because the opposition players found it difficult to take the ball away from me. Even my own team-mates couldn't get much of the ball at times – which didn't always please them. But it was when that ball was at my feet that I loved the game.'

Soon one of his mates from the village decided to start a youth club and organise a football team at the same time. Thus, Halbeath Boys' Club came into being and Jim Baxter's career began to take shape, though the manner of his comeback was more than a little accidental. He left school, worked for less than a year as a cabinet-maker's apprentice and then, in common with so many of his friends, became a miner against his parents' wishes. But there was more money to be made in the pits and that is what drew the youngster into the industry that dominated the area of Fife where he had been born and had grown up. It was almost inevitable that he became a miner despite the opposition from his mother and father.

What was not inevitable was his return to football. But Malcolm Sinclair, a boyhood friend, was instrumental in luring the teenager back into the game with Halbeath Boys' Club.

Malcolm, eighteen months older than his neighbour in the miners' row at Hill o' Beath, smiles now at how their relationship began with a mutual enmity.

'The problem when we were at the primary school,' he remembers, 'was that Jim went to the Protestant school and I was at the Catholic school; we used to play football against each other and we fought all the time. Then, when we were about twelve, we started to play football together and we became more and more friendly and that kept up when we left school. I started work as a butcher before going down the pit and Jim was a cabinetmaker before he also became a miner. And we would play in these games every Sunday on the park beside the rows, and when we played together I would pretend to be Willie Bauld because I was a Hearts supporter and Jim, who was Hibs daft back then, was always Gordon Smith. Anyhow, after he had stopped playing for the Cowdenbeath Royals, Halbeath Boys' Club got a team up and the lads who ran it, Bert Murray and Tom Cochrane, asked me if I could persuade Jim to play again. He had turned them down so often and, because I was his pal, they thought I might have some influence over him. I was not as sure because he could be stubborn and when he was injured training with the Royals he wasn't too happy and, to be honest, he seemed content just playing in the Sunday kickabouts.'

However, Malcolm Sinclair decided that he would make an effort and one Saturday morning he set off on his mission to get Baxter to turn out for Halbeath, his local team. His recollection is that he found his friend playing cards in the Hill o' Beath

Institute. Which, given his later lifestyle, has more than a ring of truth to it!

'I knew he would be there, in the Institute, and I knew where I would find him there – in the card room,' he says, smiling. 'He was playing brag [a form of poker which was the major gambling game, along with pontoon, for working-class Scots]. I asked him straight away if he was going to play for Halbeath and he said that he was finished with football and that he had told the lads at the club they were wasting their time.

'I had half an hour to spare and I thought I would hang around with him and see how the game worked out – I still can't tell you why I did that. So the game went on and it became a wee bit serious until Jim eventually put the last of his money down on the table and asked to see the other lad's cards.

'He turned over three aces and that was it. Jim was skint and he turned to me and asked where the game was. I told him the match was going to be played at Kingseat and he just said: "Give me two minutes until I get my boots and I'll come with you."

'The next thing we were walking across the Hill o' Beath for nearly two miles in one and a half inches of snow to get to Kingseat. He played that day and he kept on playing, and after six months Crossgates Primrose came along and signed him and soon he was playing with them regularly, and after that he was with Raith Rovers. It was a strange thing the way it all turned out and, to this day, I believe that if Jim had turned up the three aces and won the hand of brag then Rangers and Scotland might never have had him playing for them. That's just the way he was. A turn of the cards changed his life.'

Of course, when Crossgates Primrose saw him play for his newly organised team and signed him there was another few bob available for his card schools and a handsome signing-on fee of £50 which was more money than Baxter had even seen in his life up to that point.

It was then he realised that football could kick some extra money into his pockets to add to the seven pounds a week he was collecting as he 'worked the tables' at the pit, sorting out the stones from the coal. He was never slow to admit that it was the thought of the extra cash that lured him into the game, rather than any dreams of glory. These came later in his life when he began to realise for himself the gift he possessed.

When Raith Rovers offered him £3 a week and then increased that to £9 a week when he was picked for the first team, he began to think that he could make a decent living out of kicking a ball about. Once he was able to get a regular first team place he was persuaded by the Raith manager Bert Herdman to sign as a full-time player with the £9 guaranteed weekly wage, with bonuses added when there was a good result. With Bert a special bonus for a seriously good result could mean that the players were allowed to choose from the à la carte menu at their after-match meal!

This was life in the fast lane at Kirkcaldy and Jim Baxter, while seen as having a special talent, was not cosseted, either by the straight-talking Herdman or by his tough and experienced team-mates. Herdman was a manager of the old school. He would not be seen at training and it's doubtful if he ever knew what a track-suit was.

Yet in his own rough-diamond fashion he kept Raith Rovers in the first division for many years and, even more important in these parlous financial times, he was able to keep them afloat financially by shrewd moves into the transfer market. He sold players on a regular basis and always appeared able to bring in others to fill their places until they, too, were moved on at a profit. Always, though, Herdman had a core of seasoned professionals in any of his teams and Baxter, therefore, found that no matter how precocious his skills might be he was not going to waltz his way into the first team and instant acceptance from the older and more experienced men who were now going to complete the young apprentice's football education.

For example, the half back line Rovers boasted then had the powerful Andy Young at right half, the vastly talented Willie

McNaught at centre half, and the wily Andy Leigh occupied the left half position that Baxter preferred to play.

Jimmy McEwan, the outside right in that team and one of Bert Herdman's exports to England where he went on to play for Aston Villa, remembers when Baxter, in his words, 'still just a boy', started his senior career.

Recently he explained: 'People will find it difficult to believe today but when he joined Raith Rovers he had a bit of a job getting into the first team. He was still a part-timer, of course, still working in the pits and training a couple of nights a week. And we had a well-established half back line and so Jimmy had to play at inside left when he began to get his chance in the first team. He couldn't dislodge Andy Leigh at first.

'But the trouble was, eventually, that Jimmy was not comfortable when he was pushed that little bit further forward. He had exceptional ability and a magnificent left foot and once old Bert (Herdman) was able to slot him into the left half spot he really began to blossom. That's when all the transfer speculation emerged in the newspapers.'

Before Baxter was sold to Rangers, McEwan himself had departed for Aston Villa, but he has always found it hard to reconcile the stories of 'Baxter the playboy' with the 'shy' teenager he first met at Stark's Park. At Raith he had been so quiet that when some of the younger players were going out to the dance hall in Kirkcaldy, he would be content to sit at home.

Willie Wallace, McEwan's successor in the Raith team, was one of his Stark's Park contemporaries and he was to go on to play for Hearts and Celtic. He would also play a key role in the victory over England at Wembley in 1967, and he confirms: 'Going back to the time I was with him at Rovers he was really quiet. A few of the young players would go to the dancing during the week and Jim would never come with us. He kept to himself, away from the ground, except for playing golf. He would make up a four with myself and Denis Mochan and Andy Leigh. He was a left-hander, of course, and he was a good player and he liked to gamble a bit on the games even back then when none of us had much money to throw around!'

He was also displaying his hatred of training and Wallace says, laughing: 'I think that by the time I was in the team at Raith Jim realised that he was something a little bit special and so he thought that his skill gave him a licence not to train as hard as the rest of us. But the old trainer, there, a lad called Willie Hunter, used to haul him back from the dressing room when we had finished and make him push the huge roller over the park to make up for all the skiving he had done during the training sessions. It didn't change Jim's attitude any. He went his own sweet way!'

Earlier, however, there had been signs that the young man from Hill o' Beath was willing to listen to his elders and even to take advice. McEwan claims: 'He would always listen to Willie McNaught and there were occasions when Willie and I would talk to Jim about the way he was dressing. There was no need to talk about drinking or the like because none of that had surfaced when I was playing with him. But we would see him come in wearing drainpipe trousers and long jackets, almost Teddy Boy-type clothes that were fashionable for teenagers around that time. We thought he should move away from that and, gradually, he did. You know, when he signed for the club he was a good lad and an ideal kind of youngster to have around the dressing room. Glasgow seemed to change him.

'Once he was there with the world seemingly at his feet I don't think anything that Willie McNaught or myself could have said would have made any difference.'

In a sense, however, it was McNaught's own stalled career which probably had as big an influence on Baxter's life as anything else. The defender won only five Scotland caps in the early 1950s including one against England at Hampden in 1952 when the Scots lost 2–1, and spent his whole football life with the one club. When he retired he was back working at his trade as a bricklayer. For a superb and stylish defender he was left with little to show for nearly twenty years as a full-time professional footballer. That image of his mentor rarely left Baxter and was a major factor in his thinking as he constantly looked for salary increases during his five seasons at Ibrox. It was also McNaught to whom he turned for advice when the opportunity to sign for Rangers came. Predictably the veteran told him that he should not hesitate, that he should not even quibble over a signing-on fee or even wages, but that he should grasp the chance which had never come to him. In fact the veteran had more of a hand in the transfer than has ever been known until now.

One match day Baxter invited his mate Malcolm Sinclair and another of his pals from the village to Stark's Park where they were introduced to some of the other players after the game. Sinclair claims: 'There was a whole lot of talk going on about Jim and a possible transfer and that Rangers might want to sign him from the Rovers and we were all talking about that. There was me and one of our mates George Bryce and Jim and Willie McNaught and it was either Andy Young or Andy Leigh who was also in the company. McNaught got up and excused himself and when he came back he told us that he had been on the telephone to Ibrox. He told the people there that he was a relation of Jim Baxter of Raith Rovers and that he could assure them that the laddie wanted nothing more than to play at Ibrox. His thinking was simple: if you stayed in Fife, as he had done, then you did not get the international recognition that you received as a player in Glasgow or even in Edinburgh. He spelled that out to us and said that he had learned that from his own experience. Before we knew it the transfer to Rangers had happened, and the day after Jim signed he came back up to Fife to see me and he rolled up in front of my house in his new Jaguar and took me over to Lochgelly golf course. I'll never forget that, and George Bryce and I always believed that the phone call made by Willie McNaught to Rangers helped Jim get there.'

Baxter had played senior football for just two seasons when he was sold for £17,500 which was a fair return on the so-

shrewd Bert Herdman's £200 investment, which was the fee that
was paid to the junior club, Crossgates Primrose.

He had played only eight times against Rangers – on the first
two occasions he was out of position at inside left and then at
outside left and Raith lost both these games at the end of the
1956–57 season – 4–1 at Ibrox and the following week by 3–1
at Stark's Park.

Long-serving Rangers captain Bobby Shearer still smiles when
Baxter described, later, how he felt about facing him directly in
the second of these matches.

'We would laugh about it when he was at Ibrox,' says Shearer,
'but he wasn't laughing too much before that second match. I
can't remember exactly what had happened to the fixtures but
we finished up playing each other twice within a week. He was
playing inside left at Ibrox and then in the return Bert Herdman
told him he was going to be playing on the left wing – right
against me! Well, he admitted to me that he hardly slept the
night before the match because he was convinced that I would
kick him off the park. He didn't fancy it at all when the game got
too physical and I was the old-fashioned type of full back who
liked to get in a few heavy tackles. That was the way we played
but it was never Jim's way. I don't remember too much about the
game but I don't think I kicked Jim too much. He seemed to be
happy to stay out of my way.'

Still, when he did get the step back to wing half, in the
parlance of the day, Baxter more than held his own. In the next
six games against the Glasgow club Raith won two of them, drew
two more and lost the others. That was a creditable record
against the Rangers team then and it was in one of these Rovers
victories that the transfer to Rangers was sealed, with that little
bit of help from McNaught thrown in.

Baxter's own swaggering virtuoso performance that day
convinced the usually cautious Ibrox manager Scot Symon that
his maverick talents could transform the Rangers team. The
game was on 29 November 1959 and, subsequently, when he

was signed some six months or so later, Symon revealed to him: 'When I watched you that day I knew that I had to sign you. You ran the game, the whole show. You controlled everything and that was in a Raith Rovers jersey and I wondered just what you would be capable of wearing a Rangers jersey.'

That was a question that would soon be answered after the transfer formalities were concluded. What remains a surprise, even allowing for Baxter's extravagant skills, is the determination Symon displayed in his efforts to clinch the transfer on the very eve of a Scottish Cup Final against Kilmarnock.

After all, he had a formidable left half available to him already in Billy Stevenson who had played close to a hundred first team games in the two seasons prior to the Baxter signing and had helped Rangers win one League Championship, one Scottish Cup and reach the semi-final of the European Cup. He was also built in the tradition of Rangers wing halves. Powerfully built, strong in the tackle and able to surge up and down the field as required, Stevenson was an Ibrox prototype. Yet here was Symon, always seen as careful and canny in his managerial business, risking his reputation on a slim, still relatively untried young Fifer who couldn't tackle, who rarely, if ever, headed a ball and who looked as if he could be brushed aside by opponents.

Not only did Symon take the risk, he allowed the story of Baxter's capture to be leaked to the *Daily Record* on the morning of that final when his Rangers team were due to meet Kilmarnock at Hampden Park in the game which gave them their one remaining chance of a trophy that season. Rodger Baillie, now a leading football writer with the *Sun* in Scotland, broke the story with Symon's full knowledge. Stevenson must have gone into the final knowing that his future with Rangers was in severe doubt but, clearly, the manager was willing to take that gamble because Baxter had become something of a Holy Grail during the Glasgow club's lengthy pursuit of his signature. Symon's first offer of just £12,000 had been made to the Kirkcaldy club only a week or so after that notable Raith victory at Ibrox.

That had been rejected and Symon had been sent home to think again and to brood, presumably, over his failure to get the man he so desperately wanted to have in his team. There was something of an unwritten Ibrox law of the time that once refused, the club would never raise the ante for any player they wanted. Bert Herdman must have known that and yet considered it worth the risk to hold out for more money.

This was for a player he considered to be 'real class, pure gold dust' as he was fond of telling anyone who would listen. Symon broke with tradition, returned to Herdman, made an increased offer and finalised the deal between the clubs on 22 April – though Baxter's official signing did not take place until 21 June. Rangers won the cup the day after the signing talks in Edinburgh, when they defeated Kilmarnock 2–0 with both goals being scored by Jimmy Millar.

The following season Rangers tried to accommodate both Stevenson and Baxter, with the new man being played at inside left and inside right, but it was soon obvious that his stated preference for the wing half role had to be acceded to, and for the next turbulent five seasons Baxter was to be the King, both on and off the field. They were to be years of almost unrelenting domestic success on the field and even more unrelenting drinking, gambling and partying as the city of Glasgow took him to its ever-generous and forgiving heart.

Baxter was described as 'the King' by the Rangers fans, recognised as such by even the envious Celtic support, and accepted by Glaswegians as the kind of flawed hero with whom they could so readily identify.

The party was beginning.

3 RANGERS AND A GRUDGING ACCEPTANCE

Baxter ran these games just as he controlled so many of the matches for Rangers during these glory years. And yet, though his team-mates acknowledged the impact he made on the side following his signing, there were grumbles of discontent.

These grew over the years as his lifestyle began to grate on the other more serious professionals at Ibrox. And there were often complaints that Scot Symon, who did see himself as the guardian of the Rangers tradition, allowed his wayward genius too much licence when he ignored the disciplinary code which Rangers imposed on all their players. In essence, Baxter was treated differently from the other players and that saw a festering resentment grow between him and some of his new colleagues.

It was soon clear to everyone in Scottish football why the Rangers manager Scot Symon had been so utterly determined to persuade Raith Rovers to sell Jim Baxter. When the twenty-year-old stepped into the established Ibrox first team it was as if a revolution was taking place inside that most conservative of soccer establishments. He was, in outside left Davy Wilson's opinion, the final touch of class which Symon knew he needed to turn his team into one of the finest Rangers teams of all time.

Wilson, like some of the other first team men, wondered how the new boy would fit in. Not in a football sense because they all appreciated his skills, but in terms of his off-field image, something the club placed great store in.

Says Wilson: 'My first memory of Jimmy Baxter was when we were playing a game at Stark's Park against Raith Rovers and he was just making his name with them. Our team bus was parking in the narrow road outside the ground, ready to drop us at the players' entrance, which was on the street, and while the driver was manoeuvring the bus alongside where we were going to go in, this motorbike zoomed up and there he was, the man himself. He arrived for the game on that bike and, while the pre-match preparations were a lot less formal when we were playing, this was still a bit different!

'I would have noticed it even if Jim had not been linked with Rangers but, because there had been some newspaper talk and he was getting a little bit of publicity here and there, it was even more noticeable. So that was one of my first memories and I suppose it's fairly appropriate that it would be something so unconventional because that was always the way he lived his life.

'Of course, once you saw him on the field then you knew why Rangers were interested. He was a magnificent player and when he did sign for Rangers he was the link we needed and Symon knew that. I am sure that the manager realised that the team needed one more player, one special player, to lift us to the next level and he saw Jimmy Baxter as that player. And he wasn't wrong. Billy Stevenson, who was in the team at left half, was a great player and he went on to show that at Liverpool, and he was maybe more of a Rangers-type player, but Jimmy gave us more subtlety. He gave us class!'

It was that class which saw Rangers lift the League Cup within months of the new man's arrival and then go on to win the League Championship and reach the final of the European Cup Winners' Cup. The fresh career did not start easily, however. A defeat at Ibrox in his first Old Firm game almost saw Rangers topple out of the League Cup by failing to win the qualifying section. The loss to Celtic followed a few days after the team had lost 2–1 to Third Lanark at Cathkin when Baxter, in only his second game for the club found himself fielded at inside right – he had been at inside left in the first game against Partick Thistle – moves designed to placate Billy Stevenson and allow him to continue in the position he had held for two seasons. Of course, these positions didn't suit Baxter and by the third game of the season he was in the left half position that he was to retain throughout his time with Rangers.

The defeat at the hands of Celtic, though, did not suggest the years of dominance that were to follow in football's most fiercely contested 'derby' match. Rangers lost that home game 3–2 and it was only in the final section match they were able to gain revenge – a 2–1 victory at Celtic Park gave them that – and qualify by virtue of one point more than their Old Firm rivals. Celtic had dropped unexpected points themselves when they drew at Firhill against Partick Thistle and then lost the return on their own ground. Eventually Baxter was to play eighteen times against Celtic and would be on the losing side just one more time. It remains an extraordinary record and emphasises what Celtic players of the time would readily admit – that to them

Baxter had become their tormentor-in-chief and was always the major difference between the two teams.

They felt he had the Indian sign on them and one of those who suffered over the years, John Hughes, repeatedly insisted to me, at the time: 'If Rangers didn't have Baxter then we would beat them more than they would beat us. There is something about these games that brings out the best in him and we are not always able to handle that. He just loves the big occasion and these are always the biggest games of the season. We could only win if we could stop him but we haven't found a way to do that yet.'

Nor did they. Baxter ran these games just as he controlled so many of the matches for Rangers during these glory years. And yet, though his team-mates acknowledged the impact he made on the side following his signing, there were grumbles of discontent.

These grew over the years as his lifestyle began to grate on the other more serious professionals at Ibrox. And there were often complaints that Scot Symon, who did see himself as the guardian of the Rangers tradition, allowed his wayward genius too much licence when he ignored the disciplinary code which Rangers imposed on all their players. In essence, Baxter was treated differently from the other players and that saw a festering resentment grow between him and some of his new colleagues.

There were occasions when those who resented the two levels of discipline took the law into their own hands. Harold Davis, the rugged right half, whose game relied on strength and fierce no-nonsense tackling, seemed to provide the right balance for Rangers. He was on one side of the field where he gave them their trademark power in a vital area, and while he sat back to assist the defence, Baxter was given the freedom to go forward and set up so many of the attacking moves. For the most part Davis accepted the workhorse role that, it has to be said, suited his type of game, and allowed the flamboyant Baxter to grasp the spotlight. At times, however, the normally imperturbable Davis cracked and took Baxter to task physically.

Davy Wilson remembers: 'There was one incident when big Harry hung him on one of the pegs in the dressing room. These pegs for hanging your clothes on when you were getting ready for training or for a game were very high off the ground. And this day Jimmy had said something cheeky and you just didn't get cheeky with Harry. He lifted him up by the front of his jacket and then hung him up there and warned the rest of us that we would get the same treatment if we tried to help. No one helped – Jim got down when his jacket ripped and he fell. Harold was the only player at Ibrox who didn't have a nickname and that was because we were all too scared to give him one!'

On another occasion Davis found himself held up to ridicule during a game at a packed Ibrox and at half time he took matters into his own hands. He explains: 'I had the one major fall-out with him in public – at least it began in front of 50,000 or so supporters at Ibrox during a game there but it ended in the relative privacy of the dressing room. He had shouted for the ball when I had possession and I had passed it to someone else, which he didn't like – he never did like anyone else getting the ball if he thought that he was in the clear to accept a pass. He always wanted to have the ball.

'So he stood there in the middle of the field shouting at me and letting the fans know that, in his opinion, I had let him down.

'Naturally they were on his side and so I started to get some stick which was not very pleasant. I was furious when we went in at half time and before Symon reached the dressing room I had him pinned against the wall and I told him that he had never to do that to me again. He didn't.'

The team captain at that time was Bobby Shearer and his version adds a little more detail: 'Really he was trying to make a fool of big Harry that day by making it very clear to the supporters that Harry's passing was not up to the standards that

Jim expected. Now that was unfair because Harry contributed a lot of other things to the team and it has to be said that he worked a whole lot harder during games than Jim ever did!

'Anyhow, having a go at Harry like that was not the most sensible of things to do. We were just in the dressing room when Harry went for him – none of us could have stopped him. He grabbed him by the front of the jersey and pinned him against the wall. And he told him straight never to do that to him again. Then he added for good measure: "Just think yourself lucky we will have the second half to play – because that's all that has saved you." Jim got the message. Actually when the big man was in that kind of mood then you did understand very quickly what he was telling you. Jim was frightened of Harry after that. He used to try to keep out of his way in training games in case the big fellow was looking for revenge.'

Davis admits that there were occasions when he did look for revenge – all with the support of the long-suffering trainer Davie Kinnear who was Baxter's bête noire at Ibrox.

Davis told me: 'He and I had a few run-ins as you might expect. But there were times when he could be great company off the field. He was a Jekyll and Hyde character and Mr Hyde arrived when he had had too much to drink and when he had an audience of his cronies egging him on. He could be great fun until that happened and then he turned into a headbanger. I didn't like that side of him and he knew it. Also I didn't fancy it too much when he would report for training obviously still hungover or maybe even still a little bit drunk from the night before.

'That was when I would look for him and I would ask Davie Kinnear, who was in charge of the training, to pair me with Jim when we were working in squares.

'What happened then was that you put two players inside the square with the ball and one of them had to try to keep possession while the other put in tackles. If I reckoned Jim had had a bad night then I would give Davie the nod and he would put us together. Just the two of us in a very enclosed space and it was amazing how skill could succumb to fear in those circumstances!

'Mainly, I did that because I thought he was taking liberties as far as the rest of us were concerned. He was out on the booze night after night when the rest of us were trying to stay fit and I felt he should show his team-mates more respect than he did. It was my way of trying to get him to work hard and to train hard. But, while it made him think about what he was doing for that short spell, nothing was going to get through to him. He just didn't care about anything other than living his own life in his own way.'

Other players were less critical of Baxter's behaviour, believing that the contributions he made on the field were strong evidence in his favour. Ralph Brand and Davy Wilson both benefited because of the support Baxter gave them from the area immediately behind them. In the first season they played together in that left-wing triangle Brand scored an amazing forty goals in competitive games while Wilson added a further 22. Baxter himself, whose goals were rare, scored just once in the league and added another two in the European Cup Winners' Cup rout of Borussia Moenchengladbach when Rangers won their second leg tie against the West Germans 8–0 at Ibrox. His own meagre total apart it is very clear how influential he had become in his very first season as a Rangers player.

So it is not surprising that Brand defends him this way: 'The way he behaved off the field – and he never attempted to hide it from anyone at the club – did cause some friction in the dressing room. Big Harry Davis was not the only player to have him up against the wall in the dressing room either at half time or at the end of a game or even after training. You see, some of us had to work hard just to stay in the first team. He was different because he had all these wonderful skills he had been born with and he didn't have to work at the game at all.

'When he arrived at Rangers I was struck, not only by his

skills, which were fantastic, but also by the calm and controlled way that he had of playing the game. There was this air about him, an aura, if you like, of tremendous self-belief. He knew he could play and *we* all knew he could play within just a few games. He was truly something else and he brought something special to our team. He was never in awe, never nervous, about coming to Rangers, coming to join the biggest club in the country. That didn't affect him at all because he was always a cheeky bugger and that cheek just grew into an amazing confidence when he stepped on to the field. He always thought that he could just flick his finger and everything would work for him – and it did during his years with Rangers. And when he flicked that switch what a great player he was!

'You would watch some of the things he did with the ball and wonder how it was possible for anyone to have that kind of control. I used to get passes sent through to me when we were at Ibrox together and they were absolutely inch perfect and placed in such a way that they always allowed you good, clear scoring opportunities. When Jim was at his best he was as good as any player in the world at that time. I think everyone will tell you the same. None of us who played with him will ever forget him, nor will any of the thousands who watched him. He was a one-off and he had this charisma that set him aside from other players.'

Wilson maintains: 'We had a great combination down the left flank of the team. Eric Caldow was at full back and he had a lot of pace, which meant he could cover for Jimmy when he decided to go off on one of his wanders. So Eric would win the ball and then he would stick it forward to Baxter and that was his job done. He would never go beyond him, just give him the ball, which was the basic tactic which Scot Symon preached to us before every game. "Just give Jim the ball," he would say, and these were all the instructions we would get! Then it was up to me to get towards the bye line and Jim would send these glorious balls through for me to run on to. They were always just right for a winger, food and drink to me. I have never known service like that before or since. When we played together he was quite definitely world class.

'And it was the "claw" – that's what he called his left foot – that pushed him into that category. No one had a better left peg than he did. He was a genius, and you don't get to come across too many of them in a lifetime.'

And it was the glimpses of genius that set alight the Ibrox terracings so often during Baxter's reign there. The haul of trophies was interrupted on occasion in a league that was infinitely more competitive than the modern-day competition has been over the past decade or more. But there was not a single season in the five he spent with Rangers that Baxter was not able to boast a medal of some description. That first year, as already noted, saw the Championship trophy and the League Cup in the Ibrox trophy room. The following season the League Cup and Scottish Cup were won, then came the Championship and the Scottish Cup again and in his fourth year the club won the domestic treble – Championship, Scottish Cup and League Cup. Only in his fifth and final year did the club slip to only a single trophy success – victory coming in the League Cup. Baxter missed a dozen league games after he broke his leg in Austria when Rangers defeated Rapid Vienna in the European Cup second round.

His influence on the team was missed but there were signs during that season that all was not well between Rangers and their star player. More and more stories were surfacing about his indiscipline and with each fresh escapade the patience of the Rangers board and even that of his champion, Scot Symon, was wearing thin. The excuses offered up by the manager for the behaviour of his star player were not convincing the directors, and were alienating some of the players. It was becoming increasingly obvious that there could be only one conclusion to the turbulent relationship between Baxter and his employers.

Even the player himself was becoming less and less enamoured by life at Ibrox and, while the medals he won provided him with some solace, the wages were not up to his expectations and the failure of the team to adapt to European football had begun to frustrate him.

That nagging discontent surfaced many years after he had stopped playing when he admitted in an interview with journalist Roddy Forsyth: 'Europe was something we never conquered in the five years I was at Ibrox.

'It was a very great disappointment to me. We never really got anywhere near it. The year I broke my leg they said that was our best chance. For most of the time we didn't plan for it properly. We would play against Inter Milan the way we played against Partick Thistle or Third Lanark. We didn't change anything, but you can't do that in Europe. I know that now and Rangers do, too.

'To be fair, European football was in its early stages so it was a new dimension to the game. With Rangers, it was a case of, well, we're used to doing things our way and it usually works so we're not going to change it now. Of course, we were going around telling people we taught the world to play football. Our heads were in the sand.'

Perhaps Baxter's greatest problem was that he, too, was hiding from reality – the reality that while he was adding a fresh lustre to the Rangers first team, the club was providing him with the setting and the stage his talents deserved. They needed each other, the staid, old, establishment club and the young maverick who had revolutionised Rangers' approach to the game but who could not alter the code of conduct the directors held so dear and defended so passionately.

4 GLASGOW BELONGS TO ME!

When he had stopped playing he would boast that he had once played in an Old Firm game while still drunk. No one will confirm that but when questioned possible team-mates and opponents believe that it probably did happen. Ralph Brand admitted to hearing the story and allowed: 'I believe that because Stanley would not make up that kind of story. He didn't have to exaggerate anything he got up to. So, yes, I would probably agree that it happened.'

Billy McNeill has heard the story over the years and goes along with Brand, saying: 'He was supposed to be still drunk from the night before, or an all-night drinking session, and he was playing against us and, you know, if he said that then I would believe it. Jimmy believed that he could get away with anything at that stage of his career – and most of the time he did!

The entertainer Will Fyffe's anthem to his native city could have been written especially for Jim Baxter because, almost from the moment he signed for Rangers, Glasgow did belong to him. The people, warm and affectionate by nature, took him to their hearts, and he embraced them, all of them, without the slightest whiff of the bigotry that has so often scarred relationships between the Old Firm of Rangers and Celtic.

The chorus of Fyffe's song goes like this:

I belong to Glasgow.
Dear old Glasgow toon;
But what's the matter wi' Glasgow,
It's going' roon' and roon',
I'm only a common old workin' chap,
As anyone here can see,
But when I get a couple o' drinks on a Saturday,
Glasgow belongs to me!

The trouble with Baxter, though, was that he was never exactly happy with only a 'couple o' drinks on a Saturday', he enjoyed a 'small refreshment' to use the Glasgow parlance, any night of the week whether it was before a game or not. Nor did he restrict his intake in any way. He had a life he wanted to live and part of that life was having the very best of times that Glasgow could offer him as the Swinging 60s burst into life.

Players who were with him at Raith Rovers remember him as a 'shy youngster' when he started his senior career in Kirkcaldy. That adjective was never one that would be used when Baxter reinvented himself after his transfer made him one of Scotland's superstars.

He had suspected from the time he joined Rangers that his

footballing skills could carry him into a world that was light years away from the miners' row in Fife where he had grown up. When the opportunities to drink and gamble and party the nights away presented themselves he accepted them all.

It may have been that the city itself seduced him, though he was an ever-willing victim when temptations were spread in front of him. He was on his own a lot when he signed for the Ibrox club. Most of the other Rangers players were married and settled down into family life and several of them did not stay in Glasgow, so the new man found himself sitting in hotel rooms with none of his new team-mates around to ease his loneliness.

Raith Rovers players were surprised when they began to hear of his escapades in Glasgow. Few of them could understand how he could suddenly go off the rails, though the adulation he received from the supporters would have been difficult to resist.

Pat Crerand, who was with Celtic when Baxter arrived in Glasgow, and who was later sold to Manchester United, was one of the close-knit crowd that hung out with him after he had signed for Rangers. He explains: 'There were a few of us, Billy McNeill and Mike Jackson and Duncy McKay and myself, who became friendly with Jimmy when he first came to Glasgow. I don't know how it happened, just how it came about that we ran around together because, while Old Firm players would mix socially OK, this kind of went beyond that. Of course, most of the Rangers players were older than him and not too many of them lived in the city and so we used to get together. It got to the stage that Jimmy would come and have lunch with us at Ferrari's restaurant on Sauchiehall Street after training. Celtic always went there and he would sometimes come in, and the chairman, Bob Kelly (later Sir Robert Kelly), thought this was a great joke. He would come in and laugh about it – but I don't think there were too many people laughing about it at Ibrox. Not everyone there approved, but Jimmy didn't care what anyone thought – he never did.

'I think the Ferrari's visits emphasised that he was not

someone who was ever going to live by the expected rules. He enjoyed our company and he liked the patter and he needed that because he was shy, really just a shy lad from the Fife coalfields who was a little bit overwhelmed by the city. You only saw that side of him if you knew him really well. Certainly watching him play there was never any sign of it because out there on the field he was an arrogant so and so, with a lot to be arrogant about.

'He honestly felt that he was better than anyone else and there were times when you could not argue with that. And, then, he had that left foot – God, he could pick a lock with that!'

His friendship with the mainly Celtic group was far from the behaviour expected of players by the Rangers directors of the time. Billy McNeill, who went on to captain and to manage Celtic, looks back to those days of the 'cross-border' rapport between the emerging first team men – Crerand broke into the first team at Parkhead at almost the same time as Baxter signed for Rangers, and the others, McKay excepted, were also fledgling professionals – with affection.

'I have the feeling that Jimmy was introduced into our company by a lad called Dougie Hepburn,' he recollects. 'Dougie had been in the army with Neil Mochan and was also a pal of Dave Mackay and we used to go to the George Hotel in Glasgow on a Saturday night after the game. Jimmy started to come in there too and he was always perfectly comfortable in our company. I have to say that Jim Baxter did not have one sectarian bone in his body. It didn't matter to him that he played for Rangers and we were with Celtic. He just loved life and loved people and he and Paddy (Crerand) became very close. They shared the same nature: both were gifted players, both were as daft as a brush and both were amazingly generous. If you asked Paddy for the shirt off his back he would give it to you and Jimmy was much the same.

'He fitted into that Glasgow scene much the way Charlie Tully had ten years earlier. And while everyone talks about George Best being the football image of the Swinging 60s, Jimmy did it all before him. He arrived in Glasgow, young and single, with an extravagant gift for football, and he didn't have a care in the world. All he wanted was to be out on the field shouting: "Gie me the ball", and then come away from the ground and the game and enjoy himself. Yes, he drank a lot and the rest of us weren't drinking as much and, yes, he could be a pest when he took too much but you couldn't dislike him. There he would be in the middle of a party, shirt loosened and tied across the front – the way Harry Belafonte used to do it – and his tie was round his head like a bandana and he would be singing away and be quite happy until something happened to upset him and that meant trouble and we all knew it.

'Then, of course, he would not let it go. He was like a dog with a bone and would just go on and on about whatever it was that had annoyed him and you couldn't shut him up and before long he would want to fight. And, believe me, Jimmy couldn't fight sleep! One night he decided that he would have a go with Cowboy McCormack who was one of the best boxers Scotland has ever produced. He was friendly with us and a good pal of Jimmy's as well but it made no difference that night. Jimmy wanted to fight him. Fortunately John was a laid-back guy and he just laughed it off until the whole thing was calmed down. Of course, Jimmy collected a few sore faces over the years because he could be cheeky. But when you think about it, it was crazy. He might have been a lot of things, he might have been a great footballer, he might have been a great lover, he might have been a great drinker, but he was never any kind of a fighter.'

The 'sore faces' and the close attentions of Harold Davis never did convince Baxter that when it came to fighting then he should most definitely have stuck to football. It was as if he courted trouble on occasions, as if the risks he took gave him a certain thrill. Throughout his life he took risks. He did it on the field where his mastery of the ball rescued him most of the time. He did it with Rangers, always pushing the club that little bit further whether over wage demands or discipline. He did it with his career and ended up finished with football when he should have been at his peak. He did it in the gambling clubs he frequented and on the racecourses he visited, dropping thousands of pounds over the years. Eventually, too, he risked his health and paid for that with his life. Whatever inner demons plagued him they appeared to surface when he found himself faced with authority or when he thought he was being treated unfairly. There were times, too, when he stepped out of line just for the hell of it!

It might seem to be stepping back into Victorian times when you look at how Rangers handled their business just forty years ago and it is little wonder that Jim Baxter, a maverick by nature, would rail against the traditions which had existed for decades and which held no apparent relevance for his times. The Ibrox club held firm to a strict sectarian signing policy which was only broken when Graeme Souness became manager in the late 1980s. When Baxter signed, his background would have been investigated thoroughly beforehand.

And the transfer would only have been completed when Rangers were completely satisfied that Jim Baxter was a Protestant. The directors would not brook the signing of a Roman Catholic and so, given that policy, it is easy to imagine the anger in the Blue Room when their star player had Pat Crerand as his closest friend and, more, that there were even newspaper stories linking him romantically with the Celtic player's sister. This was not what the directors wanted. They frowned upon this more than they did on the drinking escapades that were being brought to their notice. After all, only a few years earlier one of the first-team players had been called to the manager's office and warned that the club would sack him if he persisted in plans to become engaged to his Catholic girlfriend. The romance was ended and the player remained, but Baxter was not one to toe any kind of party line and every little infraction of the Rangers rules brought him closer to all-out conflict with the club.

Naturally the constant friction between himself and the Rangers trainer, Davie Kinnear, who was a fellow Fifer, did not help long-term relationships. The two men did not get on and, when Kinnear was trying to do his job, he found his star charge unwilling to carry out any instructions, sometimes for the simple reason that Baxter was physically unable to train with the other players either because he was suffering a massive hangover or because he was still drunk when he reported in the morning.

As club captain, Bobby Shearer was sometimes caught up in the disputes. Even now he shakes his head at what went on. 'There were certain rules back in the 50s and 60s which were still looked on as sacred at the club,' he points out. 'You were expected, as players, to be ambassadors for Rangers Football Club at all times. That meant that when we went into training we were expected to wear the club blazer and a collar and tie. Sometimes you could miss out on the blazer – though not on match days when it was essential – but you did need the collar and tie. It was the way it had been at Rangers for many, many years and, well, we just accepted it. But not Jim. He would stroll in wearing a sports shirt, but casual was not a word in the club dictionary and so Davie Kinnear would tell him that he was not being allowed to train that day because he was improperly dressed when he reported at the stadium. Now, a lot of the time, when Kinnear and he were falling out, the manager Scot Symon would take Jim's side.

'But not on this issue, and so he would be sent home to change. And he didn't like that one bit. Missing the training wasn't a problem, but losing face to Kinnear was. You could understand a young lad being unimpressed by the dress code and some of the other bits of tradition around the club then but there were times when I was just not able to fathom him. He was a world-class player and one of the best, if not *the* best player Rangers have ever had, but he was a real problem off the field. Sometimes he would come into the dressing room before a game on Saturday and he would be reeking of booze and I would have to tell him not to breathe on the manager when he came in to give us a team talk before kick off. Honestly, if he had gone near Symon the smell of drink would have knocked him over. That was a regular occurrence. Now this was a top player, with the biggest club in the country, and he was out on the tiles on a Friday night when the rest of the players would be off to bed early. We could all take a drink but we kept it to the Saturday night after the match was over. But Jim would be drinking all the time. He did not believe in allowing the matches to get in the way of his social life. OK, I was the captain and maybe people thought I should have done something about the way he carried on, but I didn't. I just let him get on with his life because I knew that I would be wasting my breath trying to offer him any advice. He thought he knew it all. By the way, he didn't just turn up like that on match days – he was the same when he came into training most mornings. He had been up half the night in Glasgow and then he would report and he would be wrecked.'

The St Enoch Hotel, which was the Rangers team hotel, became Baxter's own private night club. He invited friends back there for late-night drinking sessions, held parties in his room, and all of it was placed on the Rangers tab. Champagne, Bacardi, the best Havana cigars, smoked salmon and caviar were all available and no one questioned the player when the bills arrived on manager Scot Symon's desk. There were times, of course, when Baxter would mischievously sign another player's name and when that happened the supposed miscreant would be summoned to the office at the top of the marble staircase in Ibrox where Symon would be waiting to demand an explanation for this over-spending. On one such occasion Davy Wilson found himself being questioned about a bill that carried his name.

There were three bottles of Bacardi, three bottles of champagne and so many cases of beer written on the hotel room service receipt that the poor left-winger was being told by the manager that he would have to pay for the various items. When he pointed out that first of all he did not drink and secondly that the signature did not remotely resemble his own, Symon shook his head and suggested that he get Jimmy to make the signature a bit more authentic and then the bill would probably be 'acceptable'. A bewildered Wilson returned to the dressing room realising that once again the manager was prepared to turn a blind eye to his top player's extravagances whereas, if the bill had been his, he would have had to pay for it out of his own pocket. The bills, of course, continued to flow into Ibrox, Symon continued to ignore them and the St Enoch Hotel continued as Baxter's main Glasgow base.

While the longer-serving professionals at Ibrox frowned upon his lifestyle, there were younger players coming into the team who had more than a sneaking admiration for the manner in which he brushed aside the suffocating conventions which surrounded the club. When Willie Henderson signed as a teenager he broke into the first team swiftly and so found himself one of the wing half's protégés and the pair were close with an element of hero-worship coming from the little winger.

He grins now: 'He ran the St Enoch Hotel as if it was his own private club. Rangers had an account at the hotel, the directors used it for pre-match meals and whenever there was a cup win to celebrate that's where the banquet was held. It was also where there were meals for visiting foreign sides when we played in the European tournaments – it was the normal occurrence that the teams would get together for a special dinner after the games. There was a head waiter there who was Polish, I remember, and he looked out for Jimmy. You might be coming into the hotel and when you walked across the foyer there was Johnny with a trolley laden with bottles of champagne and Bacardi and he would be on his way up to Jim's room. He would just smile and say: "Mr Baxter doesn't feel like eating in the dining room tonight so he has ordered room service, the drinks first and then the meal!" And that was it, and the whole cost of this was down to Rangers Football Club. He didn't stint himself when he was ordering.

'There were no set menus for him, he ordered the very best because that was his way of getting a bit extra from the club when they were always refusing to pay him better wages. I'm sure he ate better and drank more than any of the directors. He was a law unto himself. I think, by this time, he was very conscious of the ability he possessed and that gave him massive self-confidence. That, in turn, saw him ignore all the rules which applied to the rest of the players because he did not reckon that they applied to him. That can happen with people who are out of the ordinary – and Jimmy Baxter was well out of the ordinary. There was not an ordinary bone in his body!

'But when you put working-class lads from mining villages out there on a world stage where they are earning more money than their fathers had seen in their whole working lives, then it is not very surprising that they can go off the rails. Could you really expect anything else? Did people honestly expect that footballers with that kind of background – and most of us were in the same boat – were going to be able to handle the whole thing correctly? Clubs did nothing to prepare you for the instant fame that followed you when you played football for a top club. Remember, we were travelling the world with the club and the national team and seeing places we would never have dreamed we would visit. It took some adjustment. I know what I am talking about here because while I came from a village in Lanarkshire and Jimmy was from Fife you can forget the geography because we were really from the same place. There was no difference in the way we grew up, all these mining areas were the same when you examined them.'

Jim Forrest and Alex Willoughby were cousins who joined Rangers at virtually the same time as Baxter did – though they were some years younger. They, too, saw the 'cult' of the St Enoch Hotel as it developed. It was something that was beyond their reach because, as two Glasgow boys, they were expected to find their way home to Townhead and Springburn respectively. That was a discipline that, as Rangers supporters as well as players, they accepted. It was not one which Baxter would have recognised for a moment.

Willoughby, who remained close to the Ibrox star until his death, claims: 'Neither the manager nor the board of directors would have allowed Jim Forrest or Alex Willoughby to stay the night at the St Enoch. But it was a different story for Stanley [Baxter was nicknamed 'Stanley' after the Scottish comedian; it was Ralph Brand who christened him and several of the players still use that tag], because he did more or less what he wanted to do. There's a nightclub in Glasgow, now, Victoria's, well, the St Enoch was the Victoria's of the 1960s as far as Stanley was concerned. That was his own special nightclub. When he was ordering drinks or meals there then he simply signed for them and the bills went straight back to Ibrox. It was incredible. He would have his mates in, and they wouldn't have to pay a penny. Naturally these nights didn't end until the early hours – and if this was after a midweek match then they would carry on until dawn!

'So on Thursday you could expect him to come into training with a serious hangover. He wouldn't try to hide it either. He would stroll into Ibrox with the Alka Seltzers sticking out of his top pocket because he was not going to be able to function without taking them first. Even after he took his cure he would not train as hard as the rest of us. Now Stanley is often criticised because he never showed any interest in training – and it's true that didn't like the hard work the rest of us had to put in every morning. But I believe that if the work we were given had been a little more stimulating, if he had been allowed more of the ball, for example, then he might have responded. Instead, all we were told to do was run round the track or do sprints and that was not for him.'

Adds Forrest: 'The club was stuck in the past. There was no coaching, no tactics of any kind, and if you happened to develop as a player then you did so through your own efforts. Before a game all the advice we were ever given was "Give the ball to Jim", and you needed to have more of a game plan than that for the way the game was progressing in the 60s. We didn't get it. We were not coached as a team and we were never told how we should evolve as a team. It was all done off the cuff during the games.

'I agree that Baxter might have applied himself more at training if the routine had moved away from the running that was the norm at Ibrox when we were playing. The trouble with him was that he set out to enjoy life to the full and to hell with the consequences. The club allowed him too much licence. For a long time they turned a blind eye to his drinking and his whole off-field lifestyle and his complete lack of professionalism at times.

'Everything he got up to in his social life was known. He was not in the least bit discreet. Never mind that the players in the dressing room knew what he was up to – he would regale us with stories every day at training – the whole of the city of Glasgow seemed to know. If he had kept a lid on things then he would not have gained the reputation, the bad name, if you like, which eventually affected his career for the worse. He was a Good Time Charlie guy and he let the whole world see it and the directors did not like it. They accepted it for so long and then they decided, I suppose, that enough was enough. He was not a bad influence on any of us younger players. He was self-destructive, as we all now realise. He did not hurt other people, he just hurt himself. He set out to enjoy life to the full. That's what he was all about, and that's what he did. That was his bottom line in life – it was there to be savoured to the full. I doubt if he missed out on anything. Sadly, all that living took its toll.'

Even the older players would succumb to his charm while he continued to make telling contributions to the Rangers cause. They would listen to the stories of whatever antics he had been involved in the night before and, while some remained upset that he would jeopardise their chances in the game that loomed ahead, his transgressions would be forgiven if the right results were delivered. At his peak he was able to do that, though the risks he took became more and more bizarre. When he had stopped playing he would boast that he had once played in an Old Firm game while still drunk. No one will confirm that but when questioned possible team-mates and opponents believe that it probably did happen. Ralph Brand admitted to hearing the story and allowed: 'I believe that because Stanley would not make up that kind of story. He didn't have to exaggerate anything he got up to. So, yes, I would probably agree that it happened.'

Billy McNeill has heard the story over the years and goes along with Brand, saying: 'He was supposed to be still drunk from the night before, or an all-night drinking session, and he was playing against us and, you know, if he said that then I would believe it. Jimmy believed that he could get away with anything at that stage of his career – and most of the time he did! Now, we all enjoyed ourselves because we were young guys, but he was always different. It was as if he wanted to have everything and he wanted to have it all at once.

'He wasn't able to discipline himself at all. And from all accounts he used to turn up regularly at Ibrox still suffering from the excesses of the night before. To go into a game still feeling the effects of a drinking session wouldn't have worried him over much. He wasn't prepared to take anything seriously. It would have been just another laugh as far as he was concerned, something else he had been able to get away with.'

Certainly there is no doubting the fact that he stayed up gambling all night prior to the replayed Scottish Cup Final between Rangers and Celtic back in the spring of 1963 when Rangers were attempting to clinch a league and cup double. In his own description Baxter told how he had gone to a gambling club in Fife on the eve of the Hampden Final. Roulette was on offer and chemin-de-fer and his game of choice was 'chemmy' and by breakfast time he had won £1,700 in hard cash – which was not too far off what he was earning from Rangers in a year.

At half past nine on the morning of the game he sat down to breakfast at his parents' home, then went to bed for a couple of hours before making the journey down to finalise his 'preparations' for the game.

Baxter's rationale for this behaviour was that Rangers, during his five seasons there, were invariably stronger than Celtic and that he knew the final was going to be an easily won victory. That very season the two teams had met twice in the League Championship and Rangers had won on each occasion. In the first game, during the first week in September, a goal from Willie Henderson had given Rangers their win – but only after Baxter had psyched Pat Crerand into missing a penalty.

Crerand has never forgotten the incident and says even now, almost forty years later: 'He was an absolute piss-taker especially in Old Firm games. It didn't matter that we were the best of mates off the field – and we were – when we played against each other then we were each playing to win. But it was not only a victory Jimmy wanted – he also wanted to make us suffer. Oh, and how he did that. I used to pray that the Army – he was doing his National Service then – would keep him away from games. That didn't happen and it was bad news for us because he did have the Indian sign over Celtic. Rangers had been a good enough team before he signed but when he went there he added something extra. There was always an arrogance about him. Anyhow, during a league game this day Ralphie Brand tripped me in the penalty box and we were awarded the penalty.

'I decided that I would take the kick myself and Jimmy started off giving me so much abuse and trying to say the ball was not on the spot properly and all the rest of it. He never stopped talking, and I knew he was trying to put me off, but even knowing that I couldn't ignore him. It wasn't directed far enough away from Billy Ritchie, the Rangers goalkeeper and he shoved it away round the post and we lost the game. Going home that night I got terrible stick from the Celtic supporters, as if I didn't feel bad enough. I was raging about what Jimmy had done to me but I knew it would all be forgotten the next time I saw him and that's how it was. You couldn't be angry with him for long.'

The next time the Glasgow rivals met Rangers won 4–0 at Ibrox in the traditional New Year's Day fixture and the goals were shared by Harold Davis, Jimmy Millar, John Greig and Davy Wilson, and then came the Cup Final. The first match was drawn 1–1 in front of 129,527 fans but Rangers had controlled much of the game and Frank Haffey, in the Celtic goal, had saved the Parkhead team. No doubt that added to Baxter's arrogance and gave him the belief that, even staying out all night, he could still produce enough to help Rangers to another Scottish Cup triumph. He was right, and goals from Brand, who scored twice, and from Wilson, confirmed the Ibrox team's supremacy. Yet while Baxter did not see this particular escapade as serious risk-taking, the Old Firm fixture has had a reputation over the years for being a game where the form book can invariably be ignored.

That didn't enter Baxter's thinking. The belief in his own ability, the belief that the normal rules of behaviour were there for other, lesser mortals, were more convincing arguments as he set off for that all-night card session. Gambling was yet another of the demons he could not control. This probably stemmed from his mining background where drinking and gambling went hand-in-hand as the men attempted to escape the grim realities of their underground existence and the long hard hours they had to work to scrape the barest of livings for themselves and their families. Baxter had been a betting man since his earliest working days and he would remain one until the day he died. He loved the thrill gambling gave him, that buzz, and even when he was losing, something constantly drew him back into the action. And the bigger the bet the better he liked it even if the stakes were often a little too rich. Risk was everything – in life, in football, in his whole approach to the world – and gambling was another way of bringing him the risks he loved to take.

When players from other clubs were going with the national

team during this period they used to be surprised at the extent of the gambling which took place when the Rangers contingent got together. It did not seem to matter what they were doing in the leisure time, there had to be betting involved. Whether it was at the snooker table or in card sessions on air or rail or coach journeys, the Ibrox men, with Baxter as the instigator, were involved in gambling – and, quite often, big money was involved.

Willie Henderson was one of the regular school, as was Ronnie McKinnon, and there were rumours at the time that the little winger had lost a substantial sum of money on one international trip with Baxter coming out the winner.

Henderson's explanation, however, stresses that he was never a victim when the card games saw hundreds of pounds change hands. Looking back he points out: 'First of all, let me say that any time I lost money to Jimmy Baxter at cards it happened because I wanted to play in the game. He never had to talk me into playing, because I wanted to play and I wanted to be in his company. There were times I lost money to him – if you play cards you're not going to be winning all the time, are you? But I did not complain then and I have never complained since. I looked on all these things as a part of my education.

'It was an introduction to the real world and I did learn my lessons back then – the problem was that Jimmy didn't learn. He just kept on gambling and, while I think he regretted that later on in his life, he didn't really stop. He would bet on anything. It was a major part of his life and he was a member at several gambling clubs in Glasgow. The Chevalier was one and I think another was the Queen's Club where he would get himself involved in some heavy sessions. They were places he went to regularly because I think he got some kind of buzz from gambling whether he was winning or not. Most of the time he was losing and he would tell you that and he would admit that he wasn't very good at it. In fact he was hopeless. If you lose the amount of money he did over the years then you cannot be a good gambler!

'He was fine in card games on a team bus or on a plane when we were travelling abroad for games, or in a hotel room with other footballers. But in these clubs he was going up against professional punters, guys with a lot more money than he had and who did that kind of thing for a living. That's where he would lose a lot of money and yet he never seemed to let it worry him. He always had a sort of "easy come, easy go" attitude about his cash.'

It could scarcely be any other way when Baxter himself estimated his gambling losses over a quarter of a century or so, from the time he signed for Rangers to a point in the mid-1980s, as being around £200,000. He admitted, too, that his gambling did begin in Fife when he was still a youngster and regular 'tossing' schools and pontoon games would be organised. As well as the casinos and the card schools at Ibrox, Baxter was also a victim when it came to horse racing. But the Glasgow clubs brought him most grief.

According to Billy McNeill, 'Money didn't matter greatly to Jimmy – though he was always looking to get higher wages from Rangers – it was just a tool to him, something which would help him to further his enjoyment of life. I can remember one incident very vividly from 1963 just before I was married. Scotland had arranged a close-season tour with games against Norway, the Republic of Ireland and Spain. I had been selected for the squad and so had Jimmy and the night before we were due to fly out to Norway for the first match he phoned me from Glasgow. He was in town and there were rooms available at the North British Hotel for any of the players who were travelling to join the squad. I was only out in Bellshill but I agreed to go into Glasgow and finished up sharing a room with Jimmy. We had a bite to eat and then we went out and, bearing in mind there was too much to do in Glasgow at that time, we ended up in a gambling club where he was a member. It was a private club just off Gordon Street right in the centre of the city and you had to go upstairs to get into it.

'Now, I was an innocent abroad as far as gambling was concerned, I didn't have a clue what went on in these clubs but even to my unpractised eye it soon became obvious that Jimmy was having the kind of night when nothing could go wrong. He was playing baccarat or chemmy, I'm not sure which, and the chips were piling up in front of him. When it came time to go back to the hotel he collected £2,000 in cash to take away with him. Now, that was an awful lot of money back then and he wanted to keep it safe. I had a case with me that had good, strong locks for the outside. And, even better, it had inside pockets that could also lock and so he asked me to look after the money for him. I did that and I held on to the cash for the whole time we were away.

'We were away for just short of two weeks and after the last game in Madrid where we beat Spain 6–2 we returned to Glasgow in high spirits. So Baxter asks me for the money back when we reach the hotel. And, inevitably, we ended up back in the same club we had been in before we left. I am standing there telling Jimmy that he should get himself back up to Fife and put the money away safely and he is arguing that he wants to play cards some more and add to the money he has in his pockets. He won the argument – it was his money after all, and would you believe, in half an hour it was gone. All of it. Two thousand pounds simply vanished in front of my eyes. I couldn't do anything about it because he wouldn't listen to anyone. Now that kind of money back then would have bought you a house. But Jimmy lost it and you know what – he didn't care! It didn't matter to him one little bit. I think it mattered more to me as I watched all that money I had been looking after on the trip going back to the club. But you see, you had to understand Jimmy, and having money in his pocket never motivated him. He was motivated by enjoyment and, sadly, that eventually took over more and more as the years went past. Having a good time was more important to him than anything else.'

Losing a few thousand pounds at a time was not all that

isolated an incident. Bobby Shearer recollects that one day Baxter arrived at training looking as if he had been out on the tiles and soon he admitted that he had been up half the night and had won just short of £3,000 at one of the Glasgow casinos. He even showed the startled Shearer the wad of money he had in his pocket. A couple of days later he confessed that the money had gone. As Shearer says: 'He was skint again after having all that money in his hands. I couldn't believe it and I couldn't understand it either. It seemed to happen all the time to Jim. One day he was rolling in money and the next day he was broke.'

Baxter used to own up to betting in his Paisley Road pub on what kind or colour of shoes the next customer through the door would be wearing. Hundreds of pounds could be won or lost in this game and it was a favourite with the bar owner and his clientele. His most spectacular loss, though, was probably at a casino in Madrid after Rangers had lost 6–0 to Real in the second leg of a European Cup match back in 1963.

The Glasgow team had lost 1–0 in the first leg and the return in the Spanish capital saw them humiliated. Baxter, never the best of losers, went straight to the casino in the team hotel following the after-match banquet. Alex Willoughby, who played that night, takes up the story:

'We were staying in the Velasquez Hotel and it was late when we got back there. There was this casino in the hotel and that's where Stanley went immediately we walked into reception. When I caught up with him he was winning and he was winning a lot of money. Then the manager of the casino announced that it was time for the last bets to be placed and there was Baxter sitting at the table with something like four or five thousand pounds in front of him. He lost the lot on that last bet. A few of us tried to talk him out of it but he put some of the money on the roulette wheel, some more at one of the other tables and the rest where he had been sitting. Now we were all telling him to keep some money back and maybe bet just a few hundred pounds at the death – he ignored all of us. Remember, too, he knew that if he lost there was no comeback for him because the casino was closing and we were on a plane first thing in the morning. He ignored that. All he wanted was to make another big bet and I think, because he had been lucky up to then, he thought that was going to continue.

'I was sharing a room with him and we went up in the lift together and he was acting as if nothing had happened. Then he went off to sleep as if he hadn't a single care in the world and left me lying awake for the whole night worrying over what I had just witnessed. I was shattered but it didn't matter to him. He loved gambling and when he won he was happy and when he lost he accepted that as a part of the game.'

5 PUSHING RANGERS TO THE BRINK

When that break came it did so because the directors had finally lost patience, and even Symon was beginning to realise that the various escapades would ultimately damage the club. Essentially the problem was over money. Baxter had demanded more money at the end of every season when the clubs were bound to offer their playing staff fresh contracts. His hope, always, was that Rangers, realising his value to the team, would give him more money than the other players at the club. It was not something that was even considered by the board. Yet it became something of a matter of principle to the player.

As the various honours from the Scottish game found their way with some regularity into the Ibrox trophy room, the supporters, who had soon made Baxter their idol, knew little of the dramas being played out behind the scenes. Nor would most of them have cared that some of their hero's more senior team-mates were growing increasingly disenchanted by his behaviour and the way his breaches of discipline went largely unchecked and ignored by the manager, Scot Symon.

There were signs, too, that the directors were losing patience as the player's off-field recklessness increased. Few of his escapades made the front pages of the tabloid newspapers back then, mainly because the social scene was not as open at that time in Glasgow as it has since become. Most of Baxter's drinking took place in city centre hotels and the St Enoch with its impressive entrance was not a watering hole that welcomed the people who thronged the terracings of Ibrox to watch Baxter week after week. Sure, he made occasional forays into the ordinary pubs of the city, but these were limited and all they did was add to the legend that was growing around him.

The supporters enjoyed the fact that Baxter was something of a man about town, living the kind of life they could only dream about as they worked long hours to earn their wages in the shipyards and the factories. The dangers of his lifestyle were not yet apparent to the general public. In the dressing room and in the boardroom at Ibrox, however, there was a dawning realisation that the man whose skills had helped reshape the team on the field might also be the man to damage both the team spirit among the players and the long-held, if outdated, traditions of the club. Baxter was seen by some not as the superstar admired by the support but as a disruptive influence, and the more he pushed them the more some of the directors began to change an attitude which had been to forgive him for his lapses just so long as he continued to bring the team the success all of them craved.

His training ground nemesis Harold Davis still believes today that Symon, seen previously as something of a martinet by the players, lost the dressing room when he began to pander to his first-team favourite. 'As players we all knew what he was up to away from the ground,' Davis says simply. 'You could smell the drink off him almost every single morning he came in for training – and on match days too. If you jarred him about it he would get that cocky way he had and tell you that he could play better when he had a drink in him. Of course that was nonsense but Jim acted as if he believed it. And, actually, some of the time, when he was really suffering from the aftereffects of the booze, he delivered some really under-par performances for the team. The fans won't remember that, it's natural that they remember the good games. But, believe me, there were a lot of games when we all had to cover up for him because he was not making any kind of contribution.

'It became so bad that the centre half Bill Paterson and myself agreed that we would have to have a word with him about the whole business. We decided one day at training that after the next match we would take him aside and point out that there were things going on that the other players were not happy about. Well, of course, you have to believe that the next game Jim made up his mind that he would turn it on, took the whole ninety minutes by the scruff of the neck, and Bill and I shrugged at each other leaving the field, accepting that there was no point in talking to him. In fact none of the lads spoke to him at any length about the way he was carrying on. There would be little flare-ups but that's as far as it went and I think that was because we were all waiting for Symon to sort him out.

'When he had gone to Rangers as manager he had been faced with a situation where George Young ran things. The manager Bill Struth was getting older, had been through several operations and was in failing health and he relied on George to run the team discipline. Now George was a massive personality, club captain and Scotland captain, and yet Symon went in as the new manager and took that responsibility away from him. So, while we did talk about sorting out Jim Baxter, it was never done, because we all felt that Symon was in charge and it would be wrong of us to interfere. But the worrying thing for me was that, as a result of cutting Jim too much slack, Symon lost the dressing room. Discipline suffered and the manager lost face because we knew that he was unable to handle this one disruptive element he had brought to the club.'

Davis could understand Symon's dilemma to a certain extent and he sympathised with the plight of the man who had signed him for Rangers. He knew that the manager recognised Baxter's enormous talent and believed that he was the catalyst for the rich vein of success the club was enjoying. There was always the possibility that if he took a seriously strong line with the wayward star then the team would suffer and the trophy wins would dry up.

'If Symon had told him that he had to toe the line or else,' Davis admits, 'then Jim would just have answered, "Or else what?" and the manager would have had to back away from a real confrontation. There is no doubt that this damaged morale among the rest of the players, but when he went out and won us an Old Firm game or a cup final you just had to shake your head and own up to the fact that there were times when he was out on his own.

'But he was given preferential treatment. OK, occasionally he would be fined for one thing or another but Jim just paid the fine and then went on his own sweet way. To be fair to Scot Symon I don't know if anyone would have been capable of solving the disciplinary problems Jim brought with him. It would have been a waste of time trying to change him because he made it clear that no one was going to tell him how to run his life and that the club rules were there for the rest of us to follow and for him to break!'

That was a reasonable summing-up of Baxter's attitude at the time, and Davis was not the only senior professional to fear the damage which was being done. The manager's position was constantly undermined as the slim, young Fifer cut his own personal swathe through the city of Glasgow and the night life he was able to find there.

Eric Caldow played directly behind him and was captain of Rangers when Baxter was signed and he, too, believes that morale suffered as the new boy kicked aside so many of the old customs which had been accepted by generation upon generation of Ibrox players before him. He shrugs now: 'Once Jim settled into the team and started to play so well and to have a tremendous influence on how we approached the game on the field he was allowed to do more or less what he liked off the field. It annoyed the rest of us that Symon let him get away with so much instead of stamping down on some of his misbehaviour right at the start. He just let it drift and poor Davie Kinnear was left trying to discipline Jim but didn't have the necessary authority. That lay with the manager and he was very reluctant to place any restraints on Jim in case he upset him.

'Of course, the only tactics talk we ever heard from Scot Symon at this period was "Give the ball to Jim." He never said very much more than that. It was the major instruction given to us before we went on to the field. It indicated how important Jim became to the team – which, I think, was one of the greatest-ever Rangers teams – because he had altered the way we played the game. He was a superb attacking wing half and he brought the right balance to our team and a great mix down the left flank where I sat in behind him, and he would get the ball – as per instructions – and when he did he would release wee Davy Wilson down the wing. The understanding we all had in that area helped us win a lot of games. But we all knew the way Jim was behaving and we all knew that he was getting away with it when anyone else would have been in trouble. In fact, any other player doing what he did would have been sold immediately.'

During his time with the Glasgow club changes in the team inevitably took place and the Ibrox 'Old Guard' began to be phased out and younger players were drafted in to take their place. Most of them became disciples of the left half in one way or another. Some shared his social life, though not many, and most were in thrall to the skills he showed on the field of play. They, too, could see that the normal rules of behaviour were suspended as regards Baxter but they railed against this less than the older players had done when he first signed from Raith Rovers.

Fellow Fifer Willie Johnston was warned by Symon not to get too close to the club's most influential player. The winger was only a teenager when he broke into the first team and Baxter had taken him under his wing – something that concerned the manager. Johnston tells you now: 'Jimmy kind of looked out for me when I went to Rangers at first. I came from Cardenden and he was from Hill o' Beath and the two villages were only a few miles apart and so I think he felt it was the right thing for him to do to keep an eye out for another young lad from Fife.

'The very first day I reported for training he took me across to the Albion training ground which was across the street from the stadium. And he was always offering me advice about the game, trying to point me in the right direction – which meant when you were playing with him that you gave him the ball as often as possible! Whenever he shouted for the ball you passed it to him. If you didn't do it you were in trouble.

'That was all he wanted during any match he played – the ball at his feet. Once he had possession then he felt he could take on the world. I played with a lot of great midfield men in my career, Johnny Giles and Bryan Robson are just two of them, and they had special qualities. But when Baxter had the ball then no one could touch him. And, you know what, he worked hard too. No one ever remembers that about him. But when he looked for a pass he was always in the best possible position to accept it, he had made sure that he had found space and then he would use that left foot of his and I never saw anyone who had a left foot to even come close to Jimmy Baxter's.

'Aye, there were times when he would ask me to go out with him but I was just a youngster and I didn't really drink or anything. The first time I went into the St Enoch Hotel to the bar he asked me if I wanted "a wee Bacardi" but I asked for a lager and lime and he didn't try to talk me into having anything stronger. He wasn't like that. He did not lead me astray but there were worries at the club that he might do that to some of the younger players. When I won my first medal with Rangers we beat Celtic 2–1 in the League Cup Final in 1964 and Jimmy was captain that day. Jim Forrest scored the two goals for us that day at Hampden and there were more than 90,000 people at the game. It was only something like my fourth first team appearance and Jimmy talked me through the game.

'Then, on Monday morning after training, we were all called upstairs to the manager's office to get our bonus for winning the cup. That's the way it was done then and when it was my turn I knocked on the office door, was buzzed in, and Scot Symon was sitting behind his big desk. He gave me the envelope with the bonus and I'll never forget his words to me: "Billy you have ensured that you will have a future with this club but you have to stay away from Jimmy!" That's what he said, but it didn't make any great difference to me. I still went out with Jim every now and again but, being a good bit younger, I never really became involved in all that was going on.

'Look, he was not the best example for young players off the field but he was superb during the games. As long as he had a pitch spread out in front of him and the ball nestling at his left foot then he was happy. There were times at Ibrox when you watched him and wondered if you were seeing things properly. He was so much in control that he would just run matches. It didn't matter who the opposition was, when he was in the mood no team could stop him. He did as he liked and he was one helluva player to have pushing passes through for you. I know that OK. The service he gave to the lads playing in front of him was unbelievable.'

On the other side of that Rangers forward line was Willie Henderson, another who came into the side following Baxter's signing and another who saw him as someone to admire, as someone who personified the times they were living in. While Johnston remained in the background most of the time, Henderson was happy to join in some of his friend's excesses.

'He was tailor-made for that decade,' claims Henderson. 'Life was just one non-stop party for him. And how he liked to look the part too. He had a bit of style about him by then and he was always immaculate. Jimmy liked clothes, liked to be in fashion, and he was usually dressed better than anyone else around.'

This was part of the self-transformation Baxter undertook when he signed for Rangers and began to make more money than he had ever done before. He maintained that clothes had always been important to him and, once he moved through the 'Teddy Boy' stage which the older Raith Rovers players had disapproved of, he attempted to move up market. When he was selected for a Scotland Under-23 international while he was still a part-time player at Stark's Park he splashed out on a new suit before joining the squad. He bought an outfit in Lovat green and was embarrassed when he saw the other players at the hotel wearing the then fashionable mohair suits. He vowed then that he would never be caught in that way again – and he wasn't. Indeed he became something of a fashion icon among the other players. Style became everything for him off the field just as it had always been when he was strutting his stuff on the field out there in front of the fans that were by now his very own adoring public.

Even at the gambling tables, while he would play poker – if the truth be told he would bet on any game there was – his preferred games were baccarat and chemmy, which is just another version of baccarat, and the reason he went for these two games was because the first of the James Bond movies had been released and these were Bond's favoured games. 'Jimmy thought to himself "If it's good enough for James Bond then it's good enough for Jimmy Baxter,"' Henderson says, laughing. 'That's how he thought. He would have the best of gear on and he would sit at the tables and play against the banker as if he was Sean Connery. He loved doing that kind of thing. Having the right image was important. I think he liked to cause a stir when he walked into any of the clubs or any of the hotel bars he went to. I'll tell you what else – Jimmy Baxter never had to go looking for women. The women were out there looking for Jimmy Baxter. They were dropping out of the sky for him.'

The one-time Rangers captain and then manager, John Greig, was another of the new breed who came into the team when Baxter had established himself at Rangers. He confirms Henderson's assessment of Baxter's sense of style. 'Jim seemed to set the style in Glasgow. If he was wearing something one week then you would see other people picking up on that and a whole trend would begin – and it had started with him. To me he was something of a superstar when I started to get into the first team. He played that way and he dressed that way. Everything he did was like a fashion statement and he revelled in all of that.

'I used to watch him in training when he took possession and you could see how superbly he could control that ball. His public image would never tell you all about him because while he was full of swagger on and off the field he could be very, very helpful to young players. I know that because I was just one of those he went out of his way to assist. Before my debut in the first team he pulled me aside, got a hold of a brush and then laid it down on the dressing room floor. "Just imagine that's a net," he said and started off a game of head tennis with me and I realised that was his way of taking my mind off the game and keeping me from getting too nervous.

'It worked too – we were playing against Airdrie in a League Cup tie and I was at inside right. After only ten minutes I scored a goal and we won 4–1 in the end. When I became a permanent member of the first team I was at right half and Ronnie McKinnon was centre half and I sat in beside him and let Jimmy have his freedom and he would run things. He was a genius when he had that ball at his feet and he would have been able to take his place in any team in the world in the early 60s. He could have gone to Real Madrid or Benfica or either of the two Milan teams and he would have more than held his own in that kind of company. He had all the skill you could look for and an abundance of confidence because he knew exactly what he could do with the ball.

'His one problem was that he wouldn't train. He couldn't get his head round the running and the exercising we had to go through before we were allowed to play a practice game. He used to tell me that I would burn myself out the way I trained and the way I ran around the park during games. "You'll be finished by the time you're 25 if you don't slow down," he would say. Ironically, I was playing until I was 36 years old and Jimmy was finished by the time he reached thirty. That should never have happened, but there were times when he came into training that he couldn't bite his fingers and he would just go through and lie in the bath trying to recover. Sometimes he never made the training at all, he just could not or would not make the effort.'

Manager Scot Symon was aware of what was happening but continued to pamper the player he had bought as part of his strategy to reshape Rangers, take them away from their traditional power play, push the memories of the famed Iron Curtain defence into the past and present a more skilful side than had ever been seen at Ibrox before. Baxter was crucial to Symon's plans and the manager was willing to risk alienating those he probably saw as lesser players to keep his superstar sweet. Even Ralph Brand, a close buddy of Baxter from their time together at Rangers until his final illness and death, was angered at the stance adopted by Symon.

'The manager had a soft spot for Jim and I don't think he did him any favours by letting him off with so much,' he says. 'His normal thinking seemed to be clouded when it came to Jim. He allowed him to carry on whatever way he liked as long as he turned it on when it came to the matches. The rest of us could see what was happening and the morale in the dressing room was affected. Even when there were bust-ups in the dressing room after games and Jim was involved then it was inevitable that Symon would take his side. Anyone who lifted his hands to Stanley was liable to be in deep trouble. That was just the way it was – Symon seemed determined to protect his star player, his main investment, if you like, no matter what the rest of us thought.

'Of course, we will never know if any other approach would have changed things as far as Jim was concerned. He was such a tearaway that he didn't listen to advice from anyone. He was always intent on doing what he wanted in football and in life. Sometimes I would suggest that he should do a little bit extra training and he would look at me as if I was daft. And his answer was always the same. He would just shake his head and say: "If I trained the way you do I wouldn't be able to play in a match on a Saturday. I'd have nothing left." He believed that and therefore he wouldn't make any extra effort at getting himself even a little bit fitter. To be honest he was just given too much freedom. Now that was the right thing to do when he was playing because you could not ask him to fit himself into a team pattern. He had to be allowed to do what he wanted because that's when he was at his best. But when that freedom was extended to his off-field antics then it was wrong. That's what led to his break with Rangers and all the disappointments which came after he left Ibrox.'

When that break came it did so because the directors had finally lost patience, and even Symon was beginning to realise that the various escapades would ultimately damage the club. Essentially the problem was over money. Baxter had demanded more money at the end of every season when the clubs were bound to offer their playing staff fresh contracts. His hope, always, was that Rangers, realising his value to the team, would give him more money than the other players at the club. It was not something that was even considered by the board. Yet it became something of a matter of principle to the player. As Billy McNeill stressed earlier, money in itself was not important to Jim Baxter except as a means of buying the new suits he wanted or allowing him to drink and gamble as often as he wanted. In fact Baxter had already increased his earnings considerably by signing a contract with the *Sunday Mirror*. His deal there brought him almost as much money every week as playing for Rangers did.

The newspaper's chief Scottish football writer at the time, Rodger Baillie, reveals: 'When he started off the column he was earning £35 a week with Rangers and we were paying him almost as much. And when he left he was eventually earning £45 at Ibrox and his money from the paper had gone up to forty guineas – Fleet Street payments were in guineas back then – so you can see that he was making good money for those days. His contract with us raised eyebrows on the Scottish newspaper scene and so did the acceptance of the column by Scot Symon, who had to give his permission and who was not always too kindly disposed to that kind of thing.

'Looking back now, however, I think that Symon welcomed this extra money. He would have seen it as a way of keeping Jim happy for a little bit longer. He had not been able to persuade the board to alter the wage structure. They would not budge on that. But now, suddenly, here was a way for Jim to almost double his wages and that might, just might, be enough to keep him happy for a little while at least. He actually bent over backwards to help us work things out, even allowing Jim time off training to travel down to London to meet the paper's top brass and sign the deal. Of course Baxter was Symon's favourite player and I think he saw him as the jewel in the crown as far as his Rangers team was concerned. He didn't want to risk losing him and this was a way to give him the extra money he was always looking for. I mean the re-signing business at the end of every season became something of a soap opera because Jim was always holding out and Rangers were always refusing to give in to his demands. It was something of a saga, and the bottom line was that neither of the two parties involved wanted to be seen to lose face. Letting Baxter do the column helped solve the long-running dilemma.

'I think that Symon, on his own, would have found some way to give Baxter the extra cash he was looking for because he knew the incredible influence he had on the team and he wanted to see that continue. But, back then, the board was all-powerful and in his later years as manager Symon was particularly wary of John Lawrence, a formidable figure whom he saw as a chairman who would want to change things at the club, unlike his predecessor, Bailie John Wilson, who was much more moderate in style and would not have wanted to adopt the hands-on approach that Lawrence, a highly successful businessman in Glasgow, favoured.

'To outsiders it may have seemed that Scot Symon held one of the most prestigious managerial positions in British football, but the truth of the matter was that the real power lay in the boardroom. It was doubtful that he had the strength to oppose the directors in what they saw as a very important matter of principle. He was literally helpless when it came to trying to negotiate a fresh wage deal for Baxter. He would have had sympathy with him but that cut no ice for the men who controlled the club, and I think that Jim realised that, even as he put in transfer requests on a couple of occasions before the club did agree to sell him. By then the transfer was unavoidable even though Baxter did not want to leave.'

Part of the problem lay in Baxter's own nature. When he believed he had a grievance of any kind then he would not settle until he settled it in his favour. There was no way that he would be content, no way that he would back off from what he perceived to be a major point of principle. In this case it would have meant accepting what he considered poor wages from his major employer when his view was that he was helping earn massive amounts of cash for the men who held his destiny in their hands – and he wanted to share that wealth. He felt quite strongly and genuinely that the players were being short-changed by the people who ran the game and he wanted to see that altered.

He was an unlikely crusader and it has to be said that Baxter was not campaigning for the common good – he wanted a bigger share of the pot for himself even though he did note that his team-mates suffered too under the set-up which saw money pour into the clubs from the massive gates they drew and then be meted out to the players in remarkably slim pay packets. There was a myth around that time that the Rangers bonuses brought their players far more money than they could earn elsewhere. The reality was that the bonuses gave them greater earning power simply because they were winning more games than their rivals – not because there was more money on offer than at other clubs. Meanwhile their salaries remained stuck fast in the £40-a-week area for some years after Baxter had left the club.

Two years after he had been transferred to Sunderland, a one-time team-mate, Jimmy Millar, a long-serving first-team player, was handed a free transfer. That was in June 1967 and the previous season had seen Millar earn his highest-ever salary – it was just £45 a week. Looking back, Millar reflects: 'People kept telling me about the big money I was making at Rangers. The best wage I ever had was 45 quid a week and that was in my final season. And the bonuses weren't all that good. OK, if you won the league or one of the two cups then you were given a special bonus, but on a week-to-week basis you were getting a couple of pounds for a win and you were paid that money twice a year. You were given a few hundred quid at Christmas and then, again, at the end of the season. But you couldn't work out what you had been given in any specific game. They didn't tell you, just handed you the money. Even the manager, Scot Symon, wouldn't tell you how the club arrived at the bonus figure. It was a strange way of working.

'The directors still held on to that attitude that we should be playing for the jersey, that it was an honour to be at Rangers. So I could understand where Jimmy Baxter was coming from when he asked for a better pay deal at the end of every season. He would have these rows and there would be all the publicity and, in the end, he was forced to re-sign for the same money as the rest of us. The board would never give way on that because they knew it would open the floodgates for the rest of the players. If he was going to get a pay rise then we would all be looking for a pay rise. That's what should have happened, we should all have been handed more money. But when Jim made a serious issue of it I knew that he would be sold. It was inevitable that the club would want him out the door. The official view was always the same – that no player was bigger than Rangers Football Club and that was not going to be altered for Jim Baxter or for anyone else.'

Symon's rearguard action to keep the player as happy as possible could not last forever. The manager had given his blessing to the *Sunday Mirror* contract to allow Baxter greater earning power. He had given him so much leeway in disciplinary matters at the club that he had, in the opinion of several of the senior pros, 'lost the dressing room', and the damage was not only among those who were coming to the end of their first team lives. Younger players, too, failed to understand why there should be one law for the star player and quite another law for them.

Entering the team as teenagers, Jim Forrest and Alex Willoughby were bewildered at the way their idol was given such freedom. Even now, forty years later, they have difficulty in coming to terms with the double standards applied by Scot Symon.

Forrest left the club after carrying the can for the shock Scottish Cup defeat from Berwick Rangers in 1967 and the scars caused by that still trouble him. 'Symon could be a very strange man,' he points out, 'a distant, aloof man and someone who had been at Rangers as a player and who returned to be manager after Bill Struth stepped down. So he knew how the club operated – knew its traditions, even though a lot of them were remnants of another time – and, for the most part, he tried to maintain the discipline he had known himself in his playing days. We could not move one inch out of line but, with Jim, it was always a case of "anything goes". My own view is that he should have been disciplined like the rest of us from the moment he stepped through the front door at Ibrox. But Symon just did not know how to handle him. He had never come across a player who had the attitude that Jim Baxter had. He probably thought to himself that there were several options available to him.

'The first was that he could discipline him and risk having Jim stop trying on the field; the second was that he could just sell him on and get his money and possibly a little bit of profit back or he could soft pedal with him, give him his own way and put up with all the problems he brought because the team needed him. He went for the third and it worked out for him for five seasons. Of course, I doubt that Symon realised that the more latitude he gave Jim then the more liberties he would take. That was the way it was with him. Rangers did need him – and I needed him! He made a lot of goals for me but finally it was not down to his football skill, it was down to all that was happening in his life away from Ibrox and the demands for more money which were given a lot of publicity and which embarrassed the directors. They did not like club business being discussed in the newspapers and then, subsequently, all round Glasgow. That did not suit them. They always wanted to keep everything in-house and so when Jim began to go public and to make his unhappiness known we all knew that he was on a collision course with the club and we also knew that this meant he would be sold. The directors were not going to give way, nor were they going to let him remain a Rangers player.'

Baxter's behaviour did nothing to help the situation. It's

probably true that he would have preferred to stay with the club – John Greig is swift to point out that, while he was doubtless given many opportunities to criticise Rangers, he chose not to do so even when he might have been able to use the money on offer from the tabloids. He did not bad-mouth the club during the bad times and latterly he would agree that his best years were spent at Ibrox, but the quarrel over wages had taken on a personal note pitting the 'rebel' player against the club establishment.

Any time that happened the club was always ready to push the blame for any rift on to the player – 'spin doctoring' is not a present-day invention. Rangers had journalists they felt they could trust to put across their point of view in any such unseemly squabble, and when that happened it was done in such a way as to question the player's loyalty. That was a sure-fire method to bring the serried ranks of fans on to the side of the club they supported. The mantra was simple and lost nothing through being used so often over the years – 'no one was bigger than the club' – seven words which became a rallying call for the support, eager as always to prove their own allegiance to the Rangers cause.

The winger, Willie Henderson, a Scotland international and a club hero in his own right, suffered himself on one occasion when he dared to ask for a transfer and found that he was on the receiving end of the club's propaganda machine. It was not a pleasant experience and it was one that he had seen used before when Baxter's wage row with Rangers escalated to such a degree that there was no way back for either side.

Henderson is angry even now at how things were handled: 'If you did anything at all to rock the boat then the club just hung you out to dry. They kept a very respectable distance away from the press most of the time but when it suited them they were very good at manipulating newspapers. It happened to me when I asked for a transfer – and it happened to Jimmy Baxter too. If you were looking for a move or in his case a signing-on fee and a better salary, then you were portrayed as a "rebel", as someone who was not a "true Ranger". Believe me that was the phrase they used and a lot of the supporters went along with the party line wondering who we thought we were asking for more money from the club.

'Well, we were just working-class lads trying to better ourselves, trying to make a better life. When he had to suffer criticism from the club I think it was like a slap in the face to him. He was hurt by it. And he knew that the directors were behind it and that Symon's hands were tied. If it had been left to Symon then he would have given him the money. I am sure of that. It was a stupid, stupid decision and even after all these years I can still hardly believe what these men did to the best footballer who ever played for the Rangers.

'Baxter was such a good player and Rangers were never as good a team after he was sold. We were still OK by Scottish standards – though things started to go wrong for us. But before that, with Jimmy in the team, we were looking beyond the domestic scene. We were reaching the stage that the Old Firm clubs have reached nowadays. Quite simply, we were outgrowing the Scottish game. When he left we were back to being a force at home and not much more than that. That's how influential he was to the team.'

As regards the kernel of the dispute, Henderson remains firm in the belief that the directors blundered, holding on as they did to their policy that no one was bigger than the club. 'It was never about Jimmy Baxter being bigger than the club,' he says. 'That was something the directors hid behind. He didn't want to leave Rangers, all he wanted was some tangible signs from the board that they recognised the contribution he had made, and could still make, to the club's success. He didn't get a single sign. In reality it was about a world-class player being paid what he deserved to be paid. I handed in two transfer requests before I was able to get some kind of decent wage from the club – they should have adopted that policy earlier and given it to Stanley. Rangers looked upon themselves as a big club and yet when it came to rewarding their players they were minor league. It was decades before we saw that thinking change. Back then the club did not appreciate the prestige and the success that a player of his ability could bring. It was supposed to be enough that you had been given the chance to sign for the club – and it was the same at Celtic, too – that it was an honour and if you wanted to better yourself then all you were doing was biting the hand that fed you. It was absolutely unbelievable the way they ran things, just as if we were all still in Victorian times!'

All of the players suffered to some degree or another under the outdated regime. Bobby Shearer spent nine years with the club after being bought from Hamilton Accies for just £2,000 in December 1955. In April 1965 he was handed a free transfer after playing in more than 450 first-team games and captaining the club for several of their most successful seasons. The decision to release him then meant that the club did not have to pay him the princely sum of £750 that he was entitled to receive as a benefit after completing ten years with the one club.

'I had gone to see Symon about re-signing,' recalls Shearer, still hurt about the circumstances in which he was told. 'That was something that you did every year, and when I was talking to him I asked what the position would be regarding my benefit payment. He just looked at me and told me that I should not concern myself about the £750. I asked why that was and he replied that I would not be with the club when the money fell due. That's how I learned my career with Rangers was over. Symon could be ruthless and, to be honest, the club didn't care very much about the players. When you were doing well for them, then everything was fine, but after that you were tossed aside. They were great days when you were in the first team but they were cruel times when things started to go against you. We all knew that but, I suppose, you always hoped that it wouldn't happen to you.

'Jim was never going to win his fight with the club about money. OK, he knew that the players down south were making more money than he was and that annoyed him. He would hear all about the wages from the Scotland players who were down in England when there were international matches. Naturally he wanted to have the same standard of living as they enjoyed. But Rangers wouldn't budge. If you think about it we left the club in the same season – in April they wouldn't even give me £750 when I was seven months or so short of ten years' service so they weren't going to give Jim the ten grand he was looking for as a signing-on fee. They enjoyed all the success – but if they could get that without paying too much for it then they enjoyed it even more. I knew they would sell him because they didn't have the vision to keep him.'

Baxter himself was feeling embarrassed when he joined up with the Scotland squads and even more so when he played for the Rest of the World against England at Wembley in 1963. He mixed with the top players of Europe and South America, with Nilton Santos and Ferenc Puskas and Alfredo Di Stefano and the sole other Scot, Denis Law, knowing that the paltry £35 a week he was then earning at Ibrox was small change to the men he was playing alongside. When England won the game 2–1 his chagrin grew and on returning to Glasgow and being asked how he had enjoyed the experience, he commented typically: 'Too many chiefs and no' enough Indians.' Have no doubts that Baxter saw himself as one of 'the chiefs', even though his club would not recognise his growing stature in the game with a salary to match those of the foreign stars he was mixing with and matching on the field of play.

It was another bone of contention, another grievance on the lengthening list that Baxter was drawing up in his mind as he continued to look for a better deal. At the end of season 1964–65 the wrangling was over and Rangers agreed to transfer their greatest asset only a few months after his finest performance for the Glasgow club in a European Cup game against the Austrian champions, Rapid Vienna, in the Prater Stadium.

The timing could not have been worse for Rangers, but the

directors had had enough and Scot Symon was told that his superstar had to be sold immediately. It seemed that the matter had been taken out of the hands of the manager and Baxter's time was up.

6 THE END OF THE IBROX ERA

The Prater Stadium, though, was a setting fit for any finale, with the giant wheel featured in the film, *The Third Man*, rising above the terraces and 70,000 people there to watch a memorable performance from the midfield maestro who ran the game as he had run so many others in far less impressive surroundings. Those who were there maintain that this was a virtuoso display that eclipsed all the others he had given.

It was so utterly majestic that it gave the Rangers players and supporters a belief that victory in the European Cup, a tournament that had thrown up so many calamities for them in the past, was possible if the glorious run of form could be sustained.

It was strangely ironic that the Rangers board of directors should decide that their troublesome star was to be sold so soon after his leg had been broken in that memorable performance against Rapid Vienna. They had placed him on the list once before in December of 1962 but that rift was healed, at least temporarily, and the following season, after he had held out for some time, Baxter had signed a new one-year deal with the Ibrox club. The negotiations each close season had taken on the form of a ritual dance with Baxter insisting, initially, that he was unhappy with the offer which had been made to him for the forthcoming year, and Scot Symon insisting, on the club's behalf, that no further offer would be made. Each year, later than the rest of his team-mates, as his way of making a protest, Baxter fell into line with well-publicised reluctance.

On this occasion, however, the directors were apparently in no mood to play the annual game. It is probable they had run out of patience and probable, too, that Baxter had made up his mind that either the club paid him what he was looking for or he would move elsewhere to find the financial rewards he felt his talents deserved. He was, after all, being married that summer and he needed money to buy a house. If that was not going to be provided by Rangers then he would go to a club where he would be appreciated and where money for such items as houses would be readily available.

There should have been a stampede for his services. There had long been talk of interest from Arsenal where Billy Wright was the manager and from the other London giants Tottenham Hotspur where Baxter had an ally on the field in the club captain Dave MacKay. There had also been strong hints emanating from Italy that Inter Milan would try to tempt him to Serie A. None of these supposedly interested clubs made an offer.

The problem that Baxter now had to face up to was that his hell-raising reputation had frightened off potential buyers. At the time I asked Tommy Docherty, who was in charge at Chelsea, if he would be making a move to buy his fellow Scot.

'Leopards and spots,' he told me. 'Jim won't change his ways and he would have more chances to misbehave in London than he has in Glasgow. I'd love to have a player with his ability in my team but it's too big a risk. If Rangers can't discipline him then who can?'

That was one potential suitor gone even though Docherty had a reputation of being ready to spend big money and Chelsea were one of the highest paying clubs in England. But it was suddenly a no-go area for the unhappy Ranger. The nibbles from Inter came to nothing as well despite the player's own efforts to stimulate the interest of the Italian giants who were dominating Europe, having won the European Cup for the second successive season as Baxter was being informed that Rangers were ready to sell him.

Although Denis Law and Joe Baker had returned home from Italy chastened by their experiences there, Baxter had declared himself ready to accept the strict disciplinary code that was laid down to players in Italian football. The challenge appealed to him, but it was surely an adventure that would have ended in tears if it had ever taken place.

The lack of interest from any of the major clubs in the game must have hurt his pride, but it was an indication as to just how fearful managers and chairmen were of his off-field reputation as a troublemaker. And it could only have been the growing rumours surrounding the player's lifestyle which were well enough discussed in Glasgow and which were doubtless swirling around the board rooms in England, that made the pick of the clubs beat a hasty retreat from any proposed deal.

Certainly it could not have been his ability. Baxter had now played three times against England in the Home International Championships and been on the winning side in each game –

one of these was at Wembley in 1963 when he scored both his country's goals. And in the season which had just ended he had guided Rangers through two seriously difficult European Cup ties against Red Star Belgrade and Rapid Vienna before breaking his leg in the closing minutes of the second leg game in Austria. That was to be his last hurrah for Rangers. He was injured early in December, returned to the first team in March, and played only eight more league games and one Scottish Cup tie, a third round meeting with Hibs which Rangers lost 2–1.

The Prater Stadium, though, was a setting fit for any finale, with the giant wheel featured in the film, *The Third Man*, rising above the terraces and 70,000 people there to watch a memorable performance from the midfield maestro who ran the game as he had run so many others in far less impressive surroundings. Those who were there maintain that this was a virtuoso display that eclipsed all the others he had given.

It was so utterly majestic that it gave the Rangers players and supporters a belief that victory in the European Cup, a tournament that had thrown up so many calamities for them in the past, was possible if the glorious run of form could be sustained. Professional footballers are not often given to superlatives but all of the Ibrox men involved that day remain convinced that Jim Baxter gave one of the finest solo performances ever seen in the tournament in conditions that should have been a hindrance to the passing skills which made him so special. After severe snowfalls in the Austrian capital, the pitch had been cleared but the playing surface was heavy with mud. Nothing, though, could deter the Rangers number six on that December afternoon.

Rangers had gone into the second round tie confident that they could march on into the quarter-finals mainly because of the way they had overcome the Yugoslavian champions Red Star in the opening tie. The team from Belgrade, along with their city rivals Partizan, were seen as dangerous opponents at that period. In the first game at Ibrox an 80,000 crowd saw Baxter involved in setting up all three goals with Ralph Brand getting two and Jim Forrest the other in a 3–1 victory. In Belgrade, however, Rangers lost 4–2 and it required a last minute header from centre half Ron McKinnon to take the game into a play-off. Interestingly, a few years later, when the away goals rule was introduced, Rangers would have gone straight through, but on this occasion a third game was scheduled for Highbury where Rangers repeated their 3–1 Ibrox win. Again Baxter dominated and again Brand and Forrest shared the goals, with the young centre forward getting two this time on the Arsenal ground.

Then came Rapid in Glasgow where Baxter opened up the packed Austrian defence for Davy Wilson to get the game's solitary goal ten minutes into the second half. Despite the narrow lead Rangers were convinced they would win the return as they flew out of Glasgow Airport just short of three weeks later. Baxter himself observed: 'I had the feeling that we would win the game in Vienna. There was no way that I thought it was going to be easy because Rapid were a strong team and a very experienced team. But we were starting to learn some lessons about European football by that time and I had the feeling that if we played as well as we had in Glasgow then we would go through.'

That is how it turned out and Baxter would agree with those who thought that it was among the best games he ever played for Rangers, though he would add the rider that it was easily the most accomplished team performance during his five years with the Glasgow club.

Alex Willoughby, one of the reserves that day, declares emphatically: 'The performance Jim gave in Vienna in that second game against Rapid was one of the finest one-man performances I have ever seen in a game at that level. We are talking about the Austrian champions as opposition, and Rapid were rated as one of the top teams on the Continent then, and he was at his very best. Stanley took everything that was going that day except for the gate money – and the way he played they should have given that to him! The Austrian players could not do anything to stop him until the last minute of the game when he was tackled and we found out that his right leg was broken. He was captain that day and when the break happened Rangers were winning 2–0 on the day – which meant 3–0 on aggregate. The tie was won and all Jim had to do with the ball was lift it to the back of the terracings, get it out of play, and wait for the referee's final whistle. But he always had a different outlook from most other players. He was just so good and he was so used to inviting tackles and then stepping away from them, still keeping the ball, that it would not have occurred to him that he would be caught late. That's what happened. Off the field we didn't realise at first that the leg had been broken, we didn't even know if it was a serious injury or not.'

Jim Forrest played in the game and scored the first goal from a Baxter pass which defeated the offside trap the Austrians had adopted to stop the Rangers attacks, and he knew what had happened immediately. 'Quite a few of us who were close to the incident knew he had broken his leg,' he affirms. 'The crazy thing is that it should have been avoided and it could have been avoided. It has to be said that the injury was partly his own fault. He invited the tackle from the Austrian player when the game was over to all intents and purposes. We had won and there was maybe less than a minute to go when Jim decided to show everyone just how good he was. He had that streak in him – all really skilful players share that, to be fair – they have amazing self-confidence and they want to show people what they can do with the ball, just how good they are. On this occasion it all went terribly wrong for him.

'You know he was still lying on the ground when the referee blew for time up. It was awful and, of course, later it turned out to be a tremendously significant injury both for him and for the club. He had not returned to the first team when we played Inter Milan in the quarter-final. We lost 3–2 but with Jim in the team we could well have beaten the Italians who went on to win the trophy when the defeated Benfica in the final at their own San

Siro Stadium. That is how close I think we were that season, the closest to a European trophy I had ever been and was ever likely to be. The rest of the season petered out into an anti-climax – we finished fifth in the league, lost in the third round of the Scottish Cup to Hibs and didn't even qualify for Europe.'

Bobby Shearer was another spectator and even now you sense his frustration as he recollects: 'Jim always had that bit of arrogance, or cheek, if you like, about him, and when you played the game the way he did you needed that. Now in Vienna he had been absolutely magnificent, the best I had ever seen him play and that was saying a lot. Then he gained possession right at the end of the game and he took the ball round this poor fellow who had been trying to mark him all afternoon, then he went back and took it round him again, and when he did it for a third time the lad just cracked and lunged into the tackle. He had had enough of Jim taking the mickey out of him. Up to then Jim had always got away with that sort of thing – not just in this game but also in all manner of games – but this time the Austrian defender caught him just above the ankle and the leg was broken. It was a tragedy which he should have avoided.'

Baxter himself acknowledges that much when he discussed the incident in an interview with Roddy Forsyth: 'We were enjoying ourselves, we really were. When we went one up they couldn't cope with us. There was some slush on top of the pitch and that was absolutely made for me, believe it or not. Their defenders couldn't turn on it so I kept pinging the ball round them. You showed them the ball and once they made the commitment they couldn't stop. Their right half was Walter Skocik and he must have had the worst night of his career. I just kept nutmegging him. I don't know how many balls I put through his legs. It must have been dozens – I lost count.

'I'll tell you how good we were – the Rapid supporters were throwing snowballs at their own players. Not only that, they had started cheering us. We were nearly at the final whistle and I knew that there wasn't long to go so I started walking towards the dressing room. Something happened near me and I turned round and asked for the ball, and the next thing I knew – whack! – Skocik hit me from behind and broke my leg. I don't think he meant to do it, I really don't. I gave him a roasting that night, I'm telling you. If I had been him against me I would have kicked me much sooner, I can assure you of that. I was in scintillating form that night. Everything I was trying was coming off. But I knew at that moment that my leg was broken – I heard it break.'

While the rest of the Rangers team was taken by coach to Salzburg to enable them to get a flight home – the weather had deteriorated so badly that Vienna Airport was closed – Baxter insisted that he could not make the 200-mile journey through the snow and remained in Vienna. After the fracture had been set and a plaster put in place he returned to his hotel room – and, typically, organised a party with two of his friends from Glasgow, and a girl came along to stay the night and offer the hero of the hour some tender, loving care. Scot Symon had scarcely left his precious charge alone before he was on to room service ordering up bottles of champagne, for himself, and brandy and Black Label for his friends, and three fillet steaks all signed for with a flourish which would have been instantly familiar back in the St Enoch Hotel in Glasgow.

Nothing seemed able to break through the cocoon of confidence that Baxter wrapped round himself even at the very worst of times. While Symon fretted and his team-mates were concerned over how he might recover from this setback he was lying back enjoying himself, living his life, as always, exactly the way he wanted to live it. Storm clouds might have been gathering but they were not able to penetrate to the five-star luxury of that grand Viennese hotel where the future had been placed firmly on hold.

The immediate future was that Baxter was out of action for the next three months and in that time Rangers hit a form slump that could be traced back to the moment that the Austrian defender, Walter Skocik, lost patience with the teasing and taunting from his opponent, lashed out, and broke his leg. It was not a career-threatening fracture. Davy Wilson suffered a similar injury and came back from it without problems.

Not only that, the one-time Hibs winger and Scotland team manager Willie Ormond had the same type of break on three separate occasions and returned to action unscathed from all of them. It should have been the same for Baxter but, somehow, there was a sense that something happened that afternoon in Vienna that affected him deeply. He was to play top-level football for five years following the injury but, while there were occasions when he seemed able to return to his former glories, these became fewer and fewer. Indeed, the dismal seasons of mediocrity at Sunderland and Nottingham Forest, and then the sad return to Rangers, brought him more disillusionment than distinction. There was the wonderful Wembley of 1967 but even there he did not reach the heights that he had in the Prater Stadium.

After that game the Rapid Coach Bimbo Binder had declared: 'We were not just beaten by a very fine team but, also, by a truly world-class player in Jim Baxter.' If that was not praise enough, one of the Austrian television commentators claimed that the Scot was the best player seen in Vienna since Pele had visited the city. These accolades now take on the form of epitaphs for a career that was to end far too soon, and which would never make the permanent mark on the entire world of football in the way it should have done.

There are those who were close to him at the time of the injury who feel that it was not to blame in any physical sense for the decline that soon set in. Others believe that the injury, coming as it did just six months before Rangers decided to sell him, was a psychological blow which, coupled with the Ibrox decision to let him leave, dented the player's confidence. Another school of thought is that, after being caught by Skocik's challenge, Baxter began to perceive signs of fallibility almost as if he knew that this was a tackle he should have been able to glide away from as he had been able to do so often in other games when a similar situation arose. It is probable that there is truth in all the theories. Certainly, while the leg break itself should not have caused any lasting damage, Baxter had to cope with the problem of remaining fit when even his very limited training schedule was to be interrupted by the injury.

When Davy Wilson broke his leg he continued to exercise to maintain some level of fitness. It is unlikely that Jim Baxter did the same and so the levels of fitness that he had been able to maintain through his natural metabolism were allowed to drop. These levels were already low and Jim Forrest points out: 'When the injury in Vienna happened he was not in the best of shape – I am talking about his general fitness here – and he was never the same after that. I think, in fact, that was the beginning of the end for him. When that happened he was never able to get himself back to any real level of fitness, the kind he had to reach to continue to play at the highest level. It just wasn't there any more. Everyone knew that he was never as fit as he should have been right through his career, but then he was out for that three-month spell and when he returned to playing you could see that he was struggling. He never did get over that. Any fitness he had before the injury in Vienna vanished and when he came back into the first team he was never the same player.

'I suppose it should have been obvious to all of us that he would not work out as he should have done when he was recuperating. Because he neglected that part of his rehabilitation programme he suffered and, also, he was getting that little bit older just at the time when all the days of ducking and diving at training were starting to catch up with him. If he had trained properly then it would have stood him in good stead when the broken leg came along. But it was too late for him to change – and I doubt if he even contemplated for one minute changing his attitude.'

For some time, of course, Baxter had relied on his natural fitness to carry him through and, while much is made of his dislike of training and his over-indulgence off the field, it was always accepted that he could put in a shift to help his team-mates when they needed that. And there was one season while he was doing his National Service with the Black Watch when he played in well over one hundred games when you combined his appearances with Rangers and the various Army selects. He would not have been able to do that unless he was capable of reaching a more-than-reasonable degree of fitness.

John Greig observes: 'He worked hard in games to help the team. OK, he didn't train enough, and he was scarcely the fastest player you would ever see, but he could get around the pitch for the full ninety minutes when I first played with him. Later all the late nights and the drinking and the lack of training caught up with him. The things he could get away with when he was in his early and mid-twenties became more and more difficult as the years went by. Of course, the game was becoming faster too, and while he could sometimes slow it down to his pace, that became harder for him.

'When you are playing and you are getting that bit older then your reflexes slow a little, and if you haven't trained as you should have done over the years it all catches up, and that's what happened to Jim. It wasn't the broken leg, as such, it was all the work he should have been doing and didn't do which saw him suffer after he left Rangers.'

The psychological blow of the leg break was something which could not be ignored, and Billy McNeill was one who stressed its importance. He believes: 'When he suffered that broken leg playing for Rangers against Rapid Vienna in the European Cup it was a massive, massive blow, not just physically, but psychologically. You see, Jimmy never ever thought that could happen to him. Lesser players would be caught by a clumsy challenge but not him. He used to skip out of tackles and laugh at the guys who had made them. You would get players who would try to kick him, but he was always so aware that he would make them look foolish and he believed that he would always be able to do that. This kind of sixth sense he had when someone was coming for him was important to him – then, suddenly, he is hit with a late challenge and that damaged him.

'People who didn't really know Jimmy won't realise that one of his greatest attributes was his natural fitness. It was something he was born with, something he was blessed with, and it worked for him during his years at Ibrox. He could get about that park for the whole ninety minutes then and the myth about his tackling should be kicked into touch as well. I am not going to suggest that he was the greatest of tacklers, but he read things so well that he could nick in and make important interceptions. There was a real bravado about his play and that didn't survive the injury unscathed! To add to his troubles Rangers decided that they were going to sell him and that didn't help. As a club and as a team Rangers were perfectly suited to Baxter at that time in his life. He flourished there as he was never going to flourish again. It was the perfect setting for Jimmy and the skills he possessed. When he left he was always heading downwards.'

That was a matter of distress to many who had seen Baxter as an icon of style both on and off the field and, while so many see the afternoon in Vienna as the summit of his Rangers career, one formidable voice is raised against that. Sir Alex Ferguson, who played against Baxter and alongside him, was also a spectator at Ibrox on the night of 15 November 1960 as the Glasgow club played a European tie.

Baxter had been at Rangers a scant five months on that night when the Scottish Cup holders went out to play the second leg of their second round European Cup Winners' Cup tie against the Germans from Borussia Moenchengladbach, the team later to be the single senior side that new Scotland international team manager Berti Vogts played for in his lengthy career. The Glasgow club had beaten Ferencvaros of Hungary by a 5–3 aggregate in the first round. Then they had gone to West Germany to win 3–0 in the first leg and banish, for the moment, the memories of their dreadful European Cup semi-final defeat by an embarrassing 12–4 margin against Eintracht Frankfurt the previous season. The supporters wanted revenge at their own stadium and 50,000 of them were there and Baxter was in the mood to give them exactly what they were looking for.

Sir Alex takes up the story: 'Without any doubt the European Cup Winners' Cup game against Borussia Moenchengladbach was the best match he ever played for Rangers. There were other great games, of course, but, for me, that was the one above all the rest. That night he was unbelievable. Rangers won the game 8–0 and Jim Baxter was involved in every one of the goals. He scored the first one and he made the other seven! Believe me, he was simply magnificent. The German players did not know what had hit them. I thought he was better that night than he was in either of the two Wembley games. Yet Ibrox was like a paddy field, it was a sea of mud and he went out with rubber studs and played as if the surface was perfect. The conditions made no difference to him. I have never seen anything like that from a player. He scored early on, the first goal, after only a few minutes, and then he set up all the others. There was one own goal and even that you would put down for Jim as an assist. He ran the entire show.'

Sir Alex remains an unashamed admirer of Baxter but he is forced to admit that it was an almost inevitable managerial decision when Rangers decided to sell him. The most successful team boss in British football history and a known disciplinarian, Ferguson looks back down the years and says sadly: 'When you remember the broken leg in Vienna and I try to put myself into Scot Symon's shoes then I have to say you would be asking questions about his physical condition. First of all you have a player who has been getting himself into bother off the field and everyone knows he is not behaving properly and here he is asking for more money from the club – once again!

'So, one way is to give him the money and ask him to stop drinking – but that had been tried before and there was no way that he was ever going to do that. Now, you have to look at the injury, and while a broken leg is something that most players get over – Davy Wilson did it without a problem – most of the victims do specialised training to keep up their fitness. Jim would not work that way. That wouldn't be part of his agenda. So, in a sense, he was the maker of his own destiny as far as the situation was concerned. And so, Symon, like any other manager of a football club, would weigh it up and, being under pressure himself, would realise that a transfer was the only answer.

'I don't know why the directors acted the way that they did with Scot Symon, who had been a tremendous servant to that club. But he was under a great deal of strain when I went there a few years after this and I found out that's how things had been for several years. He used to shake like a leaf at times and he had to face all of the problems he had on his own. He had never been one to court the press and he didn't have any friends there so, when he had his problems, there was no public support. If he had kept Jim then he would have had more problems. I don't see that he could have done anything else. And no one could have changed Jim. I was going to say that maybe Big Jock (Stein) might have done but then he had his own worries at times with wee Jinky (Jimmy Johnstone) and so it's doubtful if anyone could have changed his nature or the way that he behaved or, rather, misbehaved.

'Essentially he was a man of his time and these times were far different from today. There was not the same diligence in looking at what players did, and how they lived their lives, from a management perspective. It was a part of Jim, part of his personality, part of the era in which he grew up – and other players were the same. By the time any manager got a hold of them it was too late because the bad habits had been formed. It was just a part and parcel of working-class life that when men finished their work – and this was definitely true in the Fife coalfields, I know what Fifers can be like – they went to the social club for a drink. They worked long hours and it was hard for them and that was the only relaxation they knew and Jim was born into that way of life. Now it is a whole different ball game.

In my team I have Roy Keane who has not had a drink for five years and the rest of them scarcely drink at all. One or two may have the odd beer but that's all.

'When Jim was playing there was a drinking culture which affected a lot of players and if Scot Symon, a man he had a lot of respect for, could not get through to him then no one could have done so. He would not have listened to anyone. It would be nice to think otherwise, to think he could have been disciplined, and it would be easy to do that, too, but the way Jim was, the way Jim lived his life, nothing would have changed him.'

So most of the problems had been self-inflicted and, to be fair to him, he was always the first to acknowledge that, but the transfer out of Ibrox – while he had asked for that in various salary talks – was not what he really wanted. Deep down what Jim Baxter wanted was for Rangers to pay him the wages he desired and then allow him to carry on in the same sweet way. That was where he became his own worst enemy as the club simply tired of his indiscretions and Symon's influence in the boardroom waned.

Then as the 'bad boy' reputation grew, and more and more club managers in England saw him as a tearaway who would carry too much off-field baggage with him if he was bought, then so his options lessened. From talk of Inter Milan and Arsenal and Manchester United and Tottenham Hotspur, the pursuing clubs were being identified as Stoke City and Sunderland. The other, bigger clubs had been frightened off.

While recovering from his own leg break Dave MacKay had travelled north to watch the Scottish League meet the English League at Ibrox in what was an annual fixture. He saw his mate, Jim Baxter, practically run the game and later that night when he was leaving his Glasgow hotel he bumped into his manager from White Hart Lane, Bill Nicholson, who had also been up to watch the game with the Rangers star a likely signing target as Danny Blanchflower moved towards retirement.

MacKay mused recently: 'I knew that Bill Nick [Spurs

Manager Bill Nicholson] was looking for someone to play at half back because I had this broken leg which was going to keep me out for six months. So he wanted someone right away, if you like, but he also wanted someone long term because Danny Blanchflower was coming to the end of his career. I had been at left half for Spurs because Danny was on the other side but I knew I could play on the right because that's where I had been with Hearts as John Cumming, who was a good player, was on the left side. Really it was not going to make any difference to me where I was playing.

'So when I walked into Bill Nick at the entrance to this hotel in Glasgow after the inter-League game I thought straight away that Jim and I were going to be playing together at White Hart Lane. I would have loved that and I know that Jim would have fitted right into our team. I was excited at the thought – and then nothing happened. Just nothing. The manager never spoke to me about the game nor about Jimmy and yet I knew that he would have seen straight away that night that he was a special player who would have been ideal for Spurs. I could only think that Bill Nick had done his homework and that he had found out that Jim was not exactly the best-behaved player in the world and that would have put him off. He would not have tolerated anyone stepping out of line the way Jim did. He wouldn't have stood for it for one minute. So it had to be his lifestyle that went against him and this was a year or two before the Sunderland move. It was a disappointment to me personally and it must have been a major disappointment to Jim as well.

'He knew there had been some interest and he knew that he had played well that night against the English League, but our manager walked away from any deal. If he had moved to us at that time then everything might have worked out better for him. But you can never really know that because Jim would have had to change and it might have been too late for him even then. I still wish it had happened. We could have been good together, playing week in, week out in the same team – and a very good team at that.'

Baxter did know about the possibility of a transfer to the London club and it had gone beyond the mere 'interest' that MacKay had been aware of. Baxter spoke to Nicholson, who had already entered into talks with his opposite number, Scot Symon. But any proposed deal did not go further than these preliminary discussions, and Baxter himself put the failure to reach agreement down to his lifestyle. He also felt that, at the time, the Rangers officials involved might have encouraged Nicholson's doubts. When Sunderland expressed their interest in Baxter in the summer of 1965, no one at Rangers tried to dissuade them from following through with a formal offer of £72,500. Nor was any effort made to keep the player who had played such a significant role in the club's successes over the previous five seasons.

In some strange way, that appeared to cause Baxter a deal of grief. It was all right that he should be asking to leave Rangers but not, he thought, for Rangers to sell him without making any effort to keep him at Ibrox. Of course, he wanted more money, he had always insisted that he should be paid what he believed he was worth, but if he had thought things through he would have realised that joining Sunderland from Rangers was a sharp drop in prestige, something that was always important in Baxter's thinking. He admitted that he did not want to leave, always insisting that he had been forced to move for financial reasons. Basically he did not want to lose face by re-signing once again after yet another soap-opera-style saga of newspaper speculation surrounding the 'will-he won't-he' puzzle which had become a summer staple of the sports pages. And so he made up his mind that he would make the best of things, get the money he wanted, and put a brave face on the transfer to a club that never came close to the stature of the one he was leaving behind. It must have been galling to Baxter that some of his international team-mates had been able to find their way to the very clubs he had hoped to play for himself.

His old Celtic rival, and off-field mate, Pat Crerand had been first to go some years earlier when he joined Manchester United for a transfer fee of £56,000 in February 1963. The Dundee centre half Ian Ure was sold to Arsenal the following season for £62,000 and another year down the line the Dens Park striker Alan Gilzean went to Tottenham Hotspur for £72,000. All three clubs figured high on the list of where Baxter himself would have chosen to ply his trade in England – but he was not given that opportunity. Nor did he have the luxury of choice that Gilzean had gained for himself when the Dundee manager Bob Shankly wanted him to go to Sunderland for the same fee that the Tayside team had accepted from Arsenal for Ian Ure. The forward had other ideas. He, too, had a list of priorities drawn up, the two Liverpool teams, Manchester United, Arsenal and Spurs. He threatened to give up the game and Tottenham came in, paid £10,000 more than Sunderland had offered, and Gilzean spent ten successful years at White Hart Lane.

Baxter, a better player and a bigger name than any of the talented trio mentioned, found himself with the Roker Park club as the one destination left open to him. There he would be offered a healthy signing-on fee and double his weekly wages at the same time. It was, though, a step down in status no matter what gloss he attempted to apply to the deal when it became obvious that he was not wanted by the major players in the game down south nor by any of the top clubs in Europe. He must have realised then that he was already being called to account for the lack of discipline he had shown throughout his time at Ibrox.

As almost everyone who played with him, or against him, has said – Jim Baxter wanted to live his own life in his own way. Now he was learning that there was a price to be paid for that approach. He had been able to ignore the restraints that Rangers had attempted to place on him but, while he did so, those in positions of power in the game of football had taken note. The nights of revelry in the St Enoch Hotel, the all-night gambling sessions, the drinking and carousing around the city of Glasgow where his name had become a by-word for partying, were all taken into account when decisions were being made whether signing the best player of his generation was a risk worth taking. 'Slim Jim', the nickname given to him by the press and the supporters, had now become 'Bacardi Jim'.

Sir Alex Ferguson comments: 'Jim should have been here at Old Trafford, or at Arsenal or Spurs. Tottenham would have been an ideal club for him. He would have given them what they lost when John White died so tragically and then when Danny Blanchflower retired, and he would have been perfect alongside Dave Mackay. When you are a big name player and you leave a club like Rangers then you should be looking to go to a club of the equivalent size, but that didn't happen for him and it was a shame. He should never have been at Sunderland. That was the beginning of the end.

'There were some great games, though. One of the coaches here at United, Jim Ryan, remembers playing against him at Roker Park in 1967. He still says that Baxter took them apart; he ran the show and this was United on their way to the title. In the end Sunderland lost 2–1 but Jim has never forgotten Baxter's performance. He was like that on occasions but he was at the wrong club and his next stop at Forest was even worse. That's when the decline set in and Jim could do nothing about it. It was far too late for him by then. He had made his pact with the Devil a long time before and I don't think there was ever any question in his own mind that he was destroying himself. He had such a love of life that this was the price he was prepared to pay. Unfortunately there was that streak of self-destructiveness that has plagued so many Scots and, though it's always hard to say, I really do think that Jim probably knew what was going to happen to his career. He had decided that he was going to enjoy himself and live life to the full and that on the field he was going to play the game the way he wanted to, the way he believed it should be played. You see, Jim loved them both, life and football.'

All of these things counted against him, and even the lustre of his display in Vienna or his performances for Scotland – particularly in the games against England where he reigned supreme – were not enough to calm the fears of the top clubs. They saw Jim Baxter as a threat to the stability of their own teams, and as a potential for trouble off the field. They just didn't want to take any chances with the maverick from Fife even though his abundant skills were unmatched by any other player in Britain at that time.

Sunderland, managed by his one time Scotland international team boss, Ian McColl, were ready to follow through on their interest and so the transfer was set up, the fee was agreed at £72,000 and the Baxter era at Ibrox had ended. He would never regain the success that he had enjoyed there, nor the prestige that playing for Rangers had afforded him. As Willie Henderson sadly commented: 'Leaving Rangers was a disaster for him though we didn't realise until later on just how much of a disaster it was. I mean Sunderland Football Club, with all due respect, was not in the same league as Glasgow Rangers when it came to stature or prestige or history. It was not the place for him. I think that the day Jimmy Baxter left Rangers was the day he started off on the slippery downward slope and it just became slippier and slippier for him in the few years he spent down in England. It was a terrible career move and it was a bad day for Rangers too, believe me. We were never the same team without him.'

7 SUNDERLAND – AND THE DECLINE SETS IN

The problems which struck his hoped-for new beginning and which saw Baxter begin to self-destruct at an even faster rate than had been the case in Glasgow did not stem initially from the celebrity he enjoyed in the town nor from the increased amounts of cash he now had at his disposal – his *Sunday Mirror* column had continued with an increase to match the cult status he would now have in the North-East as well as in Scotland – but from the on-field disappointments which dogged him from his very first game for his new club. It was out there on the field of play that Baxter had always enjoyed himself most and at Rangers he had been supported by a team of quality footballers. Now that was no longer the case and he was soon to find that out in the most humiliating manner, in a way he could not have foreseen, and one which he could not have enjoyed as his old Glasgow rivals, Celtic, came south to rain on his parade.

In the early 1960s the publicity surrounding Jim Baxter exceeded any that had been enjoyed – or tolerated – by footballers who had gone before him. Perhaps the Celtic winger Charlie Tully had come closest in the previous decade, but Baxter took the game away from the back pages and inside the newspapers on to the news and features sections as the public realised that there was a special aura about the Rangers player. He was invited to do fashion shoots, for example, and when he became engaged to Jean Ferguson from Coatbridge the Scottish *Daily Express* paid him a thousand pounds for the exclusive story and a picture of the happy couple with the ring. The news took up most of the then broadsheet *Express* front page. It may have become commonplace for the glossy magazines *Hello!* and *OK* to buy up such stories – back then it was unknown!

But such was Baxter's celebrity that the *Express* happily forked out for the story and the *Sunday Mirror* continued to gain in circulation as a result of the player's weekly column. When the newspaper ran a monthly competition where the winner would have lunch with Baxter the response was enormous. It was by far the most successful contest the *Mirror* staged in Scotland and it underlined just how massive a personality he had become. When he and Jean were married in the bride's home town the traffic was stopped by police to allow the happy couple to leave the church. When the wedding limousines arrived for the reception at the St Enoch Hotel in Glasgow's city centre – Baxter's bailiwick, where else? – huge crowds waited to cheer them even though they knew that the idol of Ibrox was now leaving the club to play for Sunderland. His popularity had not waned in the slightest and it never did.

Baxter had wanted financial security from the move. And while he might have been able to find that in Glasgow he knew that it was not going to come from Rangers. The Reo Stakis organisation had approached him to front a bar and restaurant in Union Street for their rapidly expanding company. It would have meant his name going above the door and, perhaps, his attendance there several times a week. They were willing to pay substantially for the right to do this and there was little work involved for the player, but it all fell through.

One reason was that he did not want his wages supplemented by outsiders to reach the level of other players down south – he felt that was simply letting the Rangers directors slip off the hook. He had never been impressed by the men in the boardroom and would shake his head in disbelief as old Bailie Wilson, the chairman, would walk down the aisle of the plane when they were travelling to a European tie speaking to the players and continually getting their names wrong. Yet, he thought, this was one of the men who didn't want to pay him a decent wage! That type of thing infuriated him and strengthened his resolve when he entered into those final wage negotiations when he was trying to boost his earnings from £45 a week – the highest money he was ever to earn at Ibrox.

There was little glamour to be found in the North-East and Sunderland had been just a year back in the first division when they bought the player they hoped would guide them to the greatness they had last glimpsed before the Second World War. In 1936 they won the First Division Championship and the following season were victorious in the FA Cup. Little had happened since. They had a brief flurry in the 1950s when they tried to buy their way to success, were nicknamed the Bank of England club as Trevor Ford and Ray Daniel and George Aitken and Willie Fraser and Charlie Fleming and others were all bought, and yet took the club nowhere. This time the spending on players was not to be as frequently high-profile and their dreams of moving onwards and upwards to join the elite of English clubs were focused on the superstar from Scotland. He had captured the imagination of the Sunderland support little more than a year earlier when the Scottish League had travelled there to take on the English League, had drawn 2–2, and Baxter had been in imperious form as he controlled the middle of the park. The directors and manager Ian McColl reckoned that luring him to Roker would be a signal to the fans that the club was truly ambitious. They also believed that they were investing in someone who would transform their team and take the club towards the kind of success they had not known in the town for thirty long years.

He completed the signing details in the North British Hotel in Edinburgh. With an irony that was perhaps lost on the player, it was the same venue where he had agreed to join Rangers five years before. And this time he gave his new club and their frustrated fans fuel for their lofty aspirations when he declared that this was the right club for him. At an impromptu press conference he insisted: 'Sunderland will suit me right down to the ground. This is one of the most famous clubs in English football, with a tremendous tradition. They are fighting to build a side equal to the great Roker teams of the past. It is now my ambition to help them do just that.'

At the time it may well have been his belief but, while he had often been described as a 'soccer sorcerer' when he had the ball at his feet, he was never going to become the alchemist Sunderland needed to turn their ordinary team into something even remotely approaching the level of their ambitions. Before too long he had realised that.

He had the solace, mind you, of the pay deal he had been looking for. He collected around £11,000 in a lump sum signing-on payment and his weekly wage soared to £80 a week which was £35 more than he had been picking up at Ibrox. There were bonuses available, too, to make the total package all the sweeter with £40 a point allowing the Sunderland players the opportunity to double their wage with every victory they could gain. On paper, in an Edinburgh hotel, it all looked even better than Baxter had been searching for. In reality the bonuses were far fewer than he had expected. His friends were surprised that he had agreed to the transfer, that he had opted to go to Sunderland. They did not realise, perhaps, that there had been little choice when the final decision had to be made.

One who failed to understand the move was Billy McNeill who, while repeating the belief that he went to the wrong club, adds: 'I never really saw Sunderland as a club – I always thought it was like some pirate ship. They just seemed to buy people from anywhere and everywhere and then expected them to come together as a team, but they never did. They spent huge amounts of money and, at one time in the 50s, they were called the Bank of England club, but the investment they made in the team didn't bring them any success at all. Nothing ever went right for that club back then and Jimmy was just dragged down by what was going on round about him.

'I think that Sunderland bought him because he had been magnificent in one of the inter-League games that had been played at Roker Park. That whole area, starved of success and starved of really big name players by then, was excited about the way Jimmy had played and the show he had put on during the game. But that was maybe eighteen months before the transfer and it was also before he suffered the broken leg in Vienna. I don't think they were getting what they had expected and I know that Jimmy most certainly got a lot worse than he had anticipated as regards the strength of the team he was joining!'

As well as the supporters and the board, who warmed themselves on the memories from that English League–Scottish League game, there was another very important man who had decided that Jim Baxter was exactly the kind of player Sunderland required to lift them out of the mediocrity that had settled around the club over the years. Ian McColl had been appointed manager that same year in succession to George Hardwick. The former England captain had won promotion with the Wearside club but the board had then decided that a change was needed to allow them to blossom in the top flight. McColl, who had been sacked by the Scottish Football Association in the middle of a qualifying campaign for the World Cup Finals in England in 1966, had been chosen to take over. He had been a Rangers player before taking on the Scotland job and he had kept a careful watch on the simmering row between his old club and their star player. Given his knowledge of the politics at the Glasgow club, McColl was convinced that Baxter would be sold, that the club would not give in no matter how important the player was to the team and its continued success. He bided his time, checking that no other club might move into the bidding ahead of him and, when he felt the time was right, he went in for the kill and made Baxter his first signing for the club.

'Sunderland had appointed me to turn them into a successful first division club,' McColl recalls. 'That is what they wanted and they made that plain to me when I was interviewed. For my part I wanted Jim Baxter to be the man I would build my team around. I thought that there were some good players at Roker Park, solid, experienced professionals, but I knew that we needed better players if we were going to achieve our ambitions and make our mark in that top league, which was very, very strong. My belief was that Jim would help us do that. He was a special player, second to none, and I had first-hand knowledge of that from the time I spent with him during my time as the Scotland manager. Now, I also knew that by this time he was desperate to get away from Rangers. His frustration over the club's wage structure had been growing year upon year.

'He thought their attitude towards him was penny-pinching and he had always hoped that one day they would take a different view. But I knew that would never happen. Rangers did not think that way. The party line at Ibrox – and I knew this from having spent sixteen years with the club as a player – would be that if Jim Baxter wanted to leave then let him go and replace him with someone from the reserve team. It was a policy that had worked for them in the past – for example, and this is only one example, Alex Scott was sold to Everton and Willie

Henderson replaced him and the team was not weakened at all. The fact that Baxter was irreplaceable, partly because of his outstanding ability and also because of his astonishing confidence, which influenced the other players, would not dawn on the directors, although I knew that Scot Symon would be aware of the major problem he would have to face when Baxter left.

'That wasn't my worry – my concern was to make my first signing for Sunderland a significant one. I saw this as an opportunity for all of us, for Sunderland, who needed a class player in the midfield, for myself to bring in a player who would excite the fans as well as ignite the team and, for Jim, it would be the opportunity to play in the English first division where he had always claimed he wanted to perform. It should have been absolutely perfect and it remains a sadness for me to this day that it did not work out as I believed it would.'

McColl was aware of the image Baxter had left behind him in Glasgow but he had a genuine belief that the player was ready to settle down. He had just been married, he was embarking on a new phase of his career, he was getting the money he had wanted, and he seemed determined to make a fresh start. After all he was still just 25 years old and at a stage where his best years should still have been stretching out ahead of him. But, before he was there very long, it seemed to dawn on the player that he had made a mistake, that he had not made the best of career moves going to Sunderland.

The problems which struck his hoped-for new beginning and which saw Baxter begin to self-destruct at an even faster rate than had been the case in Glasgow did not stem initially from the celebrity he enjoyed in the town nor from the increased amounts of cash he now had at his disposal – his *Sunday Mirror* column had continued with an increase to match the cult status he would now have in the North-East as well as in Scotland – but from the on-field disappointments which dogged him from his very first game for his new club. It was out there on the field of play that Baxter had always enjoyed himself most and at Rangers he had been supported by a team of quality footballers. Now that was no longer the case and he was soon to find that out in the most humiliating manner, in a way he could not have foreseen, and one which he could not have enjoyed as his old Glasgow rivals, Celtic, came south to rain on his parade.

Just as Baxter left Rangers, a club where his influence had been enormous, another revolution was taking place on the other side of the city of Glasgow where Jock Stein had been installed as manager. After only three months in the post he guided Celtic to a Scottish Cup win – the first trophy they had won over an eight-year period and the first success they had known during Baxter's reign at Ibrox. At the start of the next season Stein took his team to Sunderland as part of their pre-season preparations and the stage was set for a confrontation between the player who had given Rangers such domination for the first half of the decade and the manager who was about to set out on an even longer spell of supremacy in Scotland. This, then, was to be his debut, and he must have looked towards it with that ingrained self-belief reassuring him that all would be well. In his heyday, after all, he would always have chosen Celtic as opponents, knowing that the Parkhead team found it difficult to cope with his skills. He had enjoyed so much success in the Old Firm clashes – remember, in eighteen games against them he had tasted defeat just twice during that five-year spell at Ibrox – that he began to take victory for granted in the most intense derby game of them all.

Having them arrive at Roker Park then, might have appeared to be manna from heaven as he prepared to demonstrate his unique skills to a new audience. Of course, this was not Rangers he was playing with any longer; this was a middle-to-bottom-of-the-table English first division team who were unused to success. They were also unfamiliar with the challenge which Celtic would give them and Baxter himself was not yet aware of the new vibrancy which was surging through his old adversaries now that

Stein had taken over. He was soon to find out as his debut match turned into an afternoon of embarrassment for him and his new team and into ninety minutes of revenge for the Celtic players who had suffered at his hands for so many seasons and who now found themselves in the ascendancy.

Celtic scored five goals that day as they gave notice that they were ready to restore the past glories of the club and that their recent Scottish Cup win was only a start to an orgy of trophy-winning which would last until Stein stepped down from the job thirteen years later.

Billy McNeill still savours that day: 'It was our turn to give Jimmy a bit of stick and we did that. There was no malice in it, that's just the way it was between players, and in our case – Jimmy's and mine – between mates. He always had a few verbals ready for us when he was with Rangers, and they were so used to beating us because Celtic had been in something of turmoil. You always need some real experience around and we didn't have that – Bobby Collins had gone and Willie Fernie and some others. One day before a game Neilly Mochan looked round the dressing room and commented: "This is like playing for the Boys' Guild" – and he was right. So Rangers had the upper hand while Jimmy was there and he used to wind us up and, of course, I was always a victim because I rose to the bait far too easily. That day it was so different.

'We got some of our own back on Jimmy that day and afterwards he told us what had gone on in their dressing room before the game. Big Jock had only taken over a few months earlier and he had introduced a warm-up as part of the pre-match preparation. Out we went and did what we were asked to do and we worked hard – the Big Man really put us through our paces. Anyhow, some of their players were watching and they went back inside and told the others that we would be too tired for the game, that we would have nothing left to offer when the kick-off came. Now John Parke, the Northern Ireland international full back was there and he had been at Hibs when

Jock Stein was the manager at Easter Road. He warned them that this would not be the case, but not too many of his team-mates were willing to take his word. They thought they knew better.

They didn't of course, as we were soon to prove to them. John Parke was right and we scored five goals and, sadly, we saw the first signs that Jim Baxter was never going to be the force in English football that he should have been. I had suspected that he had gone to the wrong club – that game proved it to me.'

There were others who saw the decline at close quarters and Pat Crerand was just one who made a success of his own transfer south to Old Trafford and watched in disbelief as his Glasgow mate failed to hack it. 'I saw what happened to George Best and to Jimmy and it was a shame – but the difference was that no one was ever convinced in England of Jim Baxter's exceptional ability. There were glimpses of it, you caught sight of these marvellous skills in certain games, but he could not sustain his form and you had to be able to do that in the English first division. There was one game he played against us at Old Trafford and for 45 minutes he played as well as I could ever remember him playing. He ran the show the way he used to do with Rangers – and with Scotland, too, for that matter – and we could not get the ball away from him. It was an absolutely virtuoso performance but he didn't get the response from his team-mates. He made chances, they missed them, and we went in 0–0 at half time mainly because they were just unable to score. In the second half Jimmy just died, his legs gave out, and it was awful watching his reaction as we helped ourselves to five goals. He had given his team all he had but he could not keep it going. His fitness was going and you just had to be fit to play in that league. Personally I think it broke his heart when Rangers agreed to sell him. He would never admit that – but that was his home, that is where he had the best of times, and then it was all over and that was a serious blow to his self-esteem.'

Dave Mackay, who was one of the few players Baxter would ever bow the knee to, was another who witnessed his fall from superstardom in Scotland to being little more than just another player in just another team when he signed for Sunderland.

'There were occasions when he still had those special moments of magic which only he was able to produce on the field,' MacKay points out. 'The trouble, though, was that these became fewer and fewer as his fitness let him down. Quite honestly, he was drinking too much, having too many late nights and then not training as hard as he should have been doing. Look, no one enjoyed a drink more than I did. And you have to believe me when I tell you that there were nights when I would drink as much or even more than Jim did – but these nights out came after games, after the job was done. You would not get me drinking on a Monday or a Tuesday or any night before a match was due to be played. I just didn't do that. But Jim did, and the older he got then the more obvious it became that he couldn't have the kind of lifestyle he insisted upon and still be able to produce the goods out there on the field where it mattered. He would tell people how I had always preached to him about the value of training when you are a young player because it stands you in good stead later in life. You can get along without extra training when you are 21 or 22 years old. But if you have not been looking after yourself at that stage of your career then six or seven years down the line you suffer. Of course Jim didn't listen to me at the time like he should have, but he was not the only player who had that attitude.

'At Spurs Jimmy Greaves had something of the same outlook towards training. He had tremendous natural talent and so he didn't see the need to train as hard as some of the rest of us. Jim Baxter was much the same and it all went wrong for him in the end. I was able to play on until I was 37 years of age and Jim could have done the same when you think of the ability he had. But it was over for him by the time he was just thirty. It was a tragedy that he did not do better in the English first division because even though he had one or two exceptional games, he was never looked on as being a success and he should have been!

'Going to Sunderland was maybe a mistake in the sense that they were always a team who struggled a little bit. So Jim found himself playing in an ordinary side after being in one that had been strong and successful at Ibrox. That had to be something of a shock for him, suddenly finding it a battle for every single point when he had been used to winning in almost every game back home. Also you have to remember that, as well as having players around him who were not of the standard he was used to, he was coming up against much stronger opposition week after week. He should have been at a bigger club, at one of the great English clubs. Jim Baxter of Sunderland did not have the ring about it that Jim Baxter of Rangers had. It was not a marriage made in heaven.'

That had become obvious after only a few months to the man who had bought him. The manager of Sunderland, Ian McColl, had pinned his own hopes on Baxter as well as those of the club and the support. After handling him at international level he believed that he understood the wayward Fifer and that, while he had been short on discipline during his years with Rangers, he was now ready to forge a new squeaky-clean identity for himself. He had seemed genuinely pleased to be linking up with his former international team boss and McColl, to this day, harbours deep regrets that things did not work out the way he had hoped they would.

'I did believe that everything would work out for the best,' he says with regret. 'It was all there for him – he was at last getting the kind of money he felt he should always have been earning. He was just married to Jean, and he doted on her at the time, and he told me that this was the opportunity he needed to make a fresh start, to get away from the bright lights of Glasgow and to begin settling down. That was what he appeared to want from the move. Also I thought that he would appreciate the fact that, in a way, I was providing him with a lifeline as far as his career was concerned. None of the big clubs, none of the major teams in the first division, was ready to take a risk with him. They did not think he could change. I knew from my time as the Scotland manager that Matt Busby did not want him at Manchester United and that Bill Nicholson did not want him at Tottenham. They were not interested and there were others who felt the same way. Knowing him better than they did, and having met Jean, I felt that he was ready to change his ways, just as he claimed he wanted to do. It was a totally different life he was after and he intended to live up to the responsibility he had taken on when he got married. Or so he said!'

At first it did look as if Tommy Docherty would be proved wrong and the leopard would change its spots quite dramatically. Baxter even suggested to his manager that he could be happier in the North-East instead of Manchester or London because he would find it easier to get back up to Fife to see his golfing mates. He was given a club house and – that disastrous result against Celtic apart – he seemed content with his initial impressions. During the pre-season training he worked hard and was, according to McColl, as conscientious as any other player on the staff as he strove for fitness.

It was only as it gradually dawned on him that the football, the game itself, was going to be a constant struggle that he changed. When that rather grim realisation struck he soon dropped back into his old ways and rows in the dressing room did not help either his or the club's cause. His unhappiness at the plight he now found himself in manifested itself in drinking sessions which appeared, at times, to be even more prolonged and ferocious than those he had participated in towards the end of his Glasgow sojourn. And it also found release in a feud with the Sunderland captain of the time, the centre half Charlie Hurley, a Republic of Ireland international, and the hero of the Roker Park fans. 'King Charlie' they called him after he had helped them out of the second division and into what they saw as their rightful place in the top league. Baxter's view was that there was room for only one 'King' at Roker Park and he wanted that title for himself. It did not make for happy days in the dressing room.

The word came north on the football grapevine and the players he had left behind at Ibrox soon heard that among his early conversations with Hurley, Baxter, at his cheekiest, had told the burly Irishman, 'There's only room for one "King" here Charlie, and it's not going to be you.' They recognised in that the first signs of their old team-mate's disenchantment and they sat back and waited for the further squalls they knew were sure to follow that introductory notice of intent. They knew that he had made up his mind that no one was going to rule the dressing room at Roker Park except himself. Charlie Hurley might have been a hero for what he had achieved in the past but as far as the new signing was concerned he was yesterday's man no matter how much trouble he might cause in proving that and in getting his own way. Perhaps he was not able to make his mark on the field as he had hoped to do but he still aimed to prove that his power to influence players by the force of his not inconsiderable personality was as strong as it had ever been. Soon, though his performances continued to be spasmodic, he was giving the impression to many of the players that he was running the show. His reputation as a world-class midfield player still remained and his displays for Scotland at international level were enough to keep it intact for some time yet. In the meanwhile Baxter set out to impose himself on his new club and to enjoy life more or less as he had always done.

If pleasure could not be found on the field, he knew where to look for it when the training and the games were over. He had never been short on acquiring such knowledge and Sunderland, while it did not have the old-fashioned grandeur of the St Enoch Hotel to amuse him and his friends, did have a nightclub named Wetherall's and a gambling club called La Strada where he could indulge his appetites. Disillusion had set in more quickly than either McColl or Baxter could have imagined. Soon he was comparing his new club with his first club, Raith Rovers, and he would later suggest: 'There were times when I felt I was back at Kirkcaldy. The ball had a nasty habit of coming right back past me after I made a forward pass to one of our front players. And then I would be turning round to chase the game and that was never something I was comfortable with. In the first season I was just surprised that we managed, somehow, to escape relegation. That's how bad it was.'

It must have been galling for Ian McColl to watch his first major signing begin to lose interest in the 'fresh start' he had promised to make. Even now as he looks back down the years you can sense that, in a way, he blames himself for the difficulties that beset Baxter so soon after his arrival in the North-East.

'The other players at the club were just not good enough for him,' he laments, 'and I say this with all due respect to the lads who were there. To start with Jim trained like a beast and he worked hard in the matches, but then he saw that things were not going to work out for him on the field and that got to him. In another sense, Sunderland was not a big enough club for him; it just did not provide the stage he demanded. I say this with real regret because I enjoyed my own time there and I still have friends in that area. But, unhappily, that was how it was, and we were not winning games, and he hated losing, you know. He was a really bad loser. From the outside he gave the impression that there were times when he couldn't care less – but he cared OK. And when we lost it hurt him and he became very angry when the defeats came from teams who were not all that highly rated in the first division. He took these losses personally, these were blows to his pride.

'I suppose I was partly to blame for what went wrong in his career because, to be absolutely blunt, he went to the wrong club when he left Rangers. Sunderland was not the place for him. Naturally I was doing my bit for the club as manager by bringing him in, giving the supporters the high profile signing, the big name player they wanted. But he should have been at one of the glamorous sides. If he had been and he had found success then I do believe he would have settled down just as he said he wanted to do. The real worry for him was trying to handle the lack of success; he found it dispiriting to have to endure that. If he had been winning and if he had been earning not just more money, but also more applause, then he would have been a happy man. He revelled in the applause from the crowds when he was playing well. It was a shame that his skills and his enormous talent were not seen properly down south. He had his moments – with his ability you had to expect that – but they were far too few. Ultimately you had people asking why we had bought him and that made the situation worse because the answer was that we had bought Jim Baxter because he was the best midfield player in the country and, maybe, even in the whole of Europe. But when those people who posed that question watched him they couldn't see that.'

The enigma which Baxter had now become troubled one of his Scottish team-mates, Billy Hughes, younger brother of Celtic's John, who had seen him in his pomp with Rangers as he logged up one great performance after another in the tension-packed atmosphere of the Old Firm games. He was a teenager when the big new signing was unveiled and he made his own debut during that season but is now forced to own up: 'My greatest regret about these times is that no one in England, and I mean especially at Sunderland, ever saw the real Jim Baxter. The problem we had was that he was too clever for the rest of us. He was always two moves ahead of the other lads who were playing alongside him. I am not being disrespectful here because I include myself in that. It was just a fact of life. He was an exceptional player, one of these guys you come across only once in a lifetime. I had seen him play in Scotland before I signed for Sunderland so I knew what he was capable of achieving on the pitch. Then he was in an excellent Rangers team and the other players would react properly when he was making a pass, they knew instinctively where they should be moving to make the most of his skills. We did have a lot of good players at Roker Park but I don't think there was a single one of us on the same wavelength as Jim.

'That affected him and he must have become more and more frustrated, and so his own performance levels dropped and it all became something of a vicious circle. But I can still remember him one day, I can't remember now what game this was, but he was his old self, running the whole show and we won and it was all down to this one-man display because he was streets ahead of any other player on the field. When he was being sold to Nottingham Forest I was very upset that he was leaving because as far as I was concerned I had been lucky getting the opportunity to play alongside him. He was a player in the same category as Dave Mackay and Denis Law, someone who could have been, and should have been, as big a personality at Sunderland as Len Shackleton had been before him. I have never seen anyone with a left foot like him, he could do anything with it and this was at a period when his fitness was beginning to go. Even then he was incredible and I never did play with anyone better than he was.'

The football reputation he had brought south with him was becoming more than a little threadbare and, while he retained some of his swagger on and off the field, it was now being employed to disguise the doubt that must have been gnawing away at even his massive self-belief. The hell-raising reputation he had promised to leave behind him in Glasgow was not, unfortunately, tarnished in the least. Soon the stories were filtering back north that Baxter was once again on the fast lane to disaster and McColl admits that disciplining him was impossible.

'I fined Jim many, many times but it made no difference to him,' he stresses. 'I could fine him a week's wages, or even two weeks' wages and he had to pay up, something that annoyed him, but the fines would not stop him stepping out of line. Nothing I did or said could persuade him to change his lifestyle and, while it had been difficult for him to keep a low profile in Glasgow, it was impossible in Sunderland. It was a much smaller place and he couldn't pick his nose without people knowing about it. So when he was in bother – and that became far too common – the word went round the town immediately and ended in my office where I had to try to deal with all his antics. He had gone completely off the rails again and it wasn't just the drinking, it was the very heavy gambling as well. He was being paid well, which was one of the reasons he had wanted his transfer, but none of that money was being saved.

'Not a penny piece was ever finding its way into his bank account. It was going on some horse or other in the bookies or on the tables at one of the gambling clubs he had found in Sunderland. It was tragic watching him going down that road but he would not listen to any advice. He always thought that he knew best and I think, too, that he believed that the good days were going to last forever.'

As well as the fines and other attempts to bring him back into line, McColl also began to restructure his team in an effort to surround his star with players who might provide the spark to bring him back to form. If he could not surround Baxter with players of equal vision he could, at least, provide him with others who would appreciate what he was trying to do and would give him a helping hand when that was required. In came Neil Martin from Hibs, who was a front player Baxter admired, and old Ibrox buddy Ralph Brand was with him for a short spell after being with Manchester City, while George Mulhall, yet another Scot, had been there earlier. Also bought was the centre half George Kinnell, Baxter's cousin from Fife, whose reputation for wild behaviour off the field possibly exceeded that of his better-known kinsman. It was another piece of speculation by the manager and it did break up the clique that had run the dressing room before Baxter had started to place his own image on the club. The captain, Charlie Hurley, was, in time, dropped and other changes were made and soon Baxter and his own clique were in command. So much so that two other Scots, Billy Hughes and Harry Hood, later to join Celtic, tell how they were informed that they were being given a first-team chance not by the manager but by the midfielder who sometimes even passed on the bad news that they were being dropped.

Hood was appalled at what was happening. He had come south from Clyde at around the same time as Baxter had left Rangers but had sat out most of that first season because of injury. He could not play but he could see what was happening in the dressing room and shakes his head in disbelief at the memories that flood back.

'I watched what was going on and all the little factions that were being formed,' he says, 'and it was damaging for the club, though no one seemed to care about that. The whole place was a complete mess and, thankfully, I never came across a shambles like that during the rest of my time in the game. Charlie Hurley was the hero at Roker Park before Jim arrived and, basically, Jim just decided that there was no room for the two of them in the same dressing room. Big Charlie had been known as the 'King' and that title was only going to one man and so the two of them were bogeys from day one. Jim won that battle and he got so much power that there were times he seemed to think he was running the whole club!

'The atmosphere, though, was awful. The forwards didn't communicate with the midfield players who, in turn, wouldn't talk to the defenders, and the Scots lads scarcely spoke to the English players so it was little wonder that the club was struggling to avoid relegation. I was just a young boy and I could not believe what was going on. It was not a place where you could learn to be a good professional. I thought that the manager, Ian McColl, gave Jim far too much latitude, and he allowed him to get away with all kinds of bad behaviour. What happened then was that some of the other senior players, who weren't exactly model professionals either, saw what Jim was up to and they were quick to join in. Jim was not the only one at fault for the lack of discipline but he was certainly the ringleader.

'There were times when he still played well, but right from the start he was not the player he had been with Rangers, and the lack of training and the drinking were beginning to tell. It was clear that things were not going to work out for him or for the club. I think that Jim took a look around and decided early on that this was not what he had signed on for. OK, he got the money that Rangers had refused to give him, but he was not in a team that won matches the way Rangers had done in Scotland. It was a struggle all the time just to keep clear of the bottom of the table and that was not what Jim had envisaged for himself. When he moved south he was looking for a bit of glamour, hoping to hit the big time like so many of his mates in the game, and there was nothing like that available for him in the North-East. You could see that when he went out on to the big stage again, in the Scotland team for instance, that some of the ability was still there, but the flesh was weak and the appetite for the ordinary games where the team had to scuffle for survival wasn't there at all. It wasn't right for him and it wasn't right for the club; we all knew that it could not go on indefinitely. Something had to give somewhere.'

Ian McColl realised this too as more and more of his time was spent trying to cover up one scrape after another or even bailing Baxter out when he had been in trouble with the police. Late night calls from the local force had become almost the norm at the manager's home as the town's most recognisable footballer dropped into more and more trouble as the months went by. McColl's patience and that of the club, too, lasted longer than the player had any right to expect. He survived at Sunderland for two and a half years and by then McColl points out: 'He was completely out of hand again and I had learned the hard way, by now, that there was nothing you could do to change him. I would get him out of one bit of trouble with the police, fighting in a nightclub or some such, and he would be filled with remorse and would promise me it wouldn't happen again. And a few nights later my phone would ring at home and he would be in bother again.

'It got to the stage where all I wanted was to get him out of the club. He was making no contribution to the team and he was in almost constant trouble off the field. It could not go on. He had lost interest in playing for the club because he could not see what he could do to improve the side he was playing in. There were suggestions that he was not the same player after the leg break in Vienna but I won't accept that. He had made a full recovery by the time he signed for me and there was no evidence that the injury had affected him psychologically because when he was feeling good, when he was in the mood, then he could still control games. What was wrong was that the years of misbehaviour suddenly caught up with him and that happened just at the time when he found himself part of an ordinary team that was never going to be in the running for any honours. When that realisation hit him he just gave up. He virtually stopped playing, and we still had him on the books, still in the first team, and yet it was only too clear that he was no longer interested in playing for Sunderland.'

The problems soon became so enormous that the club was forced to confront them and decide what course of action had to be taken before the fabric of the team was damaged irreparably by the flaunting of authority that had become customary at Roker Park among Baxter and his cronies. As Harry Hood had seen for himself, something had to give before the malaise that gripped Sunderland could be tackled.

8   TIME RUNS OUT AT ROKER

Stories have been told and retold of the various escapades that centred mainly on their hotel, the Georgian Towers, but did spread across the continent as they travelled to fulfil their fixtures in the other cities involved in the soccer experiment. One of the ways of relieving boredom in the hotel headquarters was to go into the bar and start to drink your way along the gantry, one drink after another. The winner was the man who remained standing at the end of this exotic tasting. This competition was initiated by Baxter and Kinnell but had to be abandoned when one of the players collapsed and apparently had to be rushed to hospital suffering from alcohol-induced poisoning. Another of the party games was taken up as Baxter and his clique tried to avoid boredom.

Throughout the years at Ibrox the very obvious counterweight to Baxter's irresponsible conduct when he was out on the town was the consummate ability he was able to bring to the team and the subsequent successes that Rangers enjoyed. He was never in any sense a 'one-man team' and he would have been the first to stress that fact but, as the other Ibrox players of the period were swift to realise, he was able to add something extra in the way of skill that gave them the edge over any other team in Scotland.

Perhaps there had been a certain prescience on behalf of Rangers when they did agree to sell him. There may have been small indications that, following the leg break, he had not been looking after himself, that he had not been following the training regimes laid down for players recovering from serious injuries. In the handful of games he played on his return, for example, he was unable to change the course of Rangers season, which was well below the standards that had been set during his previous years in the side. In his first year the team won the league and the League Cup and were finalists in the European Cup Winners' Cup where they lost to the Italian side Fiorentina in a two-legged encounter when the score was 4–1 against them. A year later the team won the Scottish Cup and again lifted the League Cup. They followed that by winning the cup for the second season in succession and taking the title once more and then they took the domestic treble in season 1963–64 but following that, in Baxter's last year at the club, the trophy room was bare. Even worse they slumped to fifth place in the league, their worst position in the old Scottish first division for 39 years. The absence of Baxter for several months of the season and then his half-hearted comeback were contributory factors, and the low-key manner in which he returned might have set alarm bells ringing.

Whatever, the directors had also had their fill of his various drink-fuelled exploits and therefore they realised that it was time for him to go. Then, at Sunderland, where he looked for a new beginning, he soon became disenchanted by the lack of support afforded him by his new team-mates and the pattern that had brought about the break from Rangers began to repeat itself.

Ian McColl had held firm to the idea that he would be able to handle the problems but that faith was not enough in the face of Baxter's excesses. The manager, who had felt comfortable handling the player when they were together on international duty with Scotland, now discovered that there was little that he could do to curb the off-field antics of the man who was supposed to be the Sunderland saviour.

The superstar, who was bought to carry the unfashionable club into the limelight to glory and acclaim, and even, perhaps, the occasional trophy, was so much out of control that he was close to wrecking what little morale remained at the club. No matter what McColl did Baxter was going to go his own sweet way and he gave no public indication that he was ready to accept that the situation he found himself mired in at Roker Park was of his own making. Yes, his genius should have had him playing alongside his mates Denis Law and Pat Crerand at Old Trafford, or with the player he admired above all others, Dave Mackay at Tottenham. Or it might have been even more appropriate if he had been able to swap the marble halls of Ibrox for those of Highbury where he could have joined the Scots colony there and made up an all-Tartan half back line of McLintock, Ure and Baxter. What he was unwilling to confess – though, doubtless in private moments he would accept responsibility for his plight – was that he would have been there if he had been prepared to behave himself. If he had trained that little bit harder or if he had discarded the lifestyle which had damaged his reputation and turned him into a transfer untouchable for the major clubs then he would surely have been in the surroundings he craved. Even if he had done as he had promised to do and made a fresh start on Wearside there could still have been time for him to take his rightful place alongside his peers in the English first division.

Instead, like some wilful child, he disregarded all the advice he was given and simply paid the fines when he was in trouble with the club and went out to find more amusement away from the grind that the game had now become for him. In the past he had always been able to find some measure of comfort when he went out on the field, when he had that ball nestling at his left foot and the roar of the crowd was there to inspire him. That was gone, taken away from him by the transfer to Sunderland, and his way of coping was to drink and gamble more than ever before.

The other players knew what was happening to him, it was difficult to avoid that knowledge when he stumbled in for training still suffering the effects of the previous night's partying. They would gauge just how bad his night had been by seeing how many times he would throw up after his arrival – and that was before any work began! His ploy then was to get to the front of the pack of players when they began to do laps in the forlorn belief that by being out ahead of the others they would not be able to smell the drink from his breath. It didn't work because the players knew what was going on, just as the whole town did.

And, while he continued to harm himself on a nightly basis, his behaviour also inflamed the dressing room differences that still simmered between the rival groups. Charlie Hurley did not have the skills of the new 'King' of Roker but he was a complete professional and was appalled at how his rival conducted his life. Not that Baxter cared, he had been behaving in much the same way for years and, quite clearly, he believed that he could go on forever, and the exceptional talent he was born with, as well as his natural fitness, would see him through any difficulties. It had always worked out before so why shouldn't it work out again was the way he looked at life.

Ian McColl, though, spotted the telltale signs, little things that told him that all the years of misbehaviour were starting to catch up, just as everyone, except, apparently, Jim Baxter, knew they would do. 'For the first dozen games or so,' McColl recalls, 'he played his gut out for me and then he knew from the way the team was playing that we were going nowhere – and that he was going nowhere. Once that happened he just gave up. I suppose he thought that he would still be able to get by even if he was staying out all night because, in a way, he was something of a freak as regards fitness. Here was a guy who couldn't manage to do a single push-up in training; I used to give him hell about that. He just couldn't do it. And yet on the field he did have an engine and don't listen to anyone who tries to dispute that. Other players will tell you. Even though he was not the fastest guy around he would still get himself all over the field of play when the team needed him to do that. It was not what he wanted to do, maybe, and it was certainly not what he was best at doing, but he would work hard for the rest of the team when he had to do so.

'For instance, if a move broke down around the opposition penalty box then Jim Baxter could get himself back to defend around his own eighteen-yard line pretty damn quickly. I can remember in one game against England when he lost possession. I think it was Alan Ball who took the ball away from him and Jim was so annoyed at this, he seemed to see it as a personal insult, that he chased wee Ball and got the ball back from him. Yet this is supposed to be someone who couldn't tackle and who would never chase. He could do it when he wanted.

'Of course he wasn't a tackler like Dave Mackay was and that used to upset him. He would say to me that he wanted to go into challenges like Mackay and I would point out that he wasn't physically equipped to do that, to even attempt to play that style of game. If he had tried it he would most likely have been killed. But what he could do was get his foot in and nick the ball away from an opponent because he had the timing to do that successfully.

'Anyway, getting back to his fitness, he was a one-off because he had scarcely a muscle in his body and yet he would compensate for the deficiencies because he had a great brain and a natural stamina. It was when they began to let him down that the truth hit him. His stamina started to go and then his reflexes slowed down and, probably for the first time in his career, football became hard work for him. That's when the decline set in. He recognised the signs himself, I'm sure of that because Jim was very honest about his game. If he played badly he owned up to that, he didn't hide and he didn't make excuses, but the good performances became fewer and fewer and his great days were just memories – there were games when he was doing little more than going through the motions. It broke your heart to see him like that but there was nothing we could do to change things. We tried everything we could as a club and nothing succeeded. His career was getting to the stage where it was beyond saving.'

While the troubles in Sunderland were one thing, a six-week stay in the United States and Canada at the end of the 1967 season may have been the time when Baxter went beyond the limits as far as McColl and Sunderland were concerned. Probably lifted by the adulation which followed Scotland's win over England at Wembley and his own memorable part in that, he went with the club to Canada in the close season. Sunderland were invited to represent the city of Vancouver in the fledgling North American Soccer League while other clubs from England, Scotland, Northern Ireland and the Republic of Ireland, too, were based in different cities around the United States and Canada. For Baxter and his buddies this was party time with a vengeance.

There had been occasions at home when he had stepped out of line. Once McColl was called from his home in the early hours of the morning by the Sunderland police after complaints were made about Baxter and some of his mates from Fife as they tried to take apart one of the local hotels. And, on a train north from London to Sunderland following a midweek game in the capital, Baxter and George Kinnell, that dynamic duo, teamed up in the restaurant car and drank for almost the entire journey after being warned by the manager that their limit was to be a single bottle of beer with their lunch. That culminated in the club chairman's hat being thrown out of the window by Baxter and the two players being thrown off the train at Durham by the furious McColl. It was an unscheduled stop but the manager wanted his two most notorious troublemakers out of sight before the scheduled arrival at Sunderland where press photographers were waiting for them.

They were fined; Baxter had to pay £300 and Kinnell £200, and they did so with the money being deducted in instalments from their wages over a period of weeks. But fines were never enough to knock sense into Baxter's brain and when Canada and the States beckoned that fateful summer nothing was going to stop him having a seven-week-long party as the team crisscrossed North America. And, if the long-suffering Ian McColl thought that he had seen everything from his star buy, he was in for a few surprises, starting almost immediately on the team's arrival at their hotel in Vancouver following the near twelve-hour flight where Baxter had indulged himself with copious amounts of Bacardi to ease the strain of travelling.

The next morning he and his room-mate, Kinnell, surfaced late, ignored the call of breakfast and immediately ordered up enough booze to stock a decent-sized bar. This was to sustain them during their stay in British Columbia and the hotel porter went to the nearest liquor store and brought back a case of Bacardi, a case of Johnny Walker Black Label, a case of champagne, a case of Guinness as well as other cases of beer and mixers for the two Fifers, who began to make an immediate dent in their purchases.

'We had several large ones,' Baxter recounted later, 'and then before it was even noon we were interrupted by a knock at the room door. When we opened it there were two policemen there, in plain clothes, but obviously policemen, who went to the refrigerator, checked on our supply of booze and then pulled out a wad of ten-dollar bills. They asked if it was our money and then proceeded to explain that it was counterfeit and had been traced back from the liquor store to our room. They wanted to take us down to the police station to question us.'

Baxter talked them out of that and persuaded them to speak to the manager. McColl could not accept that his players were in trouble with the local police on their first morning in Canada – but finally he explained that they were Sunderland footballers and that the money had come from a bank at Heathrow Airport when they changed pounds into dollars for the trip. He was probably relieved that they were not guilty of any serious misbehaviour and that they had been simply innocent victims. They were not to remain that way. That was not in their nature. Nor was it on their agenda for the trip.

Baxter, being Baxter, soon had the two policemen joining them for drinks and as the stay progressed he and Kinnell found their new friends partying with them and either keeping them out of trouble or hushing up any scrapes they found themselves in. And there were plenty of these as they gradually settled into a partying routine which was so intense that today it is difficult to believe that soccer survived in Vancouver for as long as it did after Baxter and company introduced the professional game to the fans there!

Stories have been told and retold of the various escapades that centred mainly on their hotel, the Georgian Towers, but did spread across the continent as they travelled to fulfil their fixtures in the other cities involved in the soccer experiment. One of the ways of relieving boredom in the hotel headquarters was to go into the bar and start to drink your way along the gantry, one drink after another. The winner was the man who remained standing at the end of this exotic tasting. This competition was initiated by Baxter and Kinnell but had to be abandoned when one of the players collapsed and apparently had to be rushed to hospital suffering from alcohol-induced poisoning. Another of the party games was taken up as Baxter and his clique tried to avoid boredom.

This involved a group of players sitting in one of the rooms drinking and then taking pot shots from the window with the empty bottles at the hotel's neon sign trying to knock out as many of the bulbs as possible. This also had to be abandoned after a television set was thrown from the window on to the street below. There was also the morning that the club physio received a desperate telephone call from Baxter's room demanding that he come to the player's aid immediately. When he asked what was wrong he was informed that the occupants of the room could not get out of their beds. Thinking that Baxter and Kinnell were ill, he found a member of the hotel staff, who gave him a pass key, and then dashed to the room. He opened the door and found that the two players were unable to get out of bed because the floor was littered with broken glasses and bottles from the party the night before. They had gone to bed and when they wakened realised that if they took one step in their bare feet they would be badly cut and not even the physio would have been able to help them! Only after the debris had been cleared could the cousins get out of bed and try to rid themselves of their hangovers before going to training. The Roker Park ambassadors were obviously into trashing hotel rooms long before rock bands began to do the same some years later.

There was also a genuine arrest involving Baxter and, on this occasion, not his normal sparring partner, Kinnell, but the Northern Ireland international full back John Parke. This occurred in Washington, 3,000 miles from their base and from their police pals who had helped them out when the going became tough in Canada. The two players had gone out for a drink after the game in the American capital and had wandered into one of the black areas without recognising that there was a potential for trouble in doing this.

The stories vary as to what exactly happened, but Billy Hughes, who was on the tour, says: 'The way we heard it at the time was that Jim had had a few drinks and he said something to one of the guys in this bar and suddenly a whole gang of guys went for him and John Parke. They got out of there as quick as they could with a bunch of people after them. They caught up with them too and Jim was being given a bit of a doing when a police car arrived on the scene and the locals took off. Jim and John were taken into custody and the manager had to bail them out.

'There was always something going on during that tour and, as you would expect, Jim was at the heart of it all. But the whole crowd that hung out with him then was involved. I remember coming into the hotel late one night, maybe one o'clock in the morning, and hearing this racket. I tracked it down to the swimming pool and found half the team cavorting around – and this was on the day of a game!'

Another Sunderland player, Harry Hood, didn't make the Vancouver trip but caught up with the team there while on a round-the-world tour with a Scotland international select.

'I was with the Scottish squad,' he explains, 'and it was not the first-choice team because both Celtic and Rangers were playing in European finals during May and their players did not make the trip. It had been arranged before the Old Firm reached the finals of the European Cup and the Cup Winners' Cup and the Scottish Football Association went ahead with it. I was there because I had been recovering from injury at Sunderland and this looked a good opportunity to play in games and complete my recovery. Sir Alex Ferguson was there, too, and we were in Vancouver when the lads were playing a game against Shamrock Rovers who were over there representing one of the American cities. Sunderland lost and they played really badly. I was getting some stick from the Scottish lads about not being able to get a place in a team as bad as that one was. The thing was that no one was fit. It was embarrassing to watch them. We had heard about the drinking sessions and that the training was a joke and that most of the lads were just living it up night after night, but I don't think I believed how bad it had been until I saw the evidence during that match. And Jim just didn't seem to care at all.'

When the club returned for the new season the old habits remained, and on a pre-season cross-country Hood was running with one or two of the younger players who passed Baxter and his cronies en route back to the training ground. The older professionals were not making any effort at keeping up with the group in front of them. They were skiving, happy to be out of sight of the training staff for a spell. But Hood and his mates were savaged by the manager because they were a few minutes behind the front runners even though they had started off behind the squad of troublemakers. Predictably they escaped the tongue lashing.

It was very soon after that Hood decided that he had to move to another club if his career was going to go in the direction he wished. His decision to ask for a transfer was triggered by an incident that happened when Sunderland opened a special lounge at the ground for the wealthier club supporters. 'This was the forerunner of the hospitality suites,' he remembers, 'and the private boxes you get at all the grounds today. Then it was something of an event for the club and on the day of this gala opening the players were asked to attend after training. I think the idea was that we all mix with the supporters who were paying extra money to be allowed into this new area. We were there to chat to them, sign a few autographs or whatever and get the new venture off to a good start. But there were four or five of the senior lads – Jim leading the band as usual – who decided this was another opportunity for a party. Now this was at lunchtime, right after we had been training and yet they began to knock back doubles as quickly as they could be poured. I couldn't believe it and I turned round to Nick Sharkey who was standing beside me and said to him: "I have to get away from this place. It's not going to do me any good staying here." I knew that if I didn't leave then my own career would start to suffer because the club was just going down and down and no one appeared to be able to stop this plunge into deeper and deeper trouble. I went to see Ian McColl and I was transferred back to Clyde and after that I joined Celtic.

'When Jim came back to Rangers I played against him and while he had one good game when Rangers beat Celtic at Ibrox he was never going to be the force or the influence he had been before going south. It was all over for him by then and I often wonder why he went down that road. It was a shame that all that had to happen to someone who was such a great player. He should never have been at Sunderland and he should never have gone to Nottingham Forest either. These were serious career mistakes although I don't suppose he had too many choices left when it came to his departure from Sunderland.'

Hood, as a player, didn't know just how limited the choices were when Ian McColl reached the decision that his audacious signing of Jim Baxter had not worked out the way he had intended and that for the sake of morale at the club he had to go. Getting rid of him was now a major concern for the manager who had staked his own reputation on the Scottish international.

If there had been a severe lack of competition for the hard-to-handle star's signature when he was leaving Rangers there were even fewer takers now. Only a few months earlier he had dazzled the nation with his exploits against the World Cup holders, England, at Wembley, in Scotland's 3–2 victory. However, even that was not enough to convince managers in England that he was worth buying. His reputation had been in tatters when he left Rangers and the general view now was that he had reached rock bottom.

Ian McColl soon discovered that. The memories from that difficult period still clearly hurt the former Sunderland manager whose admiration for Baxter's ability was unbounded. Yet here he was hawking this unique talent around England and being rebuffed at every turn. He admits: 'There was no chance of him going to a bigger club, a better club, because the English managers had learned about his off-field problems. It had been hard for Jim to keep a low profile in Glasgow; in Sunderland the glare of publicity rarely left him. It was a depressing cycle for Jim and for the club and for me, because I did feel responsible for him, but I ran out of options and he had to be sold. That was not easy.

'I learned on the grapevine that Manchester City might have an interest though I didn't know how strong that interest was. The suggestion was that the players, Francis Lee and Mike Summerbee and one or two others were keen that the club should sign Jim. Well, Joe Mercer was the manager and Malcolm Allison was his assistant and so I called Joe and asked him straight out if he wanted to buy Baxter. He told me: "No way I want him near this club" and so that was one door closed. By this time I was ready to take thirty grand for him because I had young players such as Colin Todd coming through and I knew we could fill the gap quite easily if only we could unload him. Thirty thousand pounds, honestly, I would have accepted that. And, remember, this was for the best player I have ever seen when it came to running a game, to orchestrating matches and just controlling the entire proceedings. He was without peer at that – yet no one wanted him!

'I had just about given up hope of completing any transfer deal when out of the blue our chairman, Syd Collings, came back from either a Football Association or English League meeting in London and told me that the chairman of Nottingham Forest, a man called Tony Wood, had made an approach to him about possibly buying Baxter.

'I don't know where he had been not to know we were desperately trying to flog Jim because, by this time, as well as Joe Mercer, I had spoken to Matt Busby, Bill Nicholson and one or two others and they had all given me the same answer. It broke my heart to hear these rejections so this approach was a break for me and for the club. I had almost given up hope of selling him and, basically, I didn't know where to turn next when this interest surfaced out of nowhere. Right away I told my chairman that I was ready to do business and Forest offered us £100,000 – I could hardly believe it. We had paid Rangers nearly £30,000 less than that and here we were, at a time when the top clubs had turned their backs on him, being offered the opportunity to make a profit on a player we knew we had to sell. It was all down to Tony Wood who had just been made chairman of the club. A committee ran Forest then and everyone was given a go at being chairman and this time it was Tony Wood's turn. He was a wealthy man – I think his family had made a lot of money in the mills of the town – and he was very ambitious for the club. He wanted to attract big name players there and Jim Baxter was going to be one of them. He may have been influenced by the game against England at Wembley. I don't know, but he wanted Jim and he seemed oblivious to the worries that all the other clubs I approached had expressed. Wood did the deal himself. Johnny Carey was the manager, but I am certain that he did not want Jim, and a few months after the signing he had left the club. It was a godsend for Sunderland and also for Jim, in a financial sense. He picked up another £10,000, doubled his wages and managed to remain in the first division with a club that had finished runners-up to a very strong Manchester United side the previous season.

'This was surely another chance for him to make that fresh start he so often claimed he wanted to do, but it was too late. When he moved down to Nottingham things went from bad to worse as far as his behaviour was concerned. And when you saw him play he looked even less interested than he had done in his last few months with us at Sunderland. It didn't last long before he was given a free transfer and returned to Rangers. That finished quickly too and he was out of the game altogether by the time he was thirty years old. I spent eighteen years in the game with Queens Park and Rangers and Jim didn't come near that. That was the real tragedy. He had so much more to offer but he wasn't able to last the pace, he found himself unable to meet the demands that were placed on him when he left Rangers. The day he walked out of Ibrox was probably the turning point of his career. After that he was never the same player. All he gave us were glimpses of his genius. It was so sad.

'But I don't think anyone could have changed the direction his career took. When I was a player with Rangers we were all frightened of the manager, Bill Struth, because he held real power over the players. Once, when George Young, the biggest name in Scottish football at the time, refused to re-sign, Struth simply left him sitting in the stand and played one of the reserves, a fellow called Johnny Lindsay, who played very well, in a game against Morton. Now Morton had the likes of Jimmy Cowan, Neil Mochan and Tommy Orr in their side yet we won 2–1 down at Cappielow in the League Cup. Big George signed on the Monday and was back in the team without any rise in wages. That worked then – it wouldn't have worked with Jim Baxter. Even Struth would not have been able to handle him. I suppose it all ended up a real mess at Rangers – the club missed Baxter's influence and he missed the stability that Ibrox had offered him though he would never have admitted that. He never did say that he had made a mistake moving to England. His answer was always the same, he got the money he was looking for when Rangers would not give him that.'

And so, at the City Ground in Nottingham, the destruction of his genius continued in a last tragic postscript to his brief spell in the English first division.

9 DRUNK 'N' SOBERS IN NOTTINGHAM

When Forest played host to Manchester United, who were en route to winning the European Cup that season, Johnny Carey was still in charge. In a bid to reawaken Baxter's fading ambitions he went up to him, for a quiet – and what he hoped would be an encouraging, perhaps even inspiring – word as he was pulling on his boots. Joe Baker, sitting alongside Baxter heard Carey say: 'Listen to the crowd out there. Just listen to that. This is your type of game, your stage, just go out there and show them all what you can do.'

Baxter stood up, placed one foot on the bench to tie his bootlace and started to sing, 'Those were the days, my friend, I thought they'd never end.' Carey simply turned on his heel and walked away as he realised there was now no point in wasting any talk on the player he had not bought and had not wanted.

For anyone who did now know the nature of the beast it would have been hard to imagine things becoming any worse for the midfield icon of Scottish football than they had been during his troubled years with Sunderland. But, for James Curran Baxter, there were always fresh delights waiting in whatever city he ended up earning his living. Nottingham was no different in that respect and in an era when nightclubs were beginning to open their doors across provincial England and gambling was readily available in every city in the land it had not been left behind. Baxter settled in happily – not at the City Ground, perhaps, but in the night life where doors opened magically for the new star with Forest, the midfield great who was going to take them one step further than the season before and win them the title. That was the popular belief – the truth was more than a little different from the authorised version enjoyed by the supporters.

Baxter knew he was no longer capable of reaching the heights he had scaled so effortlessly at Wembley just six months earlier. A near-decade of dissipation had taken its toll at last – with Vancouver probably adding the coup de grace to the last remaining remnants of his fitness. Looking back in later years he would own up to his failures at Forest saying unequivocally: 'Going to Forest was a disaster. It was a disaster for me but it was a disaster for Forest and it was my fault. I let the club and the supporters down.

'It seemed that the years of self-indulgence had caught up and I knew what was happening to me. I was still confident enough and I knew what I wanted to do with the ball but I was losing that extra little bit of pace I needed. And training was becoming harder and harder. I knew from the very start that things were not going to work.'

Joe Baker was at the City Ground when the news of Baxter's

arrival was announced, to the surprise of the manager, Johnny Carey, and the players. The one-time English striker, who was at Torino with Denis Law in the 1960s and who also played for Hibs and Arsenal, smiles: 'I read about the transfer in the local newspaper at Nottingham in the morning before going into training. When the manager came into the dressing room I said to him, "I see we're signing a new player, Boss" – just like that. And you know what, he didn't even bother to answer me. He just walked away shaking his head kind of sadly. It was pretty obvious that he had not been involved in the transfer at all. The lads had all guessed that because Jim wasn't the type of character Johnny Carey would have wanted to have at the club. We all knew that it was Tony Wood who had done the business. He was a kind of a flash guy with the Rolls Royce and everything and it was his turn to be chairman and he wanted to make a big splash and get a lot of publicity by bringing in a big name player. I would doubt he even discussed the possibility of buying Jim with the manager. So it was not the best atmosphere for Jim when he did sign. It was never going to be easy for him knowing that the Gaffer didn't want him, that he had been more or less foisted on the guy who was responsible for the team.

'But it was even worse than that because Jim knew that he was just about finished by the time he was signing for Forest. It was a real shame, he was not fit and he knew that. He used to say to me – "I'm knackered. I'm finished. There's no use trying to go on because I just can't do it any more" – and this was a man of just 28 speaking. That's all the age he was when he came to the City Ground. I think he had had his 28th birthday three months or so earlier. He should have been at his peak and I kept trying to convince him that he could still keep going. But he wasn't for being kidded. He knew it was over. He knew that better than anyone else. All the years of drinking, all the parties and the late nights had caught up with him and yet, even with that realisation, he didn't let it bother him. Nothing appeared to worry Jim; nothing at all was allowed to upset him. He was so relaxed about life and it was always as if he was just happy to get up every morning and get on with whatever the day had to offer him. Most of the time that meant more of the same lifestyle he had enjoyed in Glasgow and Sunderland with a little extra thrown in. He missed nothing, believe me!'

Johnny Carey left the job of handling the unwanted Baxter mainly to his right-hand man Tommy Cavanagh, who was later to enjoy a successful spell at Manchester United as assistant to Tommy Docherty. Cav was a man who pulled no punches when dealing with players but even he was shocked by the first of the new player's many transgressions. Sitting quietly at home one night, not long after the signing, he found himself answering an emergency call to get Baxter out of trouble. It was history repeating itself as Ian McColl could have confirmed, having been summoned to perform similar rescue acts too many times in the past at Sunderland. Cavanagh can still visualise the condition Baxter was in when he drove into the centre of the city to collect him.

'He was a complete mess,' he says. 'I had, more or less, to pick him up out of the gutter because he had got himself into a fight in one of the clubs. He had been given a bit of a kicking. At the time there was a suggestion that some of the bouncers at the club had done it, but we never found out because we wanted to hush the whole thing up. I had warned him that Nottingham could be a tough city but he didn't believe me until that night. That was early on and for a week or two I kept him away from the training. His face was cut and bruised and I didn't want the other lads having a go at him. He would come in to train in the afternoons, once he had recovered from the doing he got, always when no one else was there and I would work away with him. When he rejoined the first team I told the players to say nothing to him, but they all knew – there was no way you could keep the lid on that kind of thing in a place the size of Nottingham.

'Still, they were OK, they were a good bunch of lads and they allowed him to get himself together a little bit, but I knew, and he knew, that he was never going to be one hundred per cent fit the way he should have been. To give him his due he worked hard and he tried to get there but it was too late for him when he got to the City Ground I'm afraid. I put in a lot of extra work with him but he was badly out of condition and his stamina had gone so that he could never last a full ninety minutes any longer. You know, Joe Baker, and he was another great player, he said to me, "You won't get on with Jim Baxter", because Joe knew him of old, but I liked him and I tried everything I knew to get him back to something like his best because he was such a gifted footballer. But he had a social life that had taken over and he was the kind of fellow who was always going to find mischief whether in Glasgow or Sunderland or Nottingham or anywhere you want to mention. That was just the way he was.'

A great deal of that social life, for part of the year at any rate, revolved around Nottinghamshire County Cricket Club whose Trent Bridge headquarters was close to Forest's own City Ground. There, Baxter struck up a friendship with the West Indian all-rounder Gary Sobers, one of the elements of which was cemented in a shared love of the good life. Of course that required sufficient amounts of booze to allow proceedings to go smoothly, and when the two first met they did so with a bottle of whisky placed on the table in front of Sobers, his drink of choice, and the trademark bottle of Bacardi for Baxter.

'We would go along to watch the cricket after training,' Joe Baker remembers, 'and spend the afternoon at Trent Bridge and when it was over the two of them would get at it – a bottle each – and they were known around the town as "Drunk 'n' Sobers". They were good pals and they enjoyed drinking together – I could never keep up with them. Once when I did go on the town with Jim, he drove me home, took me up to the front door and told my wife, "He's not going out with me again until he learns to drink." Thankfully I never did pass his test, which was pretty demanding!

'I used to worry about him because even then he looked

Left The youthful Jim Baxter, still with Raith Rovers and not too long after his escape from the pits, December 1959. Six months after this photograph was taken Baxter had joined Rangers in a transfer deal that valued him at £17,500. (© Empics)

Below The former Celtic captain and manager, Billy McNeill, assures us that his friend looked good in his uniform when he was called up for National Service (October 1960). But it's doubtful if Baxter, a rebel throughout his life, ever took to the discipline of the Black Watch. (© Empics)

Left A young, fresh faced Jim Baxter in his early days with Rangers poses alongside another Ibrox legend in the foyer of Glasgow's St Enoch Hotel. He is Alan Morton, the 'Wee Blue Devil' from the famous Wembley Wizards team that defeated England 5–1 in 1928. By this time Morton was a director of his former club and Baxter insisted to photographer Derek Clarkson that he be included in the picture. 'I want my wee friend in this one,' he declared and Clarkson reluctantly agreed not knowing until his father told him later who Morton was! (© Derek Clarkson)

Below The trappings of sixties success arrived soon after Baxter was sold to Rangers. Here he has just parked his Jaguar in the Ibrox car park in December 1962, light years away from the miners' rows where he was born and grew up. Not that the Rangers star ever forgot his roots. He remained a Fifer in accent and attitude for the whole of his life. (© Empics)

Above left A typical action shot of Baxter in his Ibrox heyday as he demonstrates the superb balance that set him aside from other players and added an extra dimension to his game. (© Empics)

Above right Jim Baxter with his former wife Jean only a year before their traffic-stopping marriage in her home town of Coatbridge. (© Derek Clarkson)

Left Promoted to team captain, Baxter leads the Rangers team out with goalkeeper Billy Ritchie behind him as they prepare to face Dunfermline in a League game, August 1964. (© Empics)

Left Baxter is seen here with his second team – the porters at the St Enoch Hotel who looked after his every need during his years with Rangers. If Baxter wanted late night drinking it was there for him, always at the club's expense, and always provided by the adoring staff. (© Derek Clarkson)

Right Now here's a good way to avoid all that running round the track that the other players are doing – that could be Baxter's reason for turning up in goal during a Scotland training session prior to a World Cup tie against Finland in October 1964. Scotland won the game 3–1. (© Empics)

Right A man alone. Baxter refused on this occasion to join the Cup winning celebrations with the rest of the players and the directors. He was at loggerheads over his contract and had decided he would go his own way. Next door the Scottish Cup was being filled with champagne. Baxter sat in the lounge with his trademark drink, Bacardi and Coke. (© Derek Clarkson)

The moment that some feel marked the beginning of Baxter's decline as a player. The Rangers star lies in agony in the Prater Stadium in Vienna after suffering a broken leg in the dying minutes of the game (December 1964). Within a few short months Baxter was being transferred to Sunderland. (© Empics)

Left Baxter turned himself into a fashion icon for the young men of Glasgow (November 1965). Sir Alex Ferguson says, 'He would walk down the street looking like Errol Flynn. He had real style!' (© Empics)

Below Baxter strolls away from a Rangers work-out with Willie Henderson and Willie Mathieson following him from the Albion training ground. Predictably it appears here as though Baxter was first to finish. No great surprise. (© Derek Clarkson)

Left May 1969: Rangers manager Davie White and his assistant, one time Ibrox centre forward Willie Thornton, watch as Baxter rejoins the Glasgow club after his disastrous period in England with Sunderland and Nottingham Forest. In later years the player would tell anyone willing to listen that White, soon to be sacked, paid him higher wages than any other manager he ever had. (© Empics)

Below Family man. Baxter is seen here with his sons Alan and Steven in August 1978. Even after the break-up of his marriage he remained in touch with his sons and became close to them in his last years of illness. (© Empics)

Left A frail-looking Jim Baxter emerges from Edinburgh Royal Infirmary in August 1991 following the liver transplant operation that caused so much unnecessary controversy across Scotland. (© Empics)

Below Back where he belongs ... in the Ibrox spotlight. Baxter gives a new generation a glimpse of his genius in September 1990 as he takes the field before an Old Firm game after accepting an invitation from Rangers to return to the scene of so many triumphs. (© Empics)

awful at times, really ill. After training he would be lying in the bath and his colour would be grey or even, sometimes, yellow, depending I suppose on how much he had had to drink the night before. Cav used to try to keep an eye on him, give him extra training for instance, and then we would worry about him being in the bath on his own after the rest of us were dressed and ready to head off home. We were genuinely concerned that he might be lying there and just slip under the water and drown because of the state he was in.

'Then he would come out, get himself organised, and if I was still around he would say "Jojo" – that was his name for me – "are you ready for a pint?" and I would tell him that I was heading off home. There was no way I could keep up with him. I knew that it would not be the one pint. That drink would lead to another and the likelihood was that he would keep on drinking in some club or other until the early hours and he would be in at training the next day looking a total wreck. That was the pattern during his time at the club, football was not exactly a priority by this stage of his career.'

The Celtic full back and Lisbon Lion, Tommy Gemmell, went to Forest around eighteen months after Baxter had left. When he got there he was sorry to find that the stories told in the dressing room about his fellow Scot focused on his extra-curricular activities rather than his playing ability. Gemmell confesses: 'The saddest thing down there during my spell at the club was that his ability as a player was almost never mentioned. You see, I don't think they ever saw the real Jim Baxter play, not the Baxter we saw in Scotland.

'And so all I heard were the stories of his bevvying and there were plenty of those. They had a half back line at Forest when he went there – Terry Hennessy, a Welsh international was there and, of course, you had Hennessy's brandy; then you had Bob McKinlay at centre half, and you had McKinlay's whisky and Jim was left half. In the dressing room the lads used to read out the half back line as Hennessy, McKinlay and Bacardi – Jim took that as a compliment! As for the Drunk 'n' Sobers partnership, the best story I ever heard about that was when England were playing the West Indies in a Test match at Trent Bridge. Jim and some of the other players and a couple of his mates went along as Gary Sobers' guests after the lads had finished the morning training session. Now, the steward in the clubhouse told them that there was a rule which meant they could not buy any drinks, so Gary sorted that out and told the lad to put it all on his tab. That was OK except for one thing: he went out and batted for a day and a half. Jim and his mates thought they should toast this great innings so they returned the next day and, when Gary finally came in, he found a bar bill which was about a yard long!'

The gambling continued along with the drinking and his one-time Rangers team-mate, Jim Forrest, was shocked when Baxter once revealed that he had blown nearly £6,000 in one afternoon at the races in Nottingham. Forrest claims: 'He just laughed when he told the story. It didn't mean all that much to him. He treated it as if it was a joke, which suggests that betting like that was just part of his way of life. When I was at Preston I went to see him one day and he was still the same Jim, but there were signs that the fitness was going – there was a belly there that hadn't been there at Rangers and a puffiness around his face. He knew what was happening. He had only to look in the mirror to see it. He wasn't a fool by any manner of means. He was a very bright individual but he had this philosophy that saw him just live for the moment. The worst thing of all near the end was watching him struggle during games.

'And all the time you did so knowing that not even Jim Baxter could turn that clock back as it ticked away ending his playing life far too soon.'

The well-meaning Tommy Cavanagh attempted that feat, trying to stop time running out on the former international, urging the suddenly old midfielder to do extra training and on occasion when he was dropped and found himself in the reserves the coach would make him captain. He hoped that the extra responsibility might spark a reaction, restore some degree of professionalism.

For a spell it would work but only until he returned to the first team and once he was there he was back on the old familiar road to ruin. 'I sometimes used to wish I had got a hold of him when he was younger,' Cavanagh says, 'and maybe we would have been able to work things out in a way that would have extended his career. I mean you're talking about someone who was finished when he should have been in his prime. All he had to do was to look after himself a little bit better but he never did think about the future. He had this gift, you see, and he thought it would always be there, that it would never let him down. Well, it didn't but his fitness deserted him and that, in turn, meant that his skills were no longer any use to him. He could only last fifteen or twenty minutes in any game. The whole business surrounding the transfer upset the team and the club as a whole. Instead of building on that second place position as we had planned we slid down the table. It all went wrong – not just because of Jim but also because of how it was done. Johnny Carey was undermined as the manager. That should never have happened. It had a disastrous effect and even when Matt Gillies came in to take over the job nothing was going to change the way we were heading. And a new manager wasn't going to work any kind of transformation on Jim. It reached the stage where he just had to go. There was no future left for him at Forest.'

The words Cavanagh used as Baxter's City Ground epitaph were the same as those employed by Ian McColl when the break with Sunderland was inevitable. No matter what levels of genius Baxter had reached during his time in the game, managers and clubs had run out of sympathy. McColl was one of his greatest champions; Cavanagh admits to a similar admiration for his talent and to liking him as a person despite his many faults. Neither of them, though, could see any alternative to being rid of him when his presence at both Roker Park and the City Ground began to cause problems that were on course to damaging the very fabric of the clubs and might, indeed, already have done so. It was a tragic situation for a player who had captivated a nation like no one before him had done on that April afternoon at Wembley just two years before.

As Jim Forrest and others have observed, Baxter must have known the damage he had wrought on himself and his career and yet, when others would have been in the black pit of despair, he still tossed off the easy quips as if he simply didn't care.

For example when Forest played host to Manchester United, who were en route to winning the European Cup that season, Johnny Carey was still in charge. In a bid to reawaken Baxter's fading ambitions he went up to him, for a quiet – and what he hoped would be an encouraging, perhaps even inspiring – word as he was pulling on his boots. Joe Baker, sitting alongside Baxter heard Carey say: 'Listen to the crowd out there. Just listen to that. This is your type of game, your stage, just go out there and show them all what you can do.'

Baxter stood up, placed one foot on the bench to tie his bootlace and started to sing, 'Those were the days, my friend, I thought they'd never end.' Carey simply turned on his heel and walked away as he realised there was now no point in wasting any talk on the player he had not bought and had not wanted. This was an attitude he had never encountered in a lifetime in the game and it was one he could not even begin to understand. He knew that no one could now reach Baxter and that it was pointless to believe he could be steered away from the path of self-destruction he had embarked upon. Soon after that incident Johnny Carey left Forest while Baxter survived for another year following the manager's exit.

Baker insists that Baxter meant no real malice in his response to Carey's attempt to psyche him up before the United game. 'You had to know Jim to understand him properly,' he explains. 'The manager knew he was a big occasion player and he thought that he could talk him into playing well – but Jim knew that he was asking too much. He knew that he couldn't run games the way he once did and this was just his way of owning up to that. He was being honest in his own way. He was not going to try to kid anyone. By the time he came to play for us he had just given up.'

Even, though, by his own standards of brilliance he had slipped into mediocrity and had, as Joe Baker says, 'just given up' there were sometimes moments when he cast aside the despondency which had settled on his play to produce some little gem of skill dredged from his memories of all those better times he had enjoyed.

Dave Mackay had warned his friend that the day of reckoning would arrive but even he had not believed it would come as early as it did. Yet the Spurs icon, someone for whom Baxter had unstinting admiration as a footballer, knows for a fact that there are still Forest supporters around from the 1960s who warm at the very mention of Baxter's name. He lives close to Nottingham and goes to games there.

'There are people around who still talk about him, you know,' he says. 'I have been living in this area for around thirty years now and there were Forest supporters who just loved him. Even though we all knew he was struggling when he came down to England there were still signs from him during games that had people gasping. They still remember some of the things he did on the field, still mention some of the passes he made, and while these moments lasted for maybe just a minute or two he was still able to conjure up things that other players could never have hoped to match. He was supposed to be finished when he signed for Forest but there were still these moments when he could capture the support, and the memories still remain.'

Some of them have stayed with Tommy Cavanagh for over thirty years now, and it was the knowledge that some pieces of magic still remained that had the ultra-professional working with Baxter on the training ground and attempting to encourage him as he came towards the end of his spell with the Midlands club. As Baxter was packing his gear for the last time before travelling north to rejoin Rangers, Cavanagh exhorted him, 'Keep working hard at the training. You have been doing that here and you have to keep on doing it. If you slacken off now then any benefits we might have been able to get over the past few months will be lost forever. I don't want that work wasted.'

For a short time Baxter seemed to have listened to some good advice at last, but the Ibrox comeback was blighted inside five months, as we shall see. At the City Ground the team-mates he was leaving behind were making book on whether Baxter would notch up a hat trick of sacked managers on his Glasgow homecoming.

Baker shakes his head as he points out the damning statistic which so intrigued the Forest players. 'Just after he signed for us the manager, Johnny Carey, left the club and we all knew that it was down to the fact that Jim had been signed without anyone even telling him what was going on. Then, while he was at the club, the news came that Ian McColl had been fired by Sunderland, and the way Jim had carried on up there after all that money had been paid for him led us to the conclusion that, though he had left Roker Park, the sacking was still down to him. We were waiting for Davie White, the manager of Rangers, to give him his hat trick.

'Of course, we all wanted to see him do well, particularly myself. But after what he had been telling me I just could not see it happening. He was drinking far too much by this time – one over the dozen I used to say – and it was destroying what was left of his fitness. Five or six months down the road Davie White was sacked. Jimmy had his hat trick of managerial victims and it was all over for him too. It was a shame because despite his problems he had been popular with the fans. At Forest, as I knew, and then at Sunderland as I discovered when I signed on at Roker Park – I moved in a different direction from Jim. They all had their own personal recollections of the stardust he still scattered on the odd occasions during games. So many of the fans held these dear and they will never lose them.'

They were, though, too infrequent to salvage anything further from English football and Baxter returned to Rangers. It must have seemed to him as if he was returning home, but even the emotional reunion with the Ibrox club was doomed to end in tears and recriminations and eventual humiliation for the club's greatest-ever player. Then, too, of course, there was the sacking of that third manager.

10 'THE KING IS BACK'

The fact that he was signed on a free transfer from Forest could not dampen the enthusiasm of the fans nor affect the sales of T-shirts emblazoned with the message 'The King Is Back'! Few realised, though, how fragile his hold on his skills had become or how desperately low his fitness levels had reached even though he had been trying to halt that particular deterioration with extra training before moving back to Glasgow. In spite of all the difficulties he had faced on and off the field, most of them well documented in the Scottish press, an air of optimism surrounded the signing. The 'feel good factor' White had looked to restore among the support was there in abundance. All that the manager and his players, especially his new high profile signing, had to do to maintain that was produce the on-field results. That was always going to be the tricky part.

When the Rangers manager Davie White made the decision to gamble on the signing of the club's former hero, Jim Baxter, in the summer of 1969, he could not have realised that his own future would be so swiftly and sensationally intertwined with that of the fallen idol. The Ibrox club, of course, had been in decline since the midfielder's departure for Sunderland four years before. In the seasons since he had left, Rangers had won the Scottish Cup on one solitary occasion – a stark contrast to the years of plenty enjoyed when Baxter was at his peak. What made things worse for the club and for their legions of frustrated fans was that as their own standing in the domestic game was damaged their bitter Old Firm rivals Celtic had embarked on a course of glory which was unparalleled since the club was founded the previous century. Almost at the same moment as the imperious Baxter had left the Old Firm scene, Jock Stein had been appointed manager of Celtic and soon he was dominating the ancient fixture much in the manner that the Rangers superstar had during his five seasons at Ibrox.

Before the transfer to Sunderland Stein's Celtic had won the Scottish Cup and in the intervening years had taken four successive league titles; another two Scottish Cups; four League Cups, as well as two domestic 'trebles' and the ultimate club prize – the European Cup which was won in Lisbon with a 2- victory over Inter Milan in 1967.

In that same summer Rangers had also reached the final of a European competition – the Cup Winners' Cup – but had lost to Bayern Munich by a single goal scored in extra time in a match that was played in Nuremberg, home territory for the West German club. That was all they had to show for their endeavours since their mainspring had left. Now White saw the possibility of resurrecting the player's career, bringing Rangers fresh glories as he did so, breaking the Stein stranglehold and appeasing a support that was becoming deeply disillusioned by the constant lack of success.

That was the backdrop to Baxter's reappearance, and the fact that he was signed on a free transfer from Forest could not dampen the enthusiasm of the fans nor affect the sales of T-shirts emblazoned with the message 'The King Is Back'! Few realised, though, how fragile his hold on his skills had become or how desperately low his fitness levels had reached even though he had been trying to halt that particular deterioration with extra training before moving back to Glasgow. In spite of all the difficulties he had faced on and off the field, most of them well documented in the Scottish press, an air of optimism surrounded the signing. The 'feel good factor' White had looked to restore among the support was there in abundance. All that the manager and his players, especially his new high profile signing, had to do to maintain that was produce the on-field results. That was always going to be the tricky part.

White, however, despite inevitable setbacks and some boardroom in-fighting that had preceded the deal, was confident that they could make it happen together. And Baxter himself saw the move as yet another lifeline, and this time he knew there would not be another chance for him if things went badly. He knew that his time at Forest had been a total disaster and if any confirmation of that was required then it came when the club placed him on the open-to-transfer list at just £15,000 and found no takers. Soon afterwards he was released and suffered the ignominy of discovering his fate only when he read the sports pages of the local newspaper. Therefore when he was contacted by a Glasgow-based journalist and informed that Rangers were prepared to sign him his confidence soared. As some of his Ibrox team-mates had already indicated, Baxter had not really wanted to leave the Glasgow club but was forced to do so over what he believed to be a matter of principle. When he discovered there was a route being opened up for him to make the return journey, he confessed: 'While I had fallen out with the board of directors I knew that Rangers were *the* club. I began to believe the old saying that "once a Ranger, always a Ranger" because there was just something about Ibrox, about the club, which makes you proud to be a part of it all. The thought of being welcomed back appealed to me.'

There was another signing offer made by Hearts but, while Baxter spoke to the Tynecastle manager Johnny Harvey, he had made up his mind to await the call from Davie White. That duly arrived and he travelled north to finalise a deal which would see him sign a one-year contract – though, as ever when money and Jim Baxter and Rangers were involved, there was still some serious horse trading to be done.

White takes up the story. 'It was very much my personal gamble to bring Jim back to Ibrox. And I recognised that it was a risk because he had been going through a very bad period at Forest. However, I thought that we required an injection of real class into the team and Jim was the man who could give us that. At the time we had a strong leader and a very aggressive player in John Greig, who was the team captain, but it was my view that Jim would add an extra dimension.' (It's strange that White's reasons for signing the midfield player were an exact echo of those that were credited to his predecessor in the manager's office, Scot Symon, when he bought the slim youngster from Raith Rovers. Almost a decade on and that 'new dimension' was still what was expected from Baxter no matter what travails he had suffered in the intervening period of time in England.)

White had opposition from some of the directors when he first raised the possibility of bringing back the prodigal son. He recollects: 'There were some of the directors who still used to boast at the board meetings that it had taken them just two minutes to decide to sell Jim Baxter. They were proud of that! They thought they had been clever! But I could never understand where they were coming from talking in that way about the player who was possibly the best the club had ever had. Some of them didn't want him back. There was even one of the players in the team at the time who came to see me and told me he didn't want to be in the same dressing room as Jimmy because he thought that he was going to be a disruptive influence. I chased him out of my office and I told the directors that I was in charge of team matters and so any decision on signing a player was going to be made by me. People probably wondered why I went into the deal when it appeared to be strewn with problems. Basically I still had a strong belief in Jimmy's ability and in the influence he could exert on the field. He was an exceptional player and I knew that from playing against him when he was at Rangers before and I was a wing half with Clyde. We knew each other from those days and I felt that would help strengthen my relationship with him. Possibly, I thought, a manager, closer to his own age, someone he remembered playing against, would be able to offer him a little more understanding. And I also thought that any of the baggage he brought with him could be handled if a little care and understanding could be brought into play.

'Remember we were getting him for nothing, one of the finest players you would ever see, and he was available without a transfer fee. So I thought that getting him to re-sign for the club was far more important than worrying about any of the off-field activities he had been involved in down at Nottingham. It was obvious that we would have to work on his fitness, get his weight down for a start, and also on his discipline. My feeling was that you always had to concern yourself with disciplining players, most often lesser players, so it was just another part of your job as a club manager. What I hadn't expected at the initial talks was that he would argue with me over how his signing-on fee was going to be paid. Being very aware that he was a heavy gambler it was my idea to give him a signing-on fee in kind as it were. Prior to the meeting I had a long talk with the club chairman, John Lawrence, who owned a massive building business in the west of Scotland. I had realised that Baxter would need a house for his wife and family and I wanted them back in Glasgow at the same time as he was. I didn't want a repeat of the St Enoch Hotel carry-on he had had before. The last thing I needed was for Jim Baxter to be living on his own in a Glasgow hotel!

'My idea was to give him a house which would be worth around the £10,000 or so we were thinking about as a signing inducement. The chairman agreed to make a house available in Bearsden that he could move into straight away and the club would finance this. To begin with, though, Jim was reluctant. He wanted cash, and I did not want him laying his hands on that much money in one lump sum. He took twenty-four hours to think it over and returned the next day with his lawyer, who told me that everything was perfectly acceptable, and the contract was signed.'

The irony of the whole affair could not have been lost on the player. Though he might have quibbled over the method of payment he would have realised that he was now getting what he had asked for when the club sold him at the height of his powers. He had wanted cash to enable him to buy a house – now, when his talent was clearly on the wane, he was being handed a house by the same men who had held his fate in their hands and decided what it would be in a bare two minutes. He was also returning to an Ibrox set-up where salaries had been brought more into line with those being paid in the first division in England. Not as high, but better than he could ever have believed they would be when he walked away from his pitiful £45 a week. Perhaps his stand, in part, had led to a Rangers rethink on the whole question of the dressing-room wage structure.

In any case here he was now benefiting from the more liberal approach to players' salaries, and his weekly pay was in line with what he had been earning down south, and the 'gift' of the house was a major breakthrough at a club which had been noted previously for its parsimony. In today's terms that house in Bearsden would be valued at close to a quarter of a million pounds, a fair old payday for a player who had just been dumped by an unfashionable and now struggling English first division side.

Baxter had sensed, by now, that if he was indeed standing in that Last Chance Saloon he was being well looked after and, unlike his spell at Forest, he should do something to pay back White and the club for allowing him this further opportunity to redeem himself. Yet, there was still one last flourish from the hellraiser who was claiming, once more, to be a reformed character.

The morning after the signing had taken place and Baxter had told journalists how he had turned over a new leaf and how he was dedicated to restoring Rangers to their former greatness, the telephone rang in the manager's office. Still grimacing at the memory of that call, White says: 'It was a senior police officer on the other end of the line who identified himself and then said, "David, I have some not too good news for you. Your newest signing has been in trouble over in Fife and I felt you should know about it. He has been caught drink-driving and I wanted to warn you." I thanked him and sat there for a few seconds in a bit of a daze. Here was the first sign of trouble and it was on his first day. I couldn't believe it after all the promises he had made and I decided that I would call him upstairs whenever I knew he had come in for training. I didn't have to do that. While I was preparing myself for what I was going to say to him the buzzer sounded at the door. I gave the answering buzz to tell whoever was outside that they could come in and it was Jimmy who appeared. Before I could start on at him he owned up to what had happened. He told me what had happened, that he had been in 'a bit of bother' over in Fife and he wanted to tell me before it made the newspapers.

'Then he also apologised for letting me, and the club, down and explained that he had gone back up to Fife to celebrate with some of his mates and things had got out of hand. He promised me that he would not give me any more headaches. In a way the incident worked in my favour. He was very conscious of the fact that he had come close to blowing the whole comeback and now he knew he could not step out of line again. The last thing he wanted was bad publicity about his off-field behaviour, he had had enough of that in Nottingham, and so I gave him a dressing down, told him he would be fined and then spelled out to him exactly what would be expected from him in the future. He didn't really give me any more bother after that. He was an intelligent lad and he knew that before I signed him his career had hit the skids. He was going nowhere and, now he was back where he wanted to be, he didn't want to miss out and find himself on the scrap heap.'

The directors might have been against the signing and there was that solitary player who made his feelings known about Baxter rejoining the club, but there were others in the dressing room who welcomed him and who believed he could be good for the club.

Sir Alex Ferguson was going through his own difficulties with the Ibrox hierarchy at that time, but he maintains: 'Even after all he had gone through at Forest and ending up with a free transfer there he still possessed this great confidence in his own ability. He never really lost that; no matter the circumstances he always had that belief in himself and what he could do when he had the ball at his feet. When he came back to Rangers I was a player there and I could see that his fitness had dropped, but he still had that incredible conviction, that certainty about his ability, and it never left him. That's why I believe Davie White brought him back. He wanted that kind of influence around the dressing room. Rangers were not doing well by their standards and Celtic were the team winning everything in sight. The players at Ibrox needed someone who could lift them on the field, someone who would have the ability to convince them that they were as good a team as Celtic were.

'And, while he was not the player he had been before he left Glasgow, he was still able to be influential during the biggest of games, the bigger the better as far as he was concerned, even at that difficult period in his career. He just loved the big stage, always did. That was where he shone brightest of all. He showed that in the first Old Firm game he played during that second spell with the club.

'But, even when he was away from the limelight then, he was working hard to get himself as fit as possible. He did a great pre-season and he did get rid of some of that extra weight. You could see he wanted to make a go of things. I can remember doing some circuits with him and he never shirked at all. Now as players get older that's when they start to say to the younger lads they are training with "take it easy" or "slow down a bit", stuff like that. Well, I never heard him try that on once. He certainly didn't do it with me. Possibly he did not get enough of the kind of endurance work he would get nowadays because Rangers trained over at the Albion training ground and they just didn't have enough space to do that. But on the circuits and on everything else he did all that was asked of him. I was impressed.

'Of course his reflexes were not as quick any more, they had gone a little bit and there's no doubt that the drink would have done that to him. That did affect him but he was playing OK. That game against Celtic, right at the start of the season, he was absolutely outstanding. It was almost as if he had never been away as far as the support was concerned. He gave them exactly what they wanted to see.

'I'll never forget the dressing room before that game. It was just the second match of the season, a League Cup section game. He had played a few days earlier at Stark's Park against his first senior team Raith Rovers and Rangers had won 3–2 and now it was Celtic, who were also in the qualifying group. I was bombed out, no chance of playing in the first team at all, but I was in the dressing room before the game and he was amazing. He was going around saying things like, 'Just give me the ball and then don't worry about a thing. We were fed up beating them when I was here before and we'll do that again tonight.' And these players who had been accepting that they were second best to Celtic were listening to him and you could see them responding.

'They were so short on confidence then, particularly going in against big Jock and his Celtic team, but Jim wasn't ready to play second fiddle to anyone just yet. He had something he wanted to prove and he couldn't find a better game to do it in. He was in control again; it was like a throwback to his old days, to his great days with the club. It was as if he simply took away all the pressure before the game and even when Harry Hood gave Celtic, who had been clear favourites before the game, the lead after only eight minutes he refused to allow the confidence of the other players to drop. He took over and controlled the game and Rangers scored twice early on in the second half. Orjan Persson and Willie Johnston got the goals and, while Celtic won the return 1–0, Baxter had shown that he was still capable of performing at that level. The work he had done in the pre-season had helped, and another contributory factor was that he was back in the big time, which is where he thought he should always be.'

Some of the other players, though, while still impressed by Baxter's innate skill, had nagging doubts about his physical condition. They remembered him as he had been before and the years between had not been kind to him. They applauded his efforts to push his way back to fitness but centre half Ron McKinnon, now based in South Africa, was still with the Ibrox club when Baxter arrived back there and his verdict was: 'He still had the skill, nothing could ever take that way from him, but it was as if his body had just given up on him. He'd been away just four years but it seemed a lifetime, or in his case several lifetimes. The difference in him was massive. There were some good games he played for us in that spell but he was never 100 per cent fit. He tried wearing a kind of corset thing at training to try to lose some of the weight round his middle. But it was all too late. He had never trained before and I always had the feeling when I watched him that his body was trying to tell him – 'enough is enough'.

Willie Henderson, who was to play a role, albeit unwittingly, in the affair that would end his friend's Ibrox career, remarks: 'Jimmy Baxter never came back to Rangers. It was a shadow that came back to us, nothing more than a shadow of what he had been. It wasn't really him at all. Time had caught up, the years of bad living, the bevy, everything. And I always felt that it stemmed from the time he was sold by Rangers. That hurt him and I don't think he cared as much about the game after that. Yes, he could still play well on occasion but it wasn't right what had happened to him in the years he had been away. I wish it had worked out for him because he should have had a few more years in the game. But it just seemed to be doomed. We all wanted it to go right, wanted Stanley to be back at the top, but deep down I could not see it ever happening. It was sad, awful sad, and it could have been avoided if the club had just given him what he wanted and let him stay where he was happiest.'

Alfie Conn, who starred with both Rangers and Celtic, and enjoyed a spell with Spurs in between, was a teenager when the 'King' went home, and he adds: 'I always wondered if he had been signed to change the focus away from the manager [Davie White], who was under a little bit of pressure, and give the supporters something to make them happy. Certainly it did work that way for the first few months of the season because the fans still held on to their memories of what he had done for the club the first time round. And if he gave them one or two reminders of what he had once been able to do they were fairly happy. But the reality was that he was not fit and no matter how hard he worked he was never going to be fit again. There was a terrific display against Celtic at Ibrox when Rangers won 2–1, and he was still fantastic when he had the ball at his feet. When we were training and we were going one on one and he was the guy with the ball then everyone tried to duck out of the exercise. You just could not get the ball away from him. Normally you could win the ball after a few minutes of trying, but when Jim had it then he would keep it for twenty minutes and no one could take it away. I never saw anyone who had such mastery over the ball. Willie Johnston used to tell me how he would watch him – this was in his first spell at the club – line up a few balls on the eighteen-yard line and then walk along the line hitting them towards goal. He could place them so perfectly and strike them with such perfect weight that they would hit the cross bar and then come back to where he was standing. He would do that kind of thing for fun – but the hard slog of training was a whole different ball game.'

Still, the bold and controversial initiative by White, which was backed by a willingness on the player's part to work harder than he had done at any time during his exile in England, might have succeeded if the manager had not been sacked just four months into that season – and only six months after Baxter had re-signed. When Celtic qualified from the League Cup section and went on to win the trophy, as well as defeating their Old Firm rivals in the first league meeting of the season, the pressure grew inside Ibrox. Then Rangers were dumped out of Europe by the Polish side Gornik in the second round of the Cup Winners' Cup and the knives were out for the young manager. He was not helped by the storm that erupted twenty-four hours ahead of the second leg game against Gornik at Ibrox. Looking back it is difficult to see how so much could be made of what was a relatively minor incident at the team's hotel headquarters in the seaside resort of Largs. Naturally, anything that involved Baxter was news and, when his 'partner in crime' on this occasion was Willie Henderson, then the rumour mills of Glasgow went into overdrive. Basically all that happened was that the two players slept in at the Marine and Curlinghall Hotel where the team were staying before the European tie. Yet, allied to the 3–1 home loss to Gornik, this was enough to have White sacked after only two years as manager of the Glasgow club. It also spelled an end to Baxter's hopes of reviving his career.

More than thirty years later White, still scarred by the manner of his sacking by the club, can recall every minute detail of the episode that was exaggerated to such an extent that it cost him his job.

'Apart from the two defeats from Celtic we were going along OK,' he points out, 'and, as far as I was concerned, Jim was playing his part. He had pushed himself in training, even wrapping himself in bin bags to try to get his weight down. He was giving the team the extra skill I had looked for and he was a good influence in the dressing room, giving some of the younger players a little bit of the confidence that they needed. There was the odd problem, but nothing serious, and I still say that he did a great job for me. It should not have ended the way it did with all kinds of allegations being made against him. I took enormous exception to that because none of the stories were true. It was a case where Jimmy was pilloried because of his past wrongdoings, not for anything that he did while we were staying down at Largs.

'All that occurred there was that he and his room-mate Willie Henderson slept in and missed the team bus which was taking us up to the Inverclyde Centre. That was where we did our training and, after the evening meal the night before, the players were told when the bus would leave the front door of the hotel to take us up there. The only responsibility the backroom staff had after that was to knock on each bedroom door to waken the players in the morning. After that it was up to all of them to get down for breakfast and then be on the bus at the right time. Anyhow, there we were on the bus at the appointed time and all ready to go when the coach Harold Davis and the physio Lawrie Smith did the head count. Jimmy and wee Willie were the only two players missing and big Harry growled: "Leave them to me. I'll go up and get the pair of them." That's when I made my mistake. I told Harry to stay where he was, emphasised that the two players were breaching club discipline and that the other players who were all on time were not going to be held up because of them. I added that it was now quarter to ten on my watch, and that was the time for departure, and we were going to go without them.

'To be perfectly honest, when I look back now, I see that some of the fault over what happened subsequently was mine. It was a matter of being stubborn, sticking to a point of principle when it might have been better to relax the rules a little for this one morning. None of us thought for a moment that something as trivial as two players sleeping in would cause such an impact and produce lurid headlines for the newspapers. It was not as if the training was particularly serious. All the set pieces had been worked on the day before. We had also spent time preparing the tactics we intended to adopt for the game against the Polish side. This was the day before the game and all we were going to do with the squad was give them some light training and then have a kick about. As far as the two absentees were concerned, I told the training staff that we would put them through the mill in the afternoon. There was no way that our preparations for the game were going to be affected because they weren't there. They had done the earlier work and we were set to talk through that again in the evening.

'I suppose I thought that by leaving them it would show the rest of the players that no one, not even the biggest names at the club, would be allowed to flaunt the rules. Things went horribly wrong though because there was one photographer who was at the training session taking pictures of the lads working out. He saw that there were two big names missing and alerted the various sports desks in Glasgow and all hell broke loose. The instant reaction in the newspaper offices was that the two of them had been up in Glasgow partying and drinking the night away – hence their non-appearance at training.

'Given the reputation that Jimmy had created for himself over the years it was an obvious assumption to make – but it was totally wrong. The two players had been in bed at the same time as the rest of the players and had stayed in the hotel all night. You* were one of the first journalists who called me at

---

* White is referring to the fact that I was covering the build-up to the Gornik game for the *Daily Record*.

the hotel later that day when the rumours began to fly around. I still recall explaining the whole thing to you and assuring you that there had been only a minor breach of discipline in that the two players had slept in. You covered the story accurately but other newspapers made a mountain out of a molehill, suggesting that discipline had fallen apart at Rangers. Ironically, it was because I had been a stickler for discipline that the whole affair had exploded on to some of the front pages. If I had told Harold Davis to go up and get the two players down and on to the bus then no one would have known they had spent those extra few minutes in their beds! Standing by the rules so rigidly that November morning eventually cost me my job as manager of Rangers and also saw most of the backroom staff and Jimmy Baxter himself following me out the door at Ibrox.

'The board was told that the players had not stepped out of line, that there had been no serious problem and that sleeping in was their sole offence. They must have known that when I presented my team to the chairman before the game. That was the custom and when I arrived at the stadium on the team bus I went upstairs to the boardroom and handed over the names of the players to the chairman. He then told the rest of the directors what the team was for the game that night. Jimmy and wee Willie were in it and I could see that some did not like that. They believed that there was no smoke without fire, I suppose. Essentially they had their minds made up. It was not the only reason they had for dismissing me but it was something they could point to when they announced that I was being sacked. Some of them had been against bringing Jim Baxter back and this was an opportunity for them to say "I told you so". While I had won that boardroom battle with them and several more, too, I was not going to win the war. Managers are always the losers in any showdown with directors. One or two of them had not liked the way I told them that they knew nothing about the game, so they bided their time and lay in wait for me. When we were knocked out of Europe amidst allegations of a major lack of discipline at the club they seized the moment.'

Baxter himself was never a man to hide his peccadilloes and, after accepting his punishment, he was as surprised as anyone at the stories that began to fly around Glasgow on the eve of their vital match. Some of the tales had the two of them at an all-night party in Largs, others had them in Glasgow gambling heavily, and losing, in one of the city's casinos. Still more suggested that they had not been in their room when the training staff knocked up the players in the morning. You could take your pick from all the various explanations that were on offer. The only story not doing the rounds was the true version that White had confirmed with the two supposed culprits.

Baxter always insisted: 'We went to bed after taking a sleeping pill each, that was routine when you were in a hotel and preparing for a big, important match. In the morning we heard the knock at the door and one of the backroom guys telling us to get out of our beds. OK, neither of us got up but we didn't get any reminder either. I thought that we were in plenty of time when we went down to the front door. The bus wasn't there, none of the players were there, and one of the porters told us that they had left for training. We realised that we were in trouble, that we'd probably be fined for not being there in time, but we had no idea that a simple mistake would be turned into front page news. It was unbelievable what happened and even more unbelievable when this became an excuse for the board to sack the manager.'

'We were given a bawling out from the manager,' adds Henderson, 'and we knew we deserved that. Rangers had their rules and not being downstairs in time for the bus that was to take the team to training was breaking these rules. The reaction, though, was out of proportion. We were never out of that hotel and, while we had done some daft things between us, we would never have gone out drinking eight hours before a vitally important European game. That would have been really stupid.'

Indeed, the two players accepted their punishment and in the game against Gornik they were two of the best Rangers players on show even though the team lost 3–1 on the night – exactly the same score as in the first leg game in Katowice. Baxter scored the Rangers goal after eighteen minutes but in a late collapse the Scottish side lost three goals in the final 25 minutes.

As an interesting footnote to the sleeping-in saga Sir Alex Ferguson, who had left the club to join Falkirk a week prior to the European tie, has memories of similar incidents arising from the back room staff's rigid interpretation of the club rules. He says: 'The trainer, Davie Kinnear, was always the man who insisted that there would be no reminders for any of the players after that one knock on the hotel room door in the morning. If you didn't get up and get yourself down for breakfast and then on to the bus you were left behind.

'There was one time when wee Bud [Willie Johnston] and Colin Stein were sharing a room and they slept in and Greigy [John Greig], who was the club captain, said to Kinnear that he would go upstairs and give them a knock and he was ordered not to do that. The official line was that they had been wakened once and from then on it was their responsibility. On that occasion they got someone at the hotel to give them a lift. I wouldn't blame the players; there should have been some kind of second warning for them. It was just the Rangers way and it cost Davie White his job as the manager and eventually it ended Baxter's career as well. It was a pretty costly affair for them and I honestly don't think it should have happened in that way.'

White accepts responsibility to this day and yet when he delves back into his memory it is clear that he remains almost as upset at Baxter's treatment as at his own. 'I was surprised when the whole carry-on also affected Jim Baxter's future with the club. He had played well in the months he spent in the first team and yet one little mistake was held against him and I have always felt that was wrong. I didn't feel it was the proper decision for the club or the player. Jimmy Baxter had a contribution he could have made and yet, after I left, he played only two or three games in the first team. He was frozen out. He suffered, partly, at least, because I was the man who signed him.

'In my opinion he had given us value for money after the signing was completed. He had regained his appetite for the game and that was down to the fact that returning to Rangers, knowing that he was wanted, had given him a tremendous lift. In the opening Old Firm match of the season he had been superb. Then against Steaua of Bucharest in the first round of the Cup Winners' Cup he had shown he could still compete at the highest level in Europe. We won 2–0 at Ibrox and then drew 0–0 in Romania and Jimmy was very influential in these games. It was a solid result to get against one of the better-known teams from Eastern Europe and we were just unfortunate that we drew Gornik in the next round. Polish football was strong then and in Lubanski they had an outstanding individual talent. Even then, until he ran out of steam at Ibrox, Jim was far and away our best player. And it was not lack of fitness which saw him tire, it was simply that he had worked so very, very hard in the first hour of the game to try to get us the result we needed.'

White's belief in Baxter has never been shaken. Even now he remains convinced that there was still a future for the player because, whatever he might have lost in terms of fitness, he had still been able to retain his ability to 'put the fear of death into opposing teams', in the former Rangers manager's words. Following the defeat from Gornik the Rangers directors met immediately after the match and, as White was analysing the reasons for the European exit with his players and his training staff, they were making up their minds on his future. The following day he went into Ibrox as usual for the morning training and was called in to see the board and told that he was being dismissed after two years in one of the most demanding jobs in football. He walked into Ibrox at nine o'clock and twenty minutes later he was on his way home after clearing his desk. It was as swift and as sudden as that. He was with the directors for a matter of minutes. The former Ibrox centre forward Willie Thornton, who had been White's assistant, was asked to take charge of the team until a new manager was named. Within the week Willie Waddell, who had been part of the immediate postwar forward line with Thornton, had been installed as the new manager. That hurt White deeply as Waddell, in his role as sports writer with the Scottish *Daily Express*, had been highly critical of the club's internal discipline when the storm in a teacup blew up at Largs.

Rangers played one game under Thornton, winning 3–0 at home against Raith Rovers. Baxter played at left half but was replaced by substitute Bobby Watson during the game. After Waddell took over he played only three more matches, against Hearts at Tynecastle in a 2–1 win; at home against Dundee United when another win, this time by 2–1, was recorded, and finally at Pittodrie where the Glasgow side won 3–2. But even that hat trick of successive wins could not save him. Following the Pittodrie victory he was never to play in the first team again. Both Baxter and Henderson, knowing the new manager's reputation as a strict disciplinarian, had made very public efforts to acknowledge that they were ready to live within any rules that Willie Waddell brought in, as well as respecting the traditional thinking at the club whether or not they thought, privately, that this was outdated. They had their beards shaved off, their fashionably long hair cut, and they buckled down to work as hard at their game as they knew how. Henderson survived longer than his mate, until the end of the 1971–72 season – Baxter was handed a free transfer, his second inside a year, when the end of that season came. He was only thirty years old.

White always felt that after his own sacking Baxter had been isolated. Only the other players were around to give him any support. Those directors who had been against his return in the beginning were happy to see the rebel Ranger out in the cold and Sir Alex Ferguson believes: 'It was inevitable that Jim would leave once Willie Waddell took over. As a manager before, when he had been at Kilmarnock and won the title there, he had had a reputation for being very strict with players.

'Therefore he would not have wanted to take any risks with Baxter. Look, the two players had not stepped out of line before the Gornik game, but there had been such publicity that the club would not have wanted any repeat. Willie Waddell would have looked on his action regarding Jim as cutting out any cancer in the club, getting rid of anyone he thought might bring upset into the dressing room. He was not going to take a chance on that happening under his regime and so Jim's days were numbered from the moment he took over. Jim knew that.'

In fact Baxter had heard on the grapevine as early as the turn of the year that he was going to be released. Not that it took any great feats of deduction to grasp what was going on when he found himself being left out of the team so consistently. It was a bad time for Baxter, especially as the comeback had begun so positively. Instead of being feted as he had been when the season kicked off, Baxter found himself more or less ostracised by the new man in charge. When he was called upstairs to the manager's office at the end of April, ten days after the season finished, he found himself part of a cull that had started a couple of weeks earlier. Then it was the turn of the backroom staff as Harold Davis, Lawrie Smith and Davie Kinnear were all axed and Jock Wallace moved from Hearts to become Waddell's right-hand man. Along with Baxter, Norrie Martin, Erik Sorensen and Davie Provan were freed and Swedish international winger Orjan Persson was placed on the transfer list. As anticipated Willie Waddell was placing his own stamp on the Ibrox club. Baxter accepted the news without any show of emotion although he must have been hurting inside. But, then, he had been the same during the six months he had suffered as a non-person at Rangers.

'You would not have known from Jim that there was anything wrong,' Alfie Conn explains, 'because he would never allow anyone to see that they were getting to him. Being out of the team, right out of the picture, in fact, must have been hard for him to take, but it didn't seem to make any difference to him. You would not have known he was being badly treated from looking at him in training or even speaking to him at the ground. He seemed able to accept whatever life was throwing at him and just get on with things. I suppose he was too old to change his ways entirely and he would still have been drinking a little bit when he came back. That was his lifestyle, wasn't it?'

While he brought back to the supporters memories of his previous spell at Rangers, when he enjoyed the best of times, there were other less appealing traits still surfacing from time to time. After the drink-driving episode he kept a low profile, but there were occasions when his old devils were unleashed. When Rangers drew with Steaua in the Romanian capital of Bucharest the players went out to celebrate after an after-the-match banquet where the two teams had been together. Somehow Baxter was able to steal fairly substantial quantities of drink from the dining room and led a group of team-mates to a nearby nightclub where they proceeded to drink the lot.

The management, naturally, took exception to this and the bouncers descended on the Rangers players' tables. One of them has described the scene this way: 'It was as if World War Three had broken out. Jimmy had wanted to drink the bevy we had brought from the banquet and he did it. So there were a few words after that and one or two punches were thrown and at the end of it all we were lucky to get out of the place without any of the lads being seriously hurt. Jim thought it all a great laugh, that's the way he looked on life, but it could have been serious. Romania was not the kind of place where you went looking for trouble. He did though, just for a wee bit of fun.'

Waddell had been on that trip as a journalist and doubtless had learned of the exploit, as it was not the best-kept secret on the flight back to Glasgow. That would have been one of the reasons for axing a player he had admired throughout his career. There were other reasons, too, and while White holds on to his belief that Baxter was still able to influence important games, and even win such games, for Rangers, the evidence from fellow players does not always support that. Davy Wilson was at Dundee United when Baxter went to Rangers for that second spell. He played against him in the first league game of that season and was forced to accept that his old pal was struggling for fitness.

'The fitness, or lack of it, plagued him latterly,' Wilson admits. 'When he came back to Rangers he played against Dundee United at Tannadice, which meant I was in opposition to him. The ball came to me when I was in the outside right position at one stage of that game and I stuck it by him and then ran on to get in a cross. He was giving me stick, some serious words, but the thing was he couldn't catch me. I knew that the writing was on the wall then. Unfortunately that told me all I had to know.

'Now I don't know whether he would have been a better player if he had trained more because you could not get much better than he was when he came to Rangers. What I do know is that he would have lasted longer in the game. If he had stayed with Rangers he would have been the biggest legend in the club's history, and he is big enough now! And he might have been able to play on for another four or five years if he had not gone to the wrong clubs down in England. That's where the serious damage was done.'

Of course, if he had not taken those extra minutes in bed on that November morning at Largs then Davie White might have remained as Rangers manager.

Perhaps the comeback could have been the success White believed it might have been. Certainly it was not entirely the failure that critics of the move suggested. In his 22 appearances in the first team he demonstrated more resolve than he had while languishing at Nottingham Forest. Anyone who had expected to see the Baxter of the early 1960s was, naturally, going to be disappointed. Even the player himself knew that the dreams of the support that saw him as their saviour were never going to become reality. Instead of being a truly exceptional player he had become a lesser footballer who could only offer the briefest hints of the magic that he had once possessed in abundance.

White went on to manage Dundee and to guide the Dens Park club to a League Cup win over Celtic in the final of that tournament four years later.

For Jim Baxter, however, the curtain came down on his career that April day when he walked up the marble staircase at Ibrox to be given a free transfer, and he was never allowed the opportunity of a return. At the age of thirty the party was over.

11 SCOTLAND – AND THE LOVE AFFAIR WITH WEMBLEY BEGINS

It was in 1963 that Baxter made his first appearance at Wembley, and when he took his first look at the home of English football he told the Scottish football writer Jim Rodger: 'This is the London Palladium. If I don't turn it on here then you can kick me up the backside after the game.'

It was the start of a love affair and you must be able to comprehend what the game against England meant to generations of Scottish football fans. This was their biggest game. It was a fixture for which they saved their money over the two-year spell between the London invasions. The English fans rarely made a similar foray north of the border to be at Hampden. A few thousand might make the trip but they were lost in the vast expanses of the great Glasgow ground. On the other hand Wembley became a sea of tartan – it was every Scottish schoolboy's dream to play against England there and to be on a winning side. Romance surrounded the game.

When Baxter's club career stumbled to its dismal and disastrous end with the humiliation of a second free transfer inside twelve months, his period as a vital member of the Scotland international team had finished even sooner. Despite the memorable display at Wembley against England less than a year after their World Cup triumph, the midfielder was destined to play just two more matches for his country. First was a mundane friendly against the USSR soon after the win in London, a game that Scotland lost by 2–0 at Hampden. That was followed by an even more mundane Home International Championship game against Wales, also at Hampden, when a late goal from the Rangers centre half Ronnie McKinnon gave Scotland a 3–2 win. That was on 22 November 1967 and was exactly 221 days after he had been hailed by the nation as a superstar.

His time with Scotland lasted only a little longer than his five years of club glory with Rangers. It started in 1961 and was over with that Hampden clash with the Welsh. He won just 34 caps, though it has to be remembered that at that time there were fewer international games and, in the main, honours were collected against the other three home nations. The Home International Championship was, in fact, used as a qualifying section for the European Nations' Cup tournament, the forerunner for the European Football Championships, which climaxed in 1968. England went forward from the two years of group play which decided who would represent Britain in the later stages. Even the World Cup was much less glamorous than it has now become.

Baxter played in two qualifying competitions during his time as a key player for Scotland. The first one saw Scotland fail to reach the finals in Chile when they lost in a play-off in Brussels against Czechoslovakia, who went on to be runners-up to Brazil in the Santiago Final. Four years later Scotland lost out to Italy when the opportunity was there to play in the finals in England. His small haul of caps by present-day standards should not be taken to mean that there were times when he was often left out by his country. Other players of that era rarely earned the fifty caps total that was later accepted by the Scottish Football Association as being the necessary number to be inducted into its Hall of Fame. Baxter's own hero, Dave Mackay, collected just 22 caps in a nine-year span with Scotland; Billy McNeill won only seven more than that over eleven years; Pat Crerand had sixteen in five years and even Denis Law scraped into the Hall of Fame with 55 caps after serving Scotland over a spell of fifteen years. And but for a late flowering of his skills being recognised by team managers Tommy Docherty and Willie Ormond in the early 1970s he would have missed out on that SFA salute.

Baxter cut his teeth in games against Northern Ireland, the Republic of Ireland and Czechoslovakia in his first season as a Scotland player. But it was the following year that he crossed swords with England for the first time and it was as memorable a victory as some of the others were to become in the country's football folklore. That opening encounter was at Hampden and Scotland won 2–0 with goals from Eric Caldow, a penalty, and Davy Wilson. It was the first Scottish win at Hampden in a quarter of a century, though it has to be remembered that the games were not played for eight years during the Second World War. Still, it had been a long time since the Scottish support had been able to celebrate a win at their own stadium and it was all the sweeter since it came a year after the country's shaming 9–3 defeat in the annual fixture at Wembley. It was little wonder that grown men cried on the terracings that day as 134,000 watched the oldest international fixture of them all. What they did not realise was that their team would now go on to enjoy the best run of success in games against England since the previous century. Starting with that Hampden success Scotland would lose only once in half-a-dozen games against the English. There was one draw in 1965 – and Baxter was missing from that game due to the leg break he had suffered against Rapid Vienna – and one defeat in 1966 when England won 4–3 at Hampden only weeks before their World Cup win on their own soil.

It is an understatement to say that Baxter enjoyed playing against England – he positively gloried in these games, especially at Wembley, which was a stage that seemed to invite him to strut his stuff, to go into show-off mode and to be as arrogant on the ball as only he could be during these years of plenty. It was his soon-to-be manager at Sunderland who picked him for Scotland for the first time and he guided him through these early years that were not always without incident.

First and foremost, however, McColl allowed Baxter the same free rein on the field of play that he enjoyed at Rangers. He did not see any necessity to change that, particularly as he was happy to utilise the left flank triangle that operated at Ibrox, with Eric Caldow at left back, Baxter in front of him and Davy Wilson surging down the wing. There had been an innate understanding between the three players almost from the moment Baxter joined the others in the Glasgow club's first team, and that had been built on in all the games they played together.

'It was clear to me, and to anyone else, I would imagine,' says McColl, 'that the little triangle that Caldow and Baxter and Wilson played in at club level was too successful to abandon when it came to the Scotland team selection. They worked tremendously well together. Eric was ahead of his time as a full back. He was not the type who simply wanted to get the ball up to the other end of the field as quickly as possible. He wanted to play the ball forward and Jim sensed that right away and he would always bring Eric into the game and wee Davy Wilson benefited from all of this going on behind him. We were fortunate that we had players available for Scotland who were very highly talented. Jim and Denis Law and Dave Mackay might have pushed their way ahead of some of the others but really we had a group of players with exceptional ability.

'What I also tried to instil in the squads I handled was the need for a strong team spirit. That was never there in the days when I played. I had fourteen caps and I always found that the lads in the team were playing for themselves and not for each other. I had been warned that this would be the case by my Rangers team-mate Willie Waddell. He told me it was not the same as playing for your club and I should concentrate on looking after number one. That went against the grain for me but I soon found out he was right. He was bloody right and I carried that message in my head when I was named as the international team manager. I can remember one international against France in Paris when two of the players were at loggerheads – Alex Forbes of Arsenal who was the left half and Billy Steel of Derby County who was at inside left. I don't know the reason for it but the two of them did not get on at all and it spread on to the field.

There was so much bad blood between them that when Forbes got the ball, wee Steely would go and stand beside his marker so that he wasn't in a position to accept a pass. Forbes kept shouting at him to move but he wouldn't do it and it was just impossible to give him the ball. He just didn't want to take a pass from his left half.

'Poor Alex Forbes had a nightmare and while we won 1–0 I don't know how we were able to do that. That stuck with me and I was always determined that it would not happen to me while I was the team manager. It never happened, I'm happy to say. Everyone pulled together although it was never too easy getting Jim to stick by any tactics you might have tried to lay down for him before the games. Not that I tried to overburden him with detail, there would not have been much point to that as he always preferred to go his own sweet way! In any case I did not believe in planning too much before matches when there were such high-quality players at my disposal. You always have a lot of talk about allocating jobs to this player or that but good players, when they are involved in a game, react instinctively and most of the time they do the right things. You don't have to tell them what to do, that comes naturally. That's the way it was with Jim and Denis and Dave Mackay, too, and for some of the others we had in the squads in that period.

'Look, I doubt if Matt Busby would ever have had a great deal to say to George Best about how to play the game when he was at his peak because George went where he knew he would be most effective and United allowed him that freedom. It worked for them and it worked for Scotland when we allowed Jim some licence on the field. He had to have a lot of freedom and he always demanded the ball, no matter how the game was going he wanted to have that ball at his feet. That's when he became alive, when you could see that he was a world-class footballer.'

The manager and his star midfielder would occasionally find themselves at odds, however, mainly because of Baxter's determination to ignore any pre-match planning. Willie Henderson once mentioned 'tactics' to him and claimed that Baxter simply laughed and asked if he could have a tenner each way on that horse. And when Ralph Brand and Jimmy Millar and Davy Wilson would spend hours on the Albion training ground working out the fine details of set pieces Baxter would refuse to join in. Worse, he would sometimes wait until they began their elaborate build up during a game and step in quickly to take the kick himself and wreck the scheme they had perfected. It was done from mischief but it was also Baxter's way of thumbing his nose at the organisation he could understand but did not enjoy. He remained a free spirit, dependent on improvisation for the moves he masterminded and the goal opportunities he created.

At Scotland get-togethers he would pay little attention to even McColl's common-sense, uncomplicated team talks. McColl kept it simple because he knew his players and recognised their ability, and he also knew them well enough to sense when Baxter was less than pleased at what the manager was asking prior to a game. Partly because he had been a member of the Iron Curtain defence at Ibrox in the postwar years and partly because his natural instincts were to be cautious, he would preach the necessity for extra care to be taken during the opening stages of any game. He felt that was essential, especially against England, and having suffered as manager at the 9–3 mauling at Wembley had every reason to be fearful. And so he would spell out how essential it was not to lose an early goal when playing against the English, that everyone had to concentrate on defence in the opening period of these games. Baxter did not like that.

'I knew that this kind of talk was not going to please Jim,' McColl admits, 'but I couldn't rid myself of the need for watchfulness going into the England games. I would stress to Jim that I did not want to see him wandering off up field until the game had settled down a little bit. Then he could have his freedom. But the game would be started for only a few minutes and I would look for him and he was as likely to be out on the right wing as in his own area of the field. The thing was if you curbed his natural tendencies to attack then you ran the chance of losing the brilliance he brought to the team. You must understand, too, that the other players accepted that. None of them ever criticised him for getting himself forward because they accepted that as being a part of his game.'

It soon became an integral part of the manner in which the Scotland teams of the 1960s performed. There was a skill and an exuberance and a sense of enjoyment about them as they delivered their best work. At times, too, there was a sense of frustration as you watched them drop below these high levels that always seemed to be there against the English when the two countries met each year. But too often their best form was missing against less powerful nations when the Scots felt they had less to prove. When that happened and the national side suffered defeat at the hands of Wales or Northern Ireland – and these accidents did occur – then you could be sure that Baxter and Law would carry the collective can for the failures. Neither of them liked that but Baxter was less upset by the criticism than the Manchester United man who had the added problem of being tagged an 'Anglo'.

That, in an era when there were still frequent requests for all-Tartan teams to be chosen, though many of the finest Scottish players were earning their livings in the English first division. It was easy to understand Law's disaffection.

Baxter, on the other hand, simply laughed it all off as he did with so many of the problems he had to face during his life. Attracting adverse comment from football writers was never going to be too high among his concerns and, mostly, it was praise that flowed his way.

It was in 1963 that Baxter made his first appearance at Wembley, and when he took his first look at the home of English football he told the Scottish football writer Jim Rodger: 'This is the London Palladium. If I don't turn it on here then you can kick me up the backside after the game.'

It was the start of a love affair and you must be able to comprehend what the game against England meant to generations of Scottish football fans. This was their biggest game. It was a fixture for which they saved their money over the two-year spell between the London invasions. The English fans rarely made a similar foray north of the border to be at Hampden. A few thousand might make the trip but they were lost in the vast expanses of the great Glasgow ground. On the other hand Wembley became a sea of tartan – it was every Scottish schoolboy's dream to play against England there and to be on a winning side. Romance surrounded the game, fans talked of the Wembley Wizards of 1928 when Scotland won 5–1 and of Jimmy Cowan's Wembley and of 'last-minute Reilly', the Hibs striker Lawrie Reilly who snatched a late victory for Scotland there. Baxter was soon to join these legends and he had given notice in his Hampden debut against England that he was more than ready to do so. Even the English commentators had admitted that following the 2–0 win by the Scots.

The *Daily Mirror's* Peter Wilson, never one to go out of his way to praise his own country's oldest football rivals, waxed lyrical in his report. 'Frankly, the game was so one-sided at times,' he wrote, 'that the English fans should have got their money back. It was staggering to see the bemused expressions grow on the faces of these much-lauded English stars as they watched Jim Baxter execute a progressive "Twist" marathon, smoothing down the divots with velvet feet before sliding into the area marked "Danger".'

Naturally the Scottish newspapers were even more ecstatic, given that this win had taken 25 years to be accomplished and that it followed on the worst defeat any Scotland team has ever had to suffer. When it came to that first 'Baxter Wembley' the hopes among the supporters and the players themselves were high. Changes had been made in the team but, as one of these saw Dave Mackay brought in for Pat Crerand, and another had Willie Henderson taking over from Alex Scott, it was clear that the Scotland side had not been weakened.

Baxter remained of the opinion that the team that won that day was stronger than the more celebrated side of four years later. That may have been, in part, because Mackay was there and he was always the man he rated as the most complete footballer he had played with or against. It was: Brown (Tottenham Hotspur); Hamilton (Dundee); Caldow (Rangers); Mackay (Tottenham Hotspur); Ure (Dundee); Baxter (Rangers); Henderson (Rangers); White (Tottenham Hotspur); St John (Liverpool); Law (Manchester United); and Wilson (Rangers).

Inside the opening six minutes all hopes of victory that Baxter and Scotland had held from the previous season appeared to be over. The Scotland captain Eric Caldow was injured when Bobby Smith hit him with a reckless tackle that broke the full back's leg. This was in the days before substitutes were allowed and the subsequent reshuffle saw Davy Wilson drop into the left back position and Scotland were left with ten men as Caldow was rushed to hospital. Somehow or other the Scotland players lifted themselves to even greater heights than they had reached at Hampden and Baxter, who would score only three goals in all his appearances for his country, scored the two which gave Scotland victory that afternoon.

Down that left side he provided the class while Davy Wilson, press-ganged into service as a defender, added the grit and the determination that defeated an English side that boasted such top names as Jimmy Armfield, Bobby Moore, playing for the first time against the Scots, Gordon Banks, also making his debut in this oldest of international fixtures, Bryan Douglas, Jimmy Greaves and Bobby Charlton. It was an impressive achievement and Baxter was the epitome of cool as he stepped forward to take the penalty kick that gave Scotland their second goal, one that lives in the memories of all who were there – including his team-mates!

They still talk in tones of reverence today of the moment that Jim Baxter first made Wembley his own personal property. He had started the surge to victory with a goal scored after half an hour had been played. Willie Henderson constantly exploited the weakness at left back where Liverpool's Gerry Byrne could not handle the twists and turns of the Rangers prodigy. So complete was Henderson's domination in that mano-a-mano with the Anfield defender that Byrne was to win only one more cap for his country – and that came three years later in a friendly with Norway. It was no surprise then that the little winger was involved in both goals. For the first he raced away from Ron Flowers and then Byrne before whipping the ball across the face of the England goal. It was Baxter, neglecting any defensive duties he might have inherited after Caldow's tragic injury, who reached the ball just a shade after the England captain Jimmy Armfield. It was at that moment he demonstrated the knack that he played down but others always claimed he possessed, of being able to take the ball away from an opponent's toe, on this occasion Armfield's, and then as Banks came out place the ball between the advancing keeper and the post. It was an exquisite finish to a marvellous move and it wasn't over yet.

There was a second goal to come and it was only a few

minutes before Henderson and Baxter were again involved as they sent Scotland surging into a lead they would not be in any danger of losing. On this occasion Henderson was sent crashing to the ground by the Wolves wing half Flowers as he cut into the England penalty box. There was no doubt in the referee's mind, nor was there any way the decision could be questioned, it was a penalty.

Nor was there any question as to which Scotland player would take the kick. In ordinary circumstances you might have expected some confusion as Eric Caldow, the captain and the acknowledged penalty taker, had by now been taken to hospital. Among the Scottish players, though, there were no concerns over which of them might step forward to take the so-important kick, one that would give the team a two-goal lead over the English.

Dave Mackay had taken on the captain's responsibilities when Caldow was stretchered off and he says: 'I think that game contains my own best memories of playing with Jim, I mean actually being there alongside him in an international for Scotland.

'It's appropriate that it was at Wembley against England because these were always the big games for any Scottish player. I wasn't any different from the others and I know it was a game Jim was always up for. Wembley was a stage he loved.

'I remember we were down to ten men – no substitutes then of course – very early in the game and little Davy Wilson had to go to left back. Jim scored the opening goal for us and then the penalty arrived a few minutes later. Now Eric Caldow had been the team captain but when he went off I just took on the role, not that anyone told me to do so, but it seemed the right thing to do and when we were awarded the penalty I picked up the ball and I just threw it to Jim and said to him – "Just you tuck that away in the net" – and that is exactly what he did. He was playing so well and the great thing about Jim was that on the field he was always so full of confidence and always so calm. I knew that he would not be nervous and he stepped forward and, cool as you like, struck the ball past Gordon Banks. Honestly, I never had the slightest doubt that he would score with that kick.'

The man who won the penalty, Willie Henderson, adds: 'He got the two goals that day, maybe the only game in his whole life when he scored twice and he was completely in command. When I was brought down for the penalty I don't think there was ever any doubt that Jim was going to take it. Dave Mackay threw him the ball and he placed it and he might have been getting ready to take the kick on a public park in a bounce game for all the emotion he showed. He was the coolest man in the whole stadium at that moment, maybe even the coolest man in the whole of Britain.

'He just stepped forward, placed the ball on the penalty spot and then sent his kick into the goal. No one had been elected to take penalties after Caldow went off but it had to be Jimmy. He was the only candidate. And if Jimmy felt any pressure then he didn't show it. He took that kick with the same expression on his face as he would have had if he was playing poker and had been dealt a good hand. He was like that, as if there was not a thing in the world which could upset him. The fact that he was playing at Wembley helped too. He loved that stadium.

'It was as if the place had been made for him. There were no mountains for him to climb when he went to play there, it was not any kind of ordeal, which it could be for some players who were affected by nerves, but never for Jimmy.

'I think he knew that this was a pitch where he could show off his skills to their best advantage. He just loved to play there and, like all of us, he recognised the importance of these Scotland–England games and all the history attached to them down through the years. I know that people might find it hard to understand today but these were the biggest games of the season as far as the country was concerned. They were bigger than World Cup games. Jimmy knew all of that and I think, too, that he maybe had a sense that he was destined to play there and to play well there and if that was the case then he fulfilled his destiny in the two games he played there against England. That was the first, and the second came in 1967 – but while he took a lot of praise for the game which followed England's World Cup win he said to me several times that the best team he played in was that one in 1963, and I'm glad that I was a part of it.'

Baxter captured the headlines with his goals, yet the contribution made by Davy Wilson was immense and the then international team manager Ian McColl is not slow to emphasise that: 'In all the three games that Jim played against England for me when I was the Scotland manager he was outstanding but in the second one, when we won at Wembley in 1963, Davy Wilson was absolutely phenomenal. I had to ask him to go to left back and he went up and down that left side throughout the game. We went 2–0 up and they pulled one back, but we deserved to win that day and wee Davy was one of our heroes. Dave Mackay made the decision about who was to take the penalty out there on the pitch. That's how it had to be done after Eric's injury.

'It would have been a mistake to ask anyone else to take it the way that Jim was performing and, in any case, I don't think that he would have allowed any of the other players near the ball!'

The hero of the hour, Davy Wilson, dragooned into playing left back, laughs at the memories of Baxter that day: 'He was in some mood that day, I can tell you. He just wanted the ball all the time and, as I'm sure other players will have told you, there was no argument about who was going to take that penalty. Poor Eric Caldow had had his leg broken and I was told to go to full back, the way I had to get up and down that side of the field I think I was probably the first wing back who played at Wembley. I had to be because Jimmy was all over the place. He didn't change because of what had happened, he still played the same way.

'Dave Mackay kept saying, "Let him go, let him go. Let him do what he likes." And I was trying to point out that I was playing that side of the field on my own at times. People have said to me that was my best game for Scotland but I never thought of it in that way. My captain, remember, was lying on the track with a broken leg and we all knew straight away that the leg had gone. It had been a terrible tackle from Bobby Smith and we all heard the crack and poor Eric was never the same player again. That challenge ended his international career and he only had one good year with Rangers after that. It was a tragedy. (Caldow, in fact, played just over forty more first-team games for Rangers before being given a free transfer in the spring of 1966.)

'To go back to the game, though, Ian McColl played left back along with me. He was running up and down that touchline, keeping me going, telling me where I should position myself and just encouraging me. Meanwhile Jimmy was telling me to pay no attention to the manager and just make sure that I gave him the ball when I had possession. That's all he wanted, the ball at his feet, and then he created some damage even though we were a man down for more than eighty minutes of the game. That team was the best Scotland team I ever played in and I know that Jimmy felt the same.'

There were signs then of the arrogance he would demonstrate four years on when he returned for a second clash with England, as he told Wilson: 'Don't you do too much running, wee man, just give me the ball and I'll make an arse of them on my own. Just leave it to me. Don't worry about a thing because we're going to win this game.'

For various reasons the team did not play together again. Soon after the Wembley game the Scots played Austria at Hampden and were winning 4–1 when the English referee Jim Finney abandoned the game because of the violent conduct from the Austrian players. He had sent off two of the visitors when he decided enough was enough. The promise of the performance in London was still in evidence and at the end of the season Scotland embarked on a short three-country tour which almost saw the end of Baxter's international career following an incident in Bergen after the team lost 4–3 to Norway in the first match of the trip which was also to take in the Republic of Ireland and Spain.

It has already been noted that he was a bad loser and when Norway, who were not seen as any kind of football power, beat the Wembley winners, Baxter reacted angrily.

The roots of the late-night confrontation that ensued long after the game between the always rebellious Baxter and the secretary of the Scottish Football Association, Willie Allan, probably lay in a brush that the official had had with Dave Mackay during the game.

Mackay had a pre-match arrangement with the Scotland manager Ian McColl that he would come off during the game if a pelvic injury he had been carrying began to trouble him. He explains: 'I had had a long discussion about the injury with Ian McColl beforehand and he agreed that if I felt this pelvic problem flare up then I was to come off. We were winning the game 3–2 when it went and I signalled to the dug-out that I had to come off and Frank McLintock was there to take over – it had all been worked out in advance. Yet when I went to walk up the tunnel to the dressing room, Willie Allan, who had come downstairs from the directors' box, began to tear a strip off me. He kept saying that I had no right just to walk off the field the way I had. I told him that I was injured, told him the nature of the injury, and how there was a real chance of aggravating it if I remained on the park. But he was livid because he looked on himself as being in charge of the party rather than the team manager. That was the way it was when I was playing for Scotland. So that night after the game that we lost 4–3, a result that did not help anyone's mood, we went out for a few drinks. When we came back to the hotel Willie Allan was sitting there with some of the other SFA officials.

'And Jim, as he was wont to do at times like that, decided to have a few words with him. They were not complimentary words, naturally, and we had to get Jim upstairs to his room and that came close to ending his career with Scotland. Willie Allan was very powerful and I think he wanted to send him home. It was typical of Jim that he had to have a go at the association secretary but that was how he behaved when he had a few drinks and he was angry about something.'

Another member of the company who went out for a drink after the Norway defeat was Billy McNeill, who confirms: 'When we got back to the hotel we sat down to have a bite to eat and Willie Allan was sitting at the other end of this long, long table with some other officials. Now Jimmy did not get on with Mr Allan, which was not surprising. So when he looked up and saw him there he got it into his mind that they were talking about him. He shouted down the table, "Aye, speak about me if you like. I don't care what any of you say, because I'm offski."

'He started to storm out of the room and one or two of us went after him to calm him down. When he got to his room and started to throw his clothes into a case I asked him what he thought he was doing. All he kept saying was that he was going back to Glasgow, and going back straight away, before they sent him home.

'We were all trying to point out to him that he was in Bergen and it was far too late to get a plane back home and if he calmed down everything would be sorted out by the morning. Eventually he saw sense but he was close to walking out and that might have meant walking out on Scotland forever. If we had been in Oslo rather than Bergen I think he would have gone to the airport. Jimmy had that thing about him where he didn't care about the long-term consequences if he thought his actions in the short term were right.

'Now, on this occasion, I doubt if Willie Allan had been talking about him, but that was not the first time I saw Jimmy with a few drinks in him react to some slight, real or imagined. Now he had not had a lot to drink, we had all had a few beers and I don't think he had started on the Bacardi at that time – a drink he almost single-handedly made popular in Glasgow, incidentally. Even if he had he would not have been able to find

Bacardi in Bergen, I wouldn't have thought there was much call for it there.'

It took McNeill and Mackay and then the combined efforts of Ian McColl and Baxter's Ibrox team-mate Jimmy Millar to finally talk him round to staying with the squad.

Shaking his head, McColl points out: 'That defeat upset Jim. We had a strong team out with Dave Mackay and Jim as our wing halves but Dave had a troublesome injury and we agreed that he would come off if he felt it bothering him. We didn't envisage any problem because Norway were not nearly as good a team as we were. We went 2–0 up and then relaxed and let them in to bring the score level. We stepped up the pace a bit, scored a third, and Dave gave me the signal that he was coming off. Frank McLintock went on in his place but, thinking it was all over late in the game, our lads relaxed, lowered their guard and they grabbed two goals. Jim went off his head. He was furious in the dressing room. When we got back to our hotel in town he walked straight out again and across the square in front to another hotel on the other side. When he got back with some of the other players he was drunk.

'Now, Jacky Husband, who was the trainer, had never seen him like that before and he didn't know what to do. I was up in my own room having a dram with the team doctor Archie Downie, discussing the fitness of some of the players, when Jacky knocked at the door and said to me that I had to come right away because Jim was threatening to go home. I told him to forget about it, that Jim was talking daft, but he came back and said that Jim wanted to have a talk with me before he left. That's when I became involved.

'We went to his room where he was lying on the bed, and Jimmy Millar was with him, and he told me that he was going home and that he would be buying his own ticket. He didn't need the SFA to pay for him because he had plenty of money of his own and who would want to stay with a team that couldn't even beat Norway. This was the way he was going on, and I sat for a little while and listened to all the moans and then I asked Jimmy Millar to look after him, and Baxter said he would see me in the morning. He never did, he never spoke to me the following day about going home. When he sobered up he probably realised that it was the wrong thing to do. I did have to speak to the secretary but Jim stayed and, though we lost in Dublin, he was there when we beat Spain 6–2 in the last game in Madrid.'

Jimmy Millar, another player who won Baxter's admiration for his sheer professionalism, spent an uncomfortable few hours with his difficult room-mate.

That night, after McColl had left the two of them alone, Baxter confided in Millar that he thought Willie Allan would have him sent home. Millar makes it plain: 'Jim thought he had messed up and he was so sorry about it. I felt for him that night. He was in tears at one point because he thought that this might be his last cap for Scotland. He was absolutely certain that Willie Allan, who was a very powerful man, would have him back in Glasgow the following day. Ian McColl had asked me to calm him down a bit but it wasn't easy. He was going on about walking out on the squad and getting a flight himself and all of that before we eventually got to sleep. He didn't go and Willie Allan didn't send him home so I always presumed that Ian McColl had been able to smooth things over with the Association. Mind you, though he was in tears, he wasn't upset enough that he was going to behave himself in the future. That was never in his plans. Basically Jim didn't have much time for authority.'

The next day, chastened though he must have been by the incident, Baxter had one more bad moment. Badly hungover, and looking ghastly when he got on to the bus for the airport, he felt ill during the journey and when he felt ill he opened the bus window and was violently sick. He picked his spot, too, a seat right behind one of the SFA Selectors, a former footballer himself, Bob Thyne, who was a director of Kilmarnock. He was one of the men who picked the Scotland team in those dark ages when the selection committee was all-powerful and he sat there staring straight ahead as this dreadful scene unfolded behind him. He didn't do anything. The team manager didn't do anything. And Willie Allan, who must surely have wanted to discipline the errant star, didn't do anything. The players and the journalists on the bus looked elsewhere and Baxter recovered before boarding a plane that was to take the party to Manchester where a connecting flight was picked up to fly them into Dublin for the second game – and the second defeat. The Scots lost 1–0 to the Irish and, while Baxter could not have enjoyed that any more than he did the loss in Bergen, there was no return to the bad behaviour which had brought him so close to being banned by his country.

For once he had heeded the warning signs although, as Millar indicated, that common-sense approach, that was so alien to him, was not to last. And over the years Millar was not the only room-mate who was going to suffer as Baxter went his own way, the only way he knew how, kicking over the traces and thumbing his nose at the football establishment as he did so.

Davy Wilson was a regular room-mate and grins: 'I used to tell people who asked about rooming with Jimmy that he had to be the fittest player in the country because he was always out and about early, wakening me when he came in with the sun shining as he climbed through the bedroom window. Curfews weren't meant for Jim. He paid no attention to them at all, except for the night immediately before a game when he knew that he had to play the next day. The rest of the nights when we were away were his own as far as he was concerned. He didn't mind playing the games, that's what life was about for him, but the training never did have its attraction. And once the game had been played then Jim wanted to go out and enjoy himself wherever we might be.

'That's usually when I would hear the knock at the window in the early hours and in he would come. He would then grab a couple of hours' sleep before we left the hotel, although there were times when he did cut it fine even for him. Over the years

I had come to expect an early morning wake-up call from him about five o'clock or thereabouts but once, when we were in Sunderland with the Scottish League team, he didn't come back to the room at all. We had played the English League at Roker Park and we had had a good result, and the manager, Ian McColl, told us we could have a night out after the game. But he also spelled out to every one of the players that there was a 2 a.m. curfew. If we were not back in by then we would be in trouble. He warned Baxter particularly, and I can still see him telling Jim: "When the hands on that clock – this was in the foyer of the hotel – are at two o'clock I want you in your room and in bed. That goes for everyone." Right enough around five minutes to two the lads are all back except for Jimmy. A little while later McColl comes to check our room and asks me where he is. I said I thought he was in one of the other rooms but he said he had checked them all and there was no sign of him. Later on he came back and this time it was four o'clock and Jim still wasn't there and the manager went off to his own bed.

'Well, the team bus was going back up the road to Glasgow at nine o'clock. I got up and went down for breakfast – still no sign of Jim. I came back to the room and started to pack – still no sign of Jim. I thought I had better put his things in his bag and I did that and took the two bags down to the foyer – still no sign of Jim. At two minutes to nine he strolled in and McColl went for him. "I told you I wanted you in this hotel when the hands on that clock reached two o'clock." At that, Jimmy went into his pocket, took out the clock hands, gave them to McColl and said: "They never got there. I took them off the clock before going out last night." That was typical of him; he just wasn't real, the way he carried on. After that party trick he then turned to me and asked if I had his bag, and when I said it was there he answered: "I hope it's packed as well as my mother usually does it." And that was all the thanks I got. He went through life being cheeky like that and usually being able to get away with it, probably because he was such a wonderful player. I do think that all geniuses have problems and Jimmy was a genius and he had more than his share of problems over the years.

'In the team we had back then Denis Law was a god but Jimmy thought he was more than that, he really did. Denis was superb and so was Jimmy, but they were not the closest of mates. They hadn't much in common off the field.

'Where Jimmy liked the bright lights and getting out on the town when he could, Denis was always at his happiest sitting in the team hotel with a cup of tea and having a blether with some of the lads. The two greatest Scottish players of their generation and yet they were so different off the field. Like chalk and cheese. It's funny that.'

Funny, too, that at their peak neither of these two world-class Scots ever graced the World Cup Finals. Baxter did not make an appearance at all and Law edged his way into the Scotland squad which went to West Germany in 1974 as a fitting reward for his efforts in helping the national side reach those finals in a momentous game against Czechoslovakia at Hampden which the Scots won and which carried them into the finals for the first time since Sweden in 1958. Law had reached the veteran stage, though, and played only a solitary group game in Dortmund when Scotland defeated Zaire. The best opportunity for Baxter had arrived during the qualifying games for the Chile Finals of 1962.

Again, the Czechs were involved, only this time they came out on top when the two countries met in Brussels in a play-off after finishing joint top of their section. The Czechs won in Bratislava 4–0, Scotland retaliated with a 3–2 win in Glasgow and then the Eastern Europeans won 4–2 in the Belgian capital and went on to be runners up to Brazil in South America. Ian McColl, who managed the team at that time, always felt that they were unlucky not to reach these finals. He believes: 'If we had had all our players available then I think we would have gone through. We lost several players before the play-off game in Belgium and that was what killed us there. The players we had then would have made an impact on these finals just as the Czechs did when they got there. I always wish that we had made it and Baxter would have been in his glory. Playing at that level would have seen him among his peers in world football. That was the stage for him and we failed at the last hurdle. I wish he had had that opportunity and the whole world could have appreciated his genius.'

Four years later when a second qualifying tournament presented Baxter with another chance, injuries again struck down the Scots in their final match against Italy in Naples.

A win over that Italian team at Hampden only a month earlier thanks to a John Greig goal gave Scotland, playing under the part-time guidance of Celtic manager Jock Stein, a belief that qualification might be possible.

Then came the call-offs prior to the Naples game. Neither Baxter nor Law made the journey to the Italian city and, at the last minute, a goalkeeping crisis saw Burnley's Adam Blacklaw drafted in for only his third cap – the others had been won three years before – and the makeshift team lost by 3–0 and the finals in England, so tantalisingly close just across the Border, went ahead without Scotland being involved.

Baxter had to make do with the annual jousts with the English and a showpiece game that was staged to mark the centenary of the Football Association and saw a FIFA Select chosen to meet England. The game took place at Wembley in October 1963, six months after Baxter's debut at the home of English football. Baxter, as has been noted earlier, was less than enamoured by the attitudes of his team-mates, who were there to play an exhibition game, while Baxter and his fiercely patriotic fellow Scot Denis Law were there to give England another defeat.

The teams certainly confirm the quality of footballer on view that day to salute the Football Association on its one hundredth birthday. They were: *England:* Banks (Leicester City); Armfield (Blackpool); Wilson (Huddersfield); Milne (Liverpool); Norman (Tottenham Hotspur); Moore (West Ham); Paine (Southampton);

Greaves (Tottenham Hotspur); Smith (Tottenham Hotspur); Eastham (Arsenal); and Charlton (Manchester United). *FIFA, Rest of the World Select*: Yashin (Russia); Nilton Santos (Brazil); Schnellinger (West Germany); Pluskal, Popluhar, Masopust (all Czechoslovakia); Kopa (France); Law (Scotland); Di Stefano (Spain); Eusebio (Portugal); and Gento (Spain). The substitutes for the FIFA team in the second half were Soskic of Yugoslavia replacing Yashin; Eysaguirre of Chile, for Nilton Santos; Baxter for Masopust; Uwe Seeler of West Germany for Kopa; and Puskas of Spain for Eusebio.

A quick glance at the substitutes bench alone makes you blink at the amount of talent available. It was not enough, though, to give the select victory. Terry Paine scored for England in the 70th minute, and while Denis Law equalised with seven minutes remaining, it was Jimmy Greaves who snapped the winner four minutes after that.

Baxter returned unimpressed and would later add to his famous 'too many chiefs' remark: 'Nobody wanted to play for the team, they all wanted to play for themselves.

'They were only there to show off, just do a few party tricks while Denis and myself were the only ones who wanted to win the game. The other players saw it as an exhibition whereas we saw it as another game against England! We could not get that through to the rest of them at all.'

An interesting behind the scenes story from that game comes from Jim McCalliog, later to play with Baxter and Law in the 1967 game at Wembley, but then still a humble ground staff youngster with Chelsea. He and another Scot, John Boyle, had been asked to help look after the World stars when they trained at Stamford Bridge.

'We were there to clean their boots after the training, which was the night before the game itself,' says McCalliog, 'and we were desperate to do that job, just to be able to say to your mates that you had been cleaning Denis Law's or Jim Baxter's boots or those of Puskas or Nilton Santos – they were all huge names.

Tommy Docherty was the Chelsea manager and he assigned John Boyle and myself to the group who were going to be watching the training and cleaning up afterwards. Before the workout the players began to come out on to the field, one or two at a time, and they were all flicking the ball about and showing these wonderful skills they had. Nilton Santos, who was a full back remember, he strolled on to the edge of the field and he knocked the ball over his head and caught it on his heel. Baxter followed him out and he did the same, as if to spell out that anything any of them could do, then he could do it just as well, if not better. When they began to train with the ball you could see that neither he nor Denis were at all out of place. It made you feel good as a young Scots kid seeing that. There was something distinctively Scottish about the way Jim played the game. He was part of the tradition of great ball players that the country used to be able to produce in generation after generation for many years. I know that he was disappointed about the attitude of the foreign players during that game because they didn't care about winning. A victory in a "friendly" was not important to them the way it was for Jim and Denis.'

Especially, of course, victories over England, and another of those, the third in succession, was to come for the Scots in 1964 when the bi-annual fixture returned to Glasgow to a sell-out Hampden Park. This time Alan Gilzean scored with a header and Scotland's run of success, after the embarrassing 9–3 defeat in London, continued.

The Scots players who took part in that Wembley disaster were scarred by it and Law and Mackay particularly, always sought revenge when they were involved against the English. For a spell Law found that and he revelled in it along with Baxter, who did not make his first international appearance until after that 9–3 humiliation. Mackay, for some reason, enjoyed a taste of revenge on only that single occasion in 1963.

The six games against England from Hampden in 1962 until Wembley in 1967 were profitable for the Scots. They suffered only a single defeat in that period and Baxter and Law were the two players the English could not tame. Baxter missed one of these games – he was recovering from the Vienna leg break when the Wembley game took place in April 1965. Law played in all of them. Strangely, the London encounter of 1965 was a dismal day for the Scottish team even though they returned home with a 2–2 draw. Of the eleven men representing their country that afternoon there were several survivors from that 2–1 Wembley victory but somehow the magic of that occasion was missing.

Six players were there from the eleven who started the game two years before, goalkeeper Bill Brown, right back Alex Hamilton, outside right Willie Henderson, centre forward Ian St John, inside left Denis Law and the outside left Davy Wilson. Those missing were Baxter, Eric Caldow, Dave Mackay, John White, tragically killed when struck by lightning on a golf course, and Ian Ure. But their replacements were no slouches. In came Pat Crerand and John Greig for the wing half positions, while Chelsea's Eddie McCreadie took over from Caldow, Billy McNeill was a straight swap for Ure and veteran Bobby Collins was recalled to the inside right berth.

From the beginning the Scottish side struggled and, within the opening 35 minutes, they were two goals behind after Bobby Charlton had given England the lead in 25 minutes and Jimmy Greaves had added a second ten minutes later. A rally by the visitors saw Denis Law score in 41 minutes. When Ray Wilson did not come out for the second half after suffering broken ribs the game seemed to be moving in Scotland's direction. The West Ham centre forward Johnny Byrne went to fill in at left back – shades of Davy Wilson for Scotland two years previously!

When the Wembley jinx struck Byrne, and the striker was stretchered off ten minutes after taking over his new position, it was difficult to see how England would hold out. Ian St John did get an equaliser for Scotland on the hour mark but that was all they could muster against their nine remaining opponents. The celebrations that the thousands of travelling Scottish supporters had been confident of enjoying over that Wembley weekend were not to be. Instead of toasting ten heroes as they had last time round they were now having to accept the fact that their full strength team could not beat an England side which had played for almost half the game without two of their players.

Afterwards it was hard to stray far from the feeling that the vital ingredient that was not there in the Wembley mix was the artistry and arrogance offered by Baxter. Instead of playing in the game, the fixture that meant more to him than any other, he had travelled south with the official Rangers party to watch the match from a seat in the Wembley stand. His rehabilitation had begun but, rightly, he had not been considered. After all, he had played just seven first team games for Rangers before the England fixture and was still tentatively finding his way back to fitness.

I sat with him in the stand that day, 'ghosting' his column for the *Sunday Mirror*. Earlier I had gone to the Rangers team hotel, the Mount Royal in Oxford Street, to liaise with him and also to collect a precious ticket that would enable me to sit next to him during the game. All these arrangements had been made before travelling south yet, predictably, Jim was still in bed when I arrived at the hotel in mid-morning. When I went to his room, bottles were strewn around and he admitted that there had been a party there until dawn. He had made no plans to get the ticket but he made a phone call to the manager, Scot Symon, and within ten minutes two tickets were delivered to the door, one for him and the other for me, demonstrating again, how, even at that late date, he was still able to charm the normally dour and unbending team boss.

At the game he kicked every ball, shouted exhortations to the Scottish players and was bitterly disappointed at the result. He knew that Scotland should have won and was furious that the winning sequence that had been established during his run in the international team had been ended. Remaining unbeaten was not enough. He had wanted to see four consecutive victories chalked up and, while fans around him offered sympathy, he was inconsolable. The threat, inherent in his response to the result, was that he was going off to drown his sorrows. The party that had run into the early hours of that day was now about to become a wake and Baxter was in the mood for just such an event. Coming out of the stand the Scottish support tried to soften the blow by telling him that if he had been playing then things would have been different. In his heart of hearts Baxter probably agreed with that but, while he was always aware of the special skills he possessed, he was always aware of the need for a team effort to attain victory. He accepted the words of the fans and the praise they showered on him but publicly he waved aside the suggestions that his presence alone would have brought victory.

Most observers agreed with those supporters, and the England team, too, must have known that they had escaped another defeat because their main scourge had been the most frustrated spectator in the 100,000 people at Wembley that day.

The following year at Hampden Baxter did play. So did Law. Yet, this was one time when the twin threats were not able to subdue their neighbours from south of the Border. This was England preparing for the World Cup Finals and they were able to win 4–3 at Hampden in a match which proved more difficult than most of those they were asked to play when the tournament began a little over three months later.

The win probably helped to give them the confidence boost they required as they headed towards the finals, where so much was expected from them, though Sir Alf Ramsey still tinkered with the selection and the formation before finalising the system he would adopt to give England their triumph. Their warm-up results until Hampden had been mixed, but there was the feeling that Ramsey was building towards having things right on the day and, after the game in Glasgow, the road towards their ultimate triumph seemed smoother than it had before.

Not that Baxter took any great pleasure in accepting defeat. His feelings that day were only marginally less sour than they were after the World Cup Final itself when England had beaten West Germany in extra time by 4–2. Unlike his national team-mate Law, who was playing golf while England conquered the world and who, if all the stories can be believed, threw his clubs into a bunker when someone told him the result, Baxter was at the game. Shortly after the final whistle I was standing in the Long Bar of the stadium with a colleague, Hugh Taylor, when Baxter came through a door from the stand. He looked at us, shook his head, and commented: 'Imagine that lot winning the World Cup! I just don't believe that this has happened. We are fed up beating them and here they are, champions of the world.' He knew then, as every Scottish player based in England knew, that they would have to live through some monumental ribbing when pre-season training began. Their English colleagues were not going to let any of them forget who were now the holders of the Jules Rimet trophy.

Baxter, who had been handing out his own opinions on England since being transferred to Sunderland, had to face the fact that he was now going to be on the receiving end and he did not like to even consider that. There was more to the reaction of Baxter and Law than any simple anti-English feelings. Both men disliked the regimentation that Sir Alf had brought to the game. Both men felt the approach to be sterile. Both men also believed that they were better players than those who were now to be hailed as world-beaters. Both men felt they had demonstrated in games against the very cream of English football that they could do more than simply hold their own – they could outplay the opposition. And both probably felt that they had missed out on a date with destiny in not qualifying for a World Cup tournament that was being played on their own country's doorstep. It was galling to be no more than spectators at the greatest soccer show on earth. Now, to make things even worse, they had to suffer as the English gloated over their historic achievement. This was not the happiest time for either player and Baxter, while he did not have the same overwhelming reason for revenge that Law had carried with him since 1961, now felt the need to prove once more when the opportunity came that his kind of football was better than anything his fiercest rivals could offer up.

12 THE VERY BEST OF TIMES

The games which stand out are those played on the biggest stages and when he kept the ball up for all of five seconds in the second half of that 3–2 win over the world champions, less than a year after they had been crowned, Baxter juggled his way into immortality. These few seconds, captured on grainy black and white film, are indelibly imprinted on the minds of every Scot who watches the game of football. Those who were there treasure the memory, those who were not often claim that they were in the 100,000 crowd that day, those who came later, after Baxter had left the game he graced for far too few years, marvel at the sheer cheek of the man and look in vain for anyone who can produce the same sorcery today. No one can, because Baxter was unique.

No matter what arguments are presented whenever discussions get around to the best game that Jim Baxter ever played, the Wembley match in 1967 remains the most memorable. Some will maintain that this was the most masterly display he ever gave, happily stressing that it came on the lush green turf of that grand old stadium that meant so much to him. Others will savour the two goals he scored against England on his debut there. Still others, those who were in Vienna on the afternoon when he broke his leg, will swear that he never controlled any game more than that European Cup tie against Rapid. Sir Alex Ferguson insists that another European game, against the West Germans of Borussia Moenchengladbach, brought out a world-class display from the midfielder. And in later years Baxter himself talked of a game against Partick Thistle in the old Scottish first division when Rangers won 4–1 and Davy Wilson, playing in front of him, scored all four goals. Thistle were something of a power in the land when that game was played, at least during that season when they finished third in the League, so a 4–1 win was convincing.

Yet, Jim Baxter's best ever game? Well, he believed that it was up there with any of the others that are talked about and he told Roddy Forsyth in an interview in 1995: 'You hear people saying about some player or other that he can't put a foot wrong? Well, that night I literally couldn't and it wasn't just a matter of me saying to myself, oh, I'll pass to wee Davy and the pass coming off. What happened was that if I wanted to pass the ball thirty feet and three and a half inches so that it landed eight inches in front of Davy's left foot that is exactly what happened. It got a bit uncanny after a while because everything – and I'm not kidding you about this – everything I wanted to do was coming off.

'I was starting to get amazed myself, making chances for the lads, sending people the wrong way when I was hardly moving at all, spinning the ball and curling it around people. I was nearly greeting at the end, I really was, and I knew how well I had played. I knew I had been fantastic and I just wished it had been against a team like England or Real Madrid because, let's face it, how many people were at Firhill? And who was going to remember a match against Partick Thistle, no matter how brilliant a game I might have had?'

Naturally, Baxter was right in that assessment. He remembered but no one else did. The games which stand out are those played on the biggest stages and when he kept the ball up for all of five seconds in the second half of that 3–2 win over the world champions, less than a year after they had been crowned, Baxter juggled his way into immortality. These few seconds, captured on grainy black and white film, are indelibly imprinted on the minds of every Scot who watches the game of football. Those who were there treasure the memory, those who were not often claim that they were in the 100,000 crowd that day, those who came later, after Baxter had left the game he graced for far too few years, marvel at the sheer cheek of the man and look in vain for anyone who can produce the same sorcery today. No one can, because Baxter was unique.

It is fairly typical of his own amused self-disparagement that would occasionally surface that when he sat down to watch a video of that historic match he would say to his two sons: 'Watch my first pass, I give the ball away. It's the game everyone talks about and look at what I do right at the start.'

Baxter apart, no one remembered that tiny flaw in a display which must rank among the best ever from any individual at Wembley. That opening pass may have been the sole mistake he allowed himself as the game unfolded and he took command. To understand the impact of the result and of Baxter's performance you have to examine the background to the bi-annual fixture and place it in context, too, to the English victory in the World Cup Final against West Germany just over seven months earlier.

The Scottish players had been unwilling spectators at the World Cup after failing to qualify from the group, which Italy eventually topped. The games were being played so close to them – in Newcastle and Middlesbrough, for example – and yet had been pushed beyond their reach by the Italians in Naples. And, following a hat trick of wins against England, the success rate had stalled in the last two encounters between the ancient rivals. A dismal and disappointing draw on the last visit to London and then defeat in Glasgow by that narrow 4–3 margin.

What's more the soccer philosophy that Baxter instinctively subscribed to was one that saw a minimum use of tactics and a maximum of entertainment. He hated any system that, in his mind, resembled a straitjacket and demanded that players follow a rigid pattern rather than rely on their own instincts. In this, Denis Law was from the same bolt of cloth. Neither of the Scots had any time for the 'wingless wonders' as Sir Alf Ramsey's teams were nicknamed when the manager decided against playing orthodox wing men in his line-ups. Nor could Baxter ever understand why Ramsey could not find a place for Jimmy Greaves in his World Cup winning team. The little striker shared with the Scot an uneasiness about the game being overcomplicated when his own forte was to get goals from positions inside the penalty box where his own intuition had taken him. Baxter felt that Ramsey was ill at ease when confronted with players who had natural ability and who wanted to express themselves.

In a sense the meetings between the two countries had become something of a clash of cultures, with the organisation of England matching up to the still almost totally off-the-cuff Scots, where Baxter and Law paid little more than lip service to any tactics laid down by the team manager, whoever he might be. Mostly the men who did take charge of Scotland during the years of Baxter and Law's ascendancy were happy enough to follow the Scot Symon method and order the players – 'Give the ball to Jim' – the one pre-match instruction that the midfielder would never have the slightest argument with.

Both Baxter and Law had points to prove, while the rest of the Scottish team wanted to carve a little niche in the history books as the first national side to beat England since they won the World Cup. To do it on their own Wembley turf, where all their World Cup ties had been staged, was going to make it even more special. Scottish club football was on a high, too. The Old Firm were both playing in European semi-finals around the same time as the match against the English was scheduled. Indeed, Celtic, who were to go on to win the European Cup in Lisbon the following month, had a home tie against Dukla Prague three days before the Wembley game. Meanwhile, Rangers were set to fly out immediately after the international to play the first leg of their European Cup Winners' Cup semi-final against Slavia Sofia in Bulgaria the following midweek.

They, too, made the final of the European Cup Winners' Cup but lost out 1–0 to Bayern Munich in extra time in Nuremberg. The original Scottish team selection reflected the European success the Old Firm were enjoying with Celtic providing four of the side and Rangers adding another two. Those were the days, of course, when the team was named a few days before the game, and manager Bobby Brown announced on the Monday the men he wanted to play against England, as follows: Simpson (Celtic); Gemmell (Celtic); McCreadie (Chelsea); Greig, McKinnon (both Rangers); Baxter (Sunderland); Johnstone (Celtic); Bremner (Leeds United); McCalliog (Sheffield Wednesday); Law (Manchester United); and Lennox (Celtic). It has long tempted fate to name Scotland teams in advance and this time it was no different from others except there was only the one change required when the Celtic winger Jimmy Johnstone was injured in the game against the Czech champions Dukla. On the Thursday afternoon he had to give up on his desperate attempts to be fit for a game which had captured the imagination of the entire country.

Although Steve Chalmers, another Celtic forward, had been named as one of the three travelling reserves – yes, that's how it was done – he was eventually overlooked and yet another Parkhead player, Willie Wallace, was drafted in. The one-time playing partner of Baxter at Raith Rovers was not only called into the squad but, when the match came around, he found himself in the team though he had flown down to London only late on the Thursday night and joined the team at their London hotel after dinner that night. The preparations, then, were not ideal. The team manager, Bobby Brown, was in charge for the first time and he had put together a team with limited international experience. The veteran goalkeeper Ronnie Simpson, deep into his thirties, had experienced Wembley before – playing for Newcastle United in two FA Cup Finals in the 1950s – but had not represented his country before. Tommy Gemmell, out of position at right back, was collecting only his fourth cap, though he had played against England at Hampden a year earlier; Jim McCalliog, still only twenty years old, was making his international debut; Bobby Lennox had played one game against Northern Ireland prior to the England game and latecomer Willie Wallace had just three caps.

It was little wonder that no one in the south gave Scotland any hope at all of coming out victorious, and even the bookmakers in Glasgow had them very clear outsiders on the eve of the meeting. England were standing at 4–7 with the Scots well out of things at 4–1. For the Scots to be winning at half-time and full time – as indeed they did – then the odds soared to 8–1. In London the odds against the Scots were even longer, and the attitude towards the team from the English press was a kind of amused tolerance, similar to the reception the thousands of fans were being given in the West End the night before the game. England, after all, were world champions, and here were the Scots putting together a team at the last minute and, somehow, expecting to be able to win. The omens were not good for the Scottish team, who had made their headquarters at their usual Wembley base, the Hendon Hall Hotel, close to where the England team also stayed. It was a major test for the one-time

Rangers goalkeeper and former St Johnstone manager, Brown, who had been appointed to the post full time after the Scots had sacked Ian McColl and then John Prentice, two men who had been Ibrox team-mates of the new man in charge.

Today Brown still smiles at the memory of that debut match as manager, exclaiming: 'Going into that game as your first in charge of the team looked on paper to be fairly daunting. I did not underestimate the size of the job in front of the team and myself. After all we were playing against the reigning world champions, who were just at the very beginning of their reign if you like. But we all knew how important it would be for Scotland if we could come away from Wembley with a good result. It was going to be a tremendous boost to Scotland's prestige if we could do that and after failing to qualify for the 1966 finals the country was looking for that kind of lift.

'I do have to say that I was fortunate to have so many exceptional players around. Jim Baxter, Denis Law, Billy Bremner, John Greig and Tommy Gemmell were all in the team and we had other quality men available too. It was a good time for the Scottish game and we had no shortage of international class men to choose from. I suppose I did surprise some people, probably most people, by picking Jim McCalliog, who was almost unknown in Scotland. He had gone south when he left school at fifteen and had played all his football there, at Leeds, afterwards at Chelsea, and then at Sheffield Wednesday.

'However, I had seen him in an Under-21 game and we had watched him in his club games and I thought he was the right type of player to go in against the English. My idea was to have him in the midfield between Billy Bremner, who was a terrier, and Jim Baxter, who was the complete stylist. Jim was there to fill in when they went forward and to use the ball himself – because he could do that. That was the blend we needed to have in the midfield where I did think we could outplay England, and it worked out that way. I also wanted a change in the way Denis

Law had been playing for his club. At Manchester United he had not been playing as an out-and-out striker but I wanted him right up there on top of Jack Charlton and Bobby Moore. If he was snapping at them throughout the ninety minutes then they were not going to have a comfortable afternoon and he would cause them problems. Again that worked.

'Things only began to go a little bit adrift when Jim started the keepy-uppy routine. He had me tearing my hair out on the touchline when he started all that nonsense. But he was always a law unto himself, Jim, and anything I was shouting was being ignored.'

Earlier, however, before Baxter began his risk-taking on the field he was the man who had calmed any nerves in the visitors' dressing room. It was as if he knew beforehand that this was to be his finest hour, that while the clock ran down on his club career he had this one last opportunity in the spotlight to underline his standing as not only a great Scottish player, nor even a great British player, but as one of the great players of his generation worldwide. He knew that the game would be shown around the globe and he recognised that if Scotland could be the first team to win at Wembley after the World Cup Final then the result would be remembered forever. There may have been times when it seemed that Baxter couldn't care less about certain aspects of life, but he had a shrewd sense of history and his place in it as well as a marvellous and innate sense of theatre. When these were combined it could easily be seen that the ingredients were perfect for producing a master class in football at one of the world's most famous venues, which is exactly what Baxter did on that gilded April day.

If ever there is any question of that, then all one has to do is listen to the verdicts of the Scottish players and some of the Englishmen who took part in the game. While there might have been some carping at the showboating, no one doubted they had seen a master in action. Here they describe how they reacted to one man's greatness on a day when the Wembley field was filled with footballers who had already achieved immortality by their exploits in the game.

Ronnie Simpson: 'I had never played with Jim Baxter before that game against England at Wembley. I knew him a little bit, but that was all. One thing anyone could tell you about Jim is that he was a remarkably confident fellow. From the moment I joined the squad for that match I could sense that he was confident that we would beat the English. To be honest, I was a little bit surprised at how sure he was that we were going to go there and win this game. Somehow, though, it was contagious and it began to rub off on the rest of us. I remember in the dressing room right before the match he came over to have a little chat with me. Now, by this time, it's fair to say that he was a little bit rotund. He was no longer the "Slim Jim" he had been during his years with Rangers. The fitness had started to go after his transfer to Sunderland and you could see that now.

'Anyhow, when he spoke to me it was just to tell me: "When you get the ball in your hands don't start kicking it up the field because I don't want to have to run for it. What you do is look for me and when I raise my hand just get the ball out to my feet. That's all I want – the ball at my feet." Of course, when he had the ball there, right at his feet, then the fitness thing didn't count for as much. He got the ball whenever he asked for it, which was all the way through the game. He could not get enough possession and I doubt if he ever stopped raising his hand to give me the signal to let him have the ball. He was still at Sunderland then and his career in England had probably not gone as well as he had hoped it would do after he left Rangers. Also he was a bit niggled that England had won the World Cup the year before, just the idea that they had been able to win such a massive prize when he genuinely felt that we had players who were every bit as good as the men they had. He saw that game as his chance to show that, a game against the World Cup holders on their own ground, it was just made for him.

'As far as I am concerned he was absolutely brilliant that day.

I know that Denis and the team manager Bobby Brown wanted to see more goals rather than all the little tricks he was getting up to, but it didn't bother me. And some of the others, including wee Billy Bremner, joined in the fun with him. Jim didn't sit on the ball, though that was alleged at the time, and for some years afterwards, and I wouldn't have approved of that. It happened once or twice in games I played in and I felt it was insulting to fellow professionals, but passing the ball around and keeping possession and playing keepy-uppy was not the same as that. These things were part of the game and you have to remember that Jim always wanted to entertain the supporters. He did it that day. No one who was there will ever forget his performance, and I was very glad to be a part of it I can tell you that!'

Tommy Gemmell: 'They had just one change from their World cup winning team when they met us. Roger Hunt was out and Jimmy Greaves took his place. Most of us felt that Greavesy should have been in the team that beat West Germany so it was scarcely weakened by his appearance. We had one or two players missing, including Jimmy Johnstone, who had been injured against Dukla when we played a European Cup semi-final a few days ahead of the Wembley date. From memory I went down to Largs after the Dukla game to join the rest of the players there before we travelled south to England the following day. We were allowed out for a drink; remember the game was a few days away, but there was a curfew to ensure that we were back in bed at a reasonable time. Naturally Jim missed that and he climbed in my bedroom window in the early hours still clutching a carry out as if he had not had enough to drink. But that was Jim and one of the ways he found to rebel against authority. It's strange to realise now that we travelled down on the Thursday to prepare for such a huge game, but things were not nearly so well organised and professional off the field as they are now.

'There wasn't even much of a team talk before the match. The new team manager Bobby Brown sketched out how he wanted the game to be played and then we were left talking among ourselves about which players we should be picking up when England had the ball and that kind of thing. Wee Billy did a lot of the talking there and then Jimmy butted in and I can still hear him saying, "Don't ask me to do any of that. I'm not coming back to pick anyone up, they can come and look for me!" Funnily enough, that struck the right tone in the dressing room and then, when we got the signal to go out on to the field, it was Baxter who said something like, "Let's get out there and show that lot how this game should be played", and that's what happened.

'For a game at that level and one with so much prestige at stake it was amazing just how often he was on the ball. He was always available, always in space, and this against the World Cup holders, a team which was built to deny opposition players any room at all. Everything we did seemed to go through him and he loved every minute of it. It became a day out for Jimmy and he revelled in the whole affair. He was just so arrogant that day, the little bit of keepy-uppy summed up his approach to the game. There was one stage in the game when I joined in with wee Billy and Jim to pass the ball around between us with little Alan Ball in the middle of the three of us, and he was running from man to man trying to get the ball. I've watched that on film and we put together fourteen passes as Bally became more and more angry. We had him doing "doggies" the way you do at training and this was at Wembley, the game that was always the biggest on the calendar each season for our supporters and us. The record books will tell you it was 3–2 at the end, but we won out of the park and if it had finished up six or seven then that would have been a score line that would have reflected the amount of possession we had. Not scoring the goals when we might have did cause some aggro right enough.

'Denis Law was a bit unhappy that Jim and wee Billy had decided to show off a bit rather than get goals and he was screaming at Baxter to get the ball forward to him and to stop messing around. But Jim wasn't listening to anyone that day; he was just out there to obey his own instincts. Like most of us he had been angry at the way the English newspapers had written us off, some of them suggesting that we didn't deserve to be on the same field as their team, so he was determined to show them just what he could do with that ball when he had it sitting at his left foot. No one could match him.'

John Greig: 'The Wembley game in 1967 is obviously the one that everyone remembers. You have to understand that the Scotland–England games were always looked on as *the* games until the World Cup and the European Championships began to take more and more of a hold on the public's imagination. But for Scottish players, in particular, the ambition was always to play against England at Wembley. Jim was no different from the rest of us in that respect, and that game came less than a year after England had won the World Cup. We were all looking to take them down a peg or two. None more so than Jim.

'I don't think I have ever seen him more determined to get a result in a game than he was that day. He was always a very confident player and he was more confident that day than I had ever seen him before. The press in England had been writing us off, not giving us the slightest chance of avoiding a heavy defeat, far less winning the game. So Jimmy was determined that he would show them and the rest of the world how well he could play at that level. You could sense that before, and then he went out and he just did it, he ran the whole match. I was one of the players who would have preferred to get a few more goals to show for all time the superiority we had. But Jimmy wasn't interested, he took charge and he wanted to show off. He had the English players running around trying to get the ball and he loved every minute of it. Wee Bally was going crazy and Jimmy was just laughing at him. Wembley was his stage, that stadium was made for him and that was never more apparent than in 1967. It was an astonishing display, I mean the whole team played well, but the day belonged to him.'

Ronnie McKinnon: 'Jim was a big occasion player and he came to life when he was in one of the great football grounds and when he was in front of a huge crowd. You didn't have to ask Jim what his favourite ground in the world was – you only had to see him walk out on to the Wembley turf and stand there looking around the stands and the terracings and you knew immediately that this was his special setting.

'He was magnificent when he played there in 1963 and then four years later I was in the team which won again. It was my one and only time there and I was very nervous before the game. Playing in this fixture was considered the top honour for any Scottish player and I could feel the butterflies from the moment we arrived. There was also a little bit of apprehension because we were going in to face the English team that had recently won the World Cup. I felt terrible and I think I was in and out to the bathroom five times before going out for the game. It was the most nervous I have ever been and yet Jim and Denis Law were behaving as if we were going out for a Sunday kick about in the local park. They were carrying on, the pair of them, as if it was all going to be very easy for us. It has to be said that Jim did not have a lot of respect for the English players. There were one or two of them he probably rated but, for the most part, he had enough self-confidence to believe that he was a better player than any of them.

'There was that air about him, the only word I suppose is arrogance, but he had the ability to back that up. No one came close to him that afternoon. He strutted around the field as if he owned it – and for ninety minutes he did own it! It was a superb team performance but Jim was out on his own. He and Denis Law were marvellous players. When Jim started all the nonsense, the keepy-uppy and all of that I enjoyed it. After all, when he was holding on to the ball, then he was keeping it away from our penalty area and we could relax a little. Denis wanted more goals and he kept shouting that, but nothing was going to get Jim to change his attitude. He was on a different planet, yet that was the last time he was to play there.'

Willie Wallace: 'It was a major shock for me that I was even in the team. Initially I had not even been one of the travelling reserves. There were no big squads for these games at that time. You had the team and two or three back-up players, and I wasn't one of them. But after the Dukla Prague game when wee Jimmy [Johnstone] was hurt, I was called in. Even then I thought that Steve Chalmers would be given the nod ahead of me, but then the team manager, Bobby Brown, told me, either on the Friday night or the Saturday morning, I can't remember which now, that I was playing. Of course, I had arrived late on the Thursday and had not been really involved in any of the planning, although I soon found out that there was not going to be too much of that!

'Bobby Brown didn't say a lot to us beforehand and it was down to wee Billy to get us organised when we went on to the field. I have to say that he did a great job that way but even he couldn't get Jim to accept any specific role. All Jim wanted was to have the ball and when he got it all he wanted to do, in his own words was to "take the piss" out of the English team. That's what he did and Denis was wanting to get more goals – and he could have had at least one more bar a wonder save from Gordon Banks when the keeper managed to stop a brilliant chip shot. It was something of an injustice that we only won by the one goal. Then Jack Charlton, who had been injured but went to centre forward, started to cause us some problems and it was touch and go in the late stages, but it would have been the biggest injustice in football history if we had not won the game. We were so far head in terms of possession and control and that was all down to Jim because of the way he orchestrated everything.

'All he wanted was the ball and it seemed to me that he had it for most of the afternoon. The English couldn't take it away from him. It's difficult to grasp the fact that this was a player whose best years were behind him. His finest spell in the game was during the years he was at Ibrox. For the two seasons leading up to the game against England he had been struggling at Sunderland but it was as if he made one supreme effort to prove to everyone what a great player he was. Certainly no one who watched him in that game could question his credentials as a truly world-class footballer. Remember, too, this was the second time he had taken over at Wembley in four years.'

Jim McCalliog: 'That was my first cap, and while I had played at Wembley in the FA Cup Final the year before when my club Sheffield Wednesday lost to Everton, I wasn't really known back home. I had scored in that game so going to Wembley wasn't as nerve-wracking as it might have been. Playing alongside Jim Baxter and Denis Law was, though. That was a wee bit scary! That was going to be whole new territory for me to be playing with two guys who had been my heroes.

'I was a bit overawed when I joined the rest of the squad before the game but Jim and Denis pulled me over and asked me to join them for a cup of tea and a blether just to make me feel at home. I hadn't really met either of them before though I had played against them. We were given no chance at all by the English newspapers, by the bookies and by their supporters, but Jim and Denis were so sure that we could win the game that their attitude rubbed off on the rest of us. Jim, especially, was convinced that we would be able to win the game. To be fair, none of us thought we were as poor as the English writers made us out to be. We did have a lot of good players and two or three exceptional players, and while everyone still talks about Jim playing keepy-uppy, there was also a lot of very good football played that day and wee Billy Bremner showed the English lads a few tricks as well. But Jim was superb. It was a special day for him, I think, a day when he wanted the whole world to see what a wonderful footballer he was. Four years earlier he had demonstrated that at the same venue, but this time he looked as if he was enjoying it even more than the first time round. Naturally, the importance of the game, and it was always of major importance to the Scots, was heightened because of England's World Cup success. No one knew that better than Jim.

'Denis wanted to get a few more goals but Jim wasn't worrying about that. I think their attitudes were always a little different but they were more marked that day because, I think, Denis had played in the 9–3 defeat and the memory of that match still hurt. Jim only wanted to show off and the supporters thought that was great. We had all been fired up because of what the English journalists had written about us. Simply reading the newspapers on the morning of the game was as effective as any team talk could have been. After the game when we were dressed Jim put his arm round my shoulder and said: "Stick with me, son, and I'll look after you." Somehow, though, we lost track of each other and I ended up sitting back at the team hotel drinking tea with Denis. It always stuck with me that Jim had looked for me afterwards and managed to think of me at such a moment. It said a lot about him as a man.

'Jim wanted to win the game as much as Denis did but he wanted to win it in style, he always wanted to do things with a flourish and that's what he did against England. OK, he never played there again but what a farewell performance he gave us all.'

Denis Law: 'We didn't feel in awe simply because the English had won the World Cup. We had a good side and we knew that. In fact we had been a little bit unlucky not qualifying for the finals, and we might have had a real chance ourselves of winning the trophy because, with the games being staged in England, it would have been like playing at home. I scored the first goal in 28 minutes and I wanted the team to get as many as possible. The memory of us being slaughtered 9–3 in 1961 was still fresh in my mind so I was screaming for us to run up a cricket score. Remember when Jim was playing keepy-uppies we were just one goal ahead! He was saying "Let's take the piss out of them" while I was shouting "Let's give them a doing." I wasn't happy at the time but I soon forgave him. He was magnificent that day. The English players were not able to handle him at all. No one could get the ball away from him.'

Bobby Lennox: 'Jim was absolutely outstanding in the game. Some of the other lads – in fact the whole team – played exceptionally well, but Baxter ran things. He was very assured before the game telling everyone that this was going to be our day and that we were going out on to Wembley to win the game. "Just give the ball to me, that's all I want," he kept repeating to us. There was a super confidence about him where his own ability was concerned. The lads who played in the English First Division, Denis and Jim and wee Billy, were desperate to get a result. Around that time there used to be a lot of talk that the "Anglos", the Scots who played down south, did not care as passionately about the national team as the home-based lads – well, that was rubbish. They knew that when they lost to England they had to suffer in dressing rooms at their clubs for a year until the next fixture when, hopefully, Scotland would win and they could get some of their own back. So they were well up for that match.

'We were all hurt and angry at some of the stuff written about us beforehand, all the nonsense about us not deserving to be on the same pitch as the world champions. It was all a bit silly because, apart from the three big name English-based players we had in the side, there were four guys from Celtic and another two from Rangers, and both clubs were involved in the semi-finals of Europe's top competitions. Celtic beat Dukla Prague a few days before the Wembley game against England while the Rangers lads were playing Slavia Sofia in Bulgaria the following week. Now, you don't get to that stage of the major European competitions if you can't play a little bit. Eventually, of course, we went on to win the European Cup while Rangers were beaten finalists in the Cup Winners' Cup. It didn't make any sense just to write us off as no-hopers before the game. All the newspaper articles did was wind us up and we were fortified by something a little bit stronger too.

'It was something of a tradition at Celtic Park, and I think it happens at other grounds as well, that there was always a little nip of whisky that was available in the showers if you wanted to be warmed up before you went on to the field. Just a taste, you understand, sometimes it was just washing your mouth out. Anyhow one of the lads – I can't remember now whether it was the reserve, Stevie Chalmers, another Celtic player, or Ronnie Simpson who brought a half bottle into the Wembley dressing room, but it appeared and we were fortified before taking the field. I got one of the goals, the second one that day, and it felt great. You know I was new to international football; I only had the one cap before playing England and that was against Northern Ireland when we won the game at Hampden. The team never played together again for one reason or another and the next time Scotland played we lost at home to Russia 2–0. Three or four of the Wembley players were missing and we never had that same special feeling that had been there in London. There has been a bond between the players who played that day, and I remember that when I had a wee spell playing in the States for the Houston team and going to play against Memphis when Eddie McCreadie was coaching them, we spent ages reminiscing about that day at Wembley. It was important for all of us and for the entire country. It became even more important, as far as Jim Baxter was concerned, because that was his day, and it will always be remembered that way and rightly so.'

When you talk to Bobby Brown, who was the manager, he admits readily that Baxter paid little attention to any instructions he attempted to give him that day. He admits: 'He paid no attention to me or to anyone else when he became involved in the game that day. It was almost as if he had choreographed the whole game in his mind and he was going to perform in the way he had visualised everything. We should have been able to win the game more convincingly than we did. Looking at a 3–2 score line in the record books suggests that it was close, but Jim controlled the entire ninety minutes. We should have had five or six goals but he was determined to show our supporters that he was better than any of the opposing players with their World Cup winners' medals.

'That day Jim Baxter gave one of the greatest displays ever

seen at Wembley. It was an absolutely virtuoso show and he was able to lift himself for the game even though his club form had been well below what we had all seen from him in his Rangers days. That game has to remain one of the great occasions in Scottish football history. With the growth of the World Cup and the European Championships the importance of the Scotland–England game has been diluted over the years but, back then, more than thirty years ago, that was the highlight of the season for Scotland and for the Scottish supporters. It was an important result for all of us involved but it was also, I believe, important for the whole nation. It proved that even a small country like Scotland was able to produce wonderful footballers. Jim Baxter went into the fans' Hall of Fame that afternoon And, you know, while I lost my temper about him messing around when we were just one goal in front, Jim couldn't understand what I was going on about after the game was over and we were back in the dressing room. You see he didn't think he was messing around. He just could not see it that way.

'Basically he always felt that the game should be played to provide entertainment for the paying public. That was his genuine belief and that's always what he tried to do. In fact he was as wonderful an entertainer in the game of football as I have ever been fortunate enough to watch. It was a privilege to be able to pick him and to play him in the team. That is not to downplay the contributions of the other players in the game. Every single player did his bit and it was without doubt the best managerial debut I could have been given. Before the game I had been a little apprehensive, but once the players were together you could sense their confidence and a lot of that was created by Jim. Wembley was made for Jim Baxter and Jim Baxter was made for Wembley, you have to believe that.

'Incidentally, don't ever sell him short, because the skills he possessed would shine in the modern game just as they did in the 60s. My only regret is that he did not last longer at the top. He should have done. I was very sorry over what happened to him, but we all have our memories and he will never be forgotten. His place in Scottish football history is secure and I'm sure he would take pleasure from that.'

You can take it as read that Baxter would enjoy his standing in Scottish soccer's folklore, particularly as he is remembered for his antics against the English. That would appeal to him hugely. When he talked about that game he would explain: 'I know that there are people who didn't like us taking the mickey but I wanted to show the English team how easily we could beat them. We kept the game on a razor's edge deliberately, stroking the ball about and attacking whenever we wanted, knowing that we could score more goals if they were needed. England had gone nineteen games without defeat before they met us but I always felt that we had better players.

'In the second half when we had established beyond reasonable doubt that we could win, looking round I indulged in keepy-uppy, which annoyed the English even more. Now and again one of us would put a foot on the ball and then walk away from it as if we were bored but we always knew that a team-mate would get to it first. We wanted the fans to enjoy the spectacle and I think they did. We were also able to give them a victory and that was important for them. But the manner of winning meant a lot to me.'

For the English it was a whole lot less enjoyable but, even that renowned 'hammer of the Scots', Sir Alf Ramsey, did praise Scotland after the match, saying: 'I warned that it would take a great team to beat us. Let's give them their due.'

And while the players suffered Baxter's jibes during the ninety minutes, few held grudges down through the years. Baxter and Bremner, for example, teased the so-combative Alan Ball mercilessly, as they constantly referred to him as Jimmy Clitheroe. (Clitheroe was a television comic of the time who specialised in mock schoolboy roles and had a high-pitched voice – as Ball does.) It was a ploy guaranteed to annoy the Englishman and had been concocted by Bremner and seized on with delight by Baxter. Yet today Ball takes a sanguine view of the events, pointing out quickly: 'I think I played in something like ten games against Scotland and I was on the winning side in most of them so there were times when I was able to take revenge for what happened in that one. It did not annoy me too much when Jim started all his tricks because I did it myself to some of their players in other games when we were on top.

'There's no argument about it, Scotland deserved to win, they had a very good day and Jim Baxter had one of those special days that only happen once or twice in a lifetime. I had played against him before and knew how talented he was. But I had never seen him play the way he did in that match. I tried very hard that day but I have to admit that I could not get near him. And he used that left foot of his to some advantage. Of course I rated him very, very highly as a player and I met him quite often socially and there were no grudges. I liked him as a person, he was great company, and it was a tragedy when he was struck by illness. He'll always be remembered in Scotland for that game and he was tremendously talented, a world-class player.'

Nobby Stiles, another of the English players who could not tame Baxter on that occasion, adds: 'Jim Baxter was like George Best. He could make the ball talk. I don't think I can pay him a higher compliment than that. He was one of the best players I ever played against and I faced a few, including Eusebio in the European Cup Final when Manchester United beat Benfica to win the trophy in 1968. I came face to face with Jim for the first time the year before that Wembley match. We went up to play the Scots at Hampden and we couldn't have asked for a more difficult game with the World Cup Finals coming up. We were able to win that match 4–3 but it was hard for us and Jim was fired up for it. He was even more fired up when he came to Wembley a year later. The Scots were after our blood because we had beaten them the year before and we were also the World Cup holders so there was a lot of prestige at stake. Jim was inspirational and that's why that particular game is always associated with his name.

'My most vivid memory is of Jim juggling with the ball and not one of us could get close enough to him to take it away. I just cannot think of any other player who would have attempted that during such an important game. Yet Jim did it and got away with it and somehow it didn't surprise me that he would do something as outrageous as that. I was calling him all the names under the sun. Yet that night we were all at a banquet after the game in the Café Royal in the West End and we had a few drinks together. Jim was as entertaining there as he'd been at Wembley in the afternoon. He was a joy to be with on and off the field. He was an extra special guy.'

Bobby Charlton believes that Baxter's best Wembley was in 1963, but of the game four years later, he says: 'Jim was the perfect player for Scottish folklore. The Scots love their heroes to be extravagant, larger than life, if you like, and they could see that in Jim. All told I played in eleven of these England v Scotland games and it was no coincidence that the four times I was on the losing end in 1962, 1963, 1964 and then 1967, Jim was there lording it over us. I knew what these games meant to the Scottish support and so did Jim and that's why he was always up for these occasions. He was arrogant and he was extravagant and these are qualities the fans loved to see and he was never more arrogant than he was when they beat us 3–2 after we had won the World Cup. That was a marvellous display but I honestly thought that he was better four years before when he scored both the Scottish goals. I remember hearing after the game that he intended to score an own goal in the last minute if Scotland held their two-goal lead until then. That way, he explained, he would have scored a hat trick at Wembley. But we got a late goal and he didn't get that opportunity. If he was still around today Jim Baxter is one player I would willingly pay money to go and watch because you could guarantee that you would be entertained by him.'

Bobby's brother Jack, however, did not feel he had been entertained during that Scottish victory. The Leeds United centre half had been injured and had played on as a makeshift centre forward – but an exceedingly dangerous one. He still claims that he scored an equalising goal in the last minute but also falls prey to allowing myth to overcome reality when he considers Baxter's performance that day.

'If I had been fully fit when he started all his nonsense in the second half then I would have done something about it,' he growls. 'Don't, please, get me wrong, because I am not saying this out of any feeling of sour grapes, or because we lost the game. I just didn't think he behaved in the right way. Sitting on the ball and then keeping it up the way he did – that was insulting to fellow professionals. What Jimmy Baxter was doing wasn't professional. You just don't do that kind of thing. It's OK keeping the ball and passing it round and he did that too, with wee Billy (Bremner) joining in, and you can accept that as being part of the game.

'Clowning around and taking the piss was never right in my book. He was out of order. I don't know why he did it. It's not something that I can begin to understand. Maybe he was trying to show everyone just what he could do, how much ability he had, because he had not been able to do that at club level since he moved south to Sunderland. He had not made any kind of impact at all in the first division. He had been the king when he was up in Glasgow with the Rangers but when he was at Roker Park and then at Forest no one paid any attention to him. He didn't impress the fans or any of the opposing players in the first division and I suppose that must have hurt him. He certainly could not have enjoyed being almost ignored in that way.'

Of course, while it was widely suggested over the years that Baxter had sat on the ball to taunt the English players even more, that did not happen. It was one of the many legends that grew up around the game, and that one was not true, though all these years later Jack Charlton still believes it happened. The man who managed the Republic of Ireland to so much success also believes that he scored a goal that was not given, insisting: 'We might have had a draw that day because I am still sure, to this day, that I had a header that went over the line and Ronnie Simpson dragged it back and the referee did not give it. But, on the day, Scotland played well and they did deserve to win. We hadn't paid any attention to the newspapers beforehand, which all said that we simply had to turn up to win, because every single one of us knew that it was always a battle when we played the Jocks. It was the same any time I played against them and we all expected it to be hard and it was. I just wish that Jim had not done what he did because it still annoys me. There was no need for it as far as I am concerned even though the Scottish supporters loved it. You just shouldn't treat fellow professionals that way.

'Anyhow, that was back then, and I feel very, very sorry for all the problems he had towards the end of his life. Away from that particular game, and his antics there, I had a few drinks with him down through the years and I found him to be a good lad, and great company. Well, when he was sober he was great company, but when he had had a few then he became a wee bit cheeky. Wee Billy Bremner, a lovely little man, was exactly the same and I used to say to him when we were at Leeds together that the English could handle their drink better than the Scots and that didn't go down too well!'

While none of the Scots would concede that Charlton's headed effort should have counted – and there was no photographic evidence that suggested that was the case – they would all agree that he was a thorn in their flesh when he was operating at centre forward. There was always an aerial threat from him and, in what turned out to be a frenzied finish to the game, the Scots flirted with defeat when they should have been winning without worry. But Baxter did like to live life on the edge and that's how it turned out. Scotland had enjoyed the cushion of the Denis Law goal after 28 minutes but, despite the enormous amount of possession they enjoyed, they did not score another until the 71st minute when Bobby Lennox increased their lead. Jack Charlton then scored the first of three goals in three minutes as the match moved towards the end of the ninety minutes. His strike came in the 85th minute and then Jim McCalliog increased Scotland's lead two minutes later with Geoff Hurst bringing the English back into a position where they were only one goal behind again, which was a little too close for comfort as far as the Scots support was concerned. The thought of having victory, a thoroughly deserved triumph, snatched away from them in the final minute was a very real fear.

Still Baxter, socks round his ankles for most of that second half, was able to rally his team-mates and see them through the closing moments and then savour the moment. It was the last time he was to do so. He played a few weeks later in the desultory friendly with the Soviet Union that the Scots lost 2–0 at Hampden. Some months after that, in November and again at Hampden, he played in a scrambled 3–2 win over Wales and it was all over. In December the £100,000 transfer from Sunderland to Nottingham Forest went through and the midfield great was never to appear in his country's colours again. As his club career collapsed disastrously, he was never again considered for the international side. His years with Scotland brought him 34 caps and three goals, one in a friendly against Uruguay at Hampden in 1962 when Scotland lost 3–2 to the South Americans. The other two were scored at Wembley, of course, in 1963, when he was part of a team he thought the best Scotland side he had ever been in. He played for Scotland for the first time in a 6–1 win over Northern Ireland in Belfast on 7 October 1961 and it was all over on 22 November 1967 against Wales just over six brief years later.

It was not nearly long enough. Indeed it was tragically and shamefully short, although the memories will always remain and in them Baxter will be forever young, forever arrogant and forever majestic. And always he will be beating England and glorying in the triumphs at Wembley, which was his spiritual home, that great old ground that is now no more but which provided the perfect backdrop to the most extravagantly gifted footballer of his time. He enjoyed the very best of times there on that famously rich and luxuriant sward and, if he had done no more than that, then he would still have been recognised as one of Scottish football's giants. His precious skills may have been frittered away at club level in England but that cannot dim their brilliance. Nothing can, just as long as those black and white images from the 1960s are still available and other generations can see the sheer impudence of the magical five seconds of keepy-uppy in 1967 that so effectively sum up the football philosophy of one man and an entire nation who identified with him for those half dozen seasons when it seemed that he could conquer the world all on his own.

13 AND THE WORST OF TIMES

As for football, that was pushed aside. The men who ran the game in Scotland had slammed shut their doors in the face of the man who had given the country so much pleasure as a player. For a time he tried to find a job as a manager. He asked journalists to help him get a job and he was ready to start at one of the lesser clubs and try to construct a new life for himself involved, again, in what he knew best. He asked his friend Jim Rodger to talk to his first senior club Raith Rovers when their manager's job became vacant. He asked me to talk to Queen of the South when there was an opening there. Not even these unfashionable clubs wanted to take a chance on handing him his first managerial position. Tragically, no one wanted him and, eventually, disillusioned by the lack of interest, he turned his back on the game. For many years he did not even go to watch the matches at Ibrox.

When the Ibrox comeback failed and, for the second time in a year, Jim Baxter faced up to fact that he had been handed another free transfer, even his 'live for today and let tomorrow take care of itself' outlook was severely jolted. From the time he left the pits and signed as a full-time professional for Raith Rovers, until that day in 1969, he had always been able to earn his living as a footballer.

Times may have grown more difficult as his talents were dissipated but, in his last two moves, even though they both turned out badly, he had made serious money. His five-figure signing-on fee at Forest did not reflect his failure at Sunderland, nor did his salary at the City Ground. And the Rangers manager Davie White has already revealed that when he returned to Ibrox he was given a house by the club to help broker the deal.

Now, though, he knew that he was no longer able to command such lucrative contracts, his playing days were over and he had to concentrate on earning a living outside the game. To do so he opened a pub in Paisley Road West – Jim Baxter's it was called, predictably enough and, placed handily for Ibrox on match days, it should have offered the man who still enjoyed the adulation of the Rangers faithful a good living. For maybe five of the thirteen years he held on to the business it did – but towards the end of his time there his old club was doing badly, gates had slumped to an all-time low, and no one was drinking in his pub en route to the games.

But if the fans were not drinking there too often, Baxter was becoming his own best customer. By his own admission he was drinking close to three bottles of Bacardi a day at this time and his gambling was as out of control as his drinking. He was betting £200–£300 on a horse and only rarely missing a race. If that were not enough he was playing cards in the pub for huge stakes, sometimes thousands of pounds would change hands, and playing pool against anyone who came in, for serious side stakes. As for football, that was pushed aside. The men who ran the game in Scotland had slammed shut their doors in the face of the man who had given the country so much pleasure as a player. For a time he tried to find a job as a manager. He asked journalists to help him get a job and he was ready to start at one of the lesser clubs and try to construct a new life for himself involved, again, in what he knew best. He asked his friend Jim Rodger to talk to his first senior club Raith Rovers when their manager's job became vacant. He asked me to talk to Queen of the South when there was an opening there. Not even these unfashionable clubs wanted to take a chance on handing him his first managerial position. Tragically, no one wanted him and, eventually, disillusioned by the lack of interest, he turned his back on the game. For many years he did not even go to watch the matches at Ibrox.

Part of the reason clubs would not take him on board was his reputation and another part was that everyone knew that Baxter had not been the most conscientious trainer in the world when he played, nor did he take kindly to either on or off field discipline. And so there was a refusal to accept him as a serious contender for jobs when they did become vacant. Yet, Sir Alex Ferguson, who saw a lot of him during these troubled years, maintains that Baxter, for all his public criticism of rigidly applied team tactics, had a deep knowledge of the game, which is not always apparent in those players whose skills have come naturally to them.

He says: 'I think because Jim played so much of his own football off the cuff so to speak, there are people who just don't realise that he had a great knowledge of the game. You know he would argue all day about football and very often the pair of us did that!

'He had a pub in Paisley Road West when he stopped playing and I had a pub right across the road from him while I was manager of St Mirren. I was doing quite well there at Love Street and Jim would come across for a cup of tea and he would sit there and start talking about football. He would get one of these dish towels we used to have on the bar and he would set it down and ask me to write my team on it. Then he would write his own and ask me how I was going to beat him. That kind of thing would go on for hours. He wasn't even going to the games by then, I think he had stopped after being freed by Rangers, but that didn't mean he had lost interest. He would have been a tremendous coach or manager, without question, because of the depth of his knowledge.

'I am not referring here to his ability as a footballer because we have all seen players of great natural ability who haven't made it as managers. I just happen to believe that he could have been different because he thought about the game quite deeply. He actually had a good tactical brain but when he was looking for a job in football then people were worried about the baggage he might bring with him. It was unfortunate that he had to carry that around because, I think, he maybe had a lot to offer. But his reputation scared directors away.

'I realised how much he thought about the game when I was with him at Ibrox for a short spell before I was sold to Falkirk. In one game against Aberdeen he was being man-marked by a lad called Tommy Wilson, who was going to go with Jim wherever he went on the field. Now the manager, Davie White, was shouting to Jim to drop deeper and to lose his marker that way. Instead Jim went right up front and started to play in the centre forward position, taking the Aberdeen player with him. At half time I was in the dressing room even though the manager had bombed me out at that time, and Davie White was on at Jim again, asking him what he thought he was doing. And, to be fair, it was the natural thing to do to drop deeper and that way lose the player who had been delegated to pick you up all the time. Well, Jim's thinking on this was fantastic. He explained that he knew that when he got the ball Tommy Wilson would be there beside him ready to make a tackle. Therefore, he said, it was better to be up in their penalty area rather than back in his own when that happened. He thought that if he lost the ball back around his own box then the team might lose a goal. On the other hand if he stayed well up field then he might manage to score one! It all sounds so simple now, but he had put some thought into the problem and had come up with a solution that was against the normal thinking of the time. He had worked that out and he was right, too.'

On another notable occasion Baxter came up with a novel and much more personal way of ridding himself of the unwanted attentions of a close-marking opponent. In a game against Dundee at Dens Park the then manager of the Tayside club, Bob Shankly, had given the job of marking the Rangers wing half to one of his younger, emerging players, who diligently took on the task, following his quarry around the field, never more than a few yards away from him. Baxter's way, in that game, of wrecking his opponent's concentration, was to drift out to the touchline and then take several steps over the touchline and on to the track. His marker duly followed and only realised where he had wandered when Baxter stood there mocking him. The Dundee player did not recover from the embarrassment and the Ibrox star found the freedom he craved.

On yet another occasion Sir Alex Ferguson was a victim of Baxter's artistry and he still admits to the humiliation he suffered when he was asked to perform a marking role on the midfielder. He says: 'I was with Dunfermline and we were going to play Rangers in the quarter-final of the League Cup at Ibrox back in 1964, and the manager, Willie Cunningham, decided just before the game that I was going to man-mark Baxter. Well, I knew all my mates in Glasgow would be at the game and I knew they would be standing in their usual place, way up between passageways twelve and thirteen at the Rangers end. So the first time he had the ball I went in to tackle him and I was determined to let him know that I was playing and I made this lunge for him and, cool as you like, he nutmegged me [placed the ball between his legs] and there I was lying on my arse and I thought "Oh no" because I could just visualise all my mates laughing at me. I had just started playing full time with Dunfermline then and while we drew with them 2–2 that night we had lost the first leg at East End Park 3–0 and they went on to win the trophy.

'Anyhow, because I was training every day in Fife now, I used to see my pals on a Sunday afternoon in Glasgow to catch up with them. We would meet outside the Odeon Cinema in Renfield Street and then we would go for a coffee to the Viking or the Cadora and then go to the movies. When I walked up the Sunday after that game, there they were waiting for me, all of them, pretending they were nutmegging each other as I walked up. I took some stick! Actually what Jim Baxter had to set him apart from everyone else was a wonderful sense of balance, he just seemed to float over the ground. That allowed him to take the ball in tight situations with people marking him without having to worry too much about the challenge that was going to come in.'

It has to be said that Baxter was unfortunate, too, when his career ended, in that television punditry had not reached the levels it has done today when so many former footballers are seen on the box giving their opinions of the games. The journalist who collaborated with him on that long-running *Sunday Mirror* column, Rodger Baillie believes: 'His accent went against him. He never lost that Fife singsong way of speaking and that would have put off some of the radio and television producers back then. But he would have been good in that role because he was never afraid to speak his mind. Several lesser players were given these jobs and they were, for the most part, rarely as controversial as Baxter would have been. He was never short of a viewpoint, never short of an opinion and never afraid to speak his mind even if that meant him landing in trouble with the football authorities. He talked a lot about ignoring tactics when he played but he always talked very intelligently about the game. It was a shame he was never given an opportunity on television or on radio.'

Ferguson has another view – he believes that he was simply in the wrong place at the wrong time: 'Jock Stein was the main man from Scotland who was used on the major television panels then. All the main pundits were from English football and so Jim missed out on that. If the situation had been the same as it is today then he might have been given a job and, believe me, he would have spoken his mind. He would be blunt, you always got the truth from Jim Baxter, and that would have made him a success. He had this knowledge as I said, and he was also able to put it all into words without talking round things. And he would not have worried about upsetting anyone or hurting anyone's feelings. He would have told it the way he saw it. Jim lost out when no one gave him a job but television lost out even more.'

While the pub was still providing him with a reasonable livelihood, he continued to gamble and drink to excess, and there were times when he would alienate his friends. That would only happen when he had taken too much to drink, and Sir Alex Ferguson admits: 'There were two sides I saw to Jim when he came into my pub. There was the lad who was really serious about his football and there was the other lad who could be a bit cheeky at times, but that was only when he had had a drink or two. When that happened he would appear in the pub the next day and apologise and want to buy all the regulars a drink to make up for anything he might have said that was out of order. I wouldn't let him do that, of course, but it did let you know that he realised that there was this other, blacker side to his personality.'

During this period his old Rangers team-mate, Willie Henderson, opened a pub in Coatbridge with Alfie Conn as one of his partners in the venture. On opening night Baxter and some of his cronies from his own Paisley Road establishment had been invited to the launch party. Conn, a teenager on the fringe of the first team, who had been in awe of the Ibrox legend when he returned to Rangers, still remembers his shock when that 'Mr Hyde' persona suddenly surfaced that night.

He says: 'I had remembered that Jim had a really caring side to his nature because one time I had been down at Ayr races and this guy had invited me up to one of the hospitality areas. So up I go, Jack the lad, and Jim is there well ensconced with a whole crowd of his mates. When he saw me he came straight over and took me aside and told me that I was too young to be involved with the kind of people who were around in this lounge and that if I wanted to make something of my career then I should remember that and be careful. He more or less told me to get on my bike and get out of there and that's what I did. Naturally, Jim stayed on, but that was exactly what I would have expected. What I had not reckoned on was that he would take time to give me a friendly warning. It was almost as if he did not want to see a young player go down the same road that he had been travelling for too many years. I thought a lot of him for doing that.

'So you can understand how surprised I was when I saw his other side. We had staged this big opening night party; a private affair, invitation only, and Jim came along and started a gambling school round one of the pool tables. Now there were signs on the wall stating quite clearly that no gambling was allowed on the premises. We could have been in trouble with the police and that could have meant losing the licence just as we were opening. Anyhow, I went over to him, told him that he would have to stop gambling and pointed out one of the signs on the wall of the pub. He just looked at me and said, "Rules are there to be broken," which I suppose summed up his lifestyle. No matter how friendly he had been to me before and no matter how long his close friendship with Willie Henderson had lasted, he couldn't care less that he might get us in bother. He wanted to play cards and, as far as he was concerned, that was that.

'Later he came over to the bar and asked for a Bacardi and coke. I served him but we didn't have any ice because the ice machine had broken, and he ordered me to go out and find some ice for his drink. It was as if he didn't know me. I couldn't believe this was the same guy who had been so kind to me at Ibrox. That was one of his bad nights and nothing we could do could please him, mainly because he had had too much to drink and could not get his own way over the card game.'

This was now the way he was living his life, often testing even the longest-running friendships when he had been drinking and when he became soured by the situation he now found himself in. As the Rangers slump continued and the gates fell, and the property in the surrounding area began to be demolished, and the local customers moved away, so the pub became less successful. Baxter held on to it for thirteen years but always reckoned he had had just five good years from the business before the problems set in. Ironically, if he had held on for another few years then he could have flourished along with his former club when Graeme Souness began his Rangers revolution in 1986. But, by then, the pub had changed hands and circumstances had conspired against Baxter yet again. The time had been wrong. As Ibrox became a sell-out week after week, Baxter was no longer running the pub that would have, once again, become a gold mine.

Willie Henderson claims: 'The pub should have been a licence to print money but then Rangers went through bad times and Jimmy sold out. Two or three years later Graeme Souness arrived, the boom times were back, and he missed out on them. That was tragic. But, you know, he never blamed anyone else for things that went wrong in his life. He took the blame for them all and I suppose you have to say that he was right when he summed things up that way. Not many lawyers would have got him off if he had been charged with messing things up! Jimmy had a wee catalogue of things in his head, a wee portfolio, where he knew what he had done wrong in his life: the break-up of his marriage, leaving Rangers when he did, all kinds of things. Losing the pub when he did was another one of them. But he never fretted publicly over them and, always, money was just a commodity, it was never important in itself. You had only to watch him gamble to realise that – Jimmy played cards the way he played football, always ready to take the risks, but while he was an absolutely fearless gambler he didn't have the skill at cards or horses that he had as a footballer.'

During this period he was not even going to watch games on any kind of regular basis. It was only in the last few years of his life that John Greig, back serving his old club, enticed him back to Ibrox, and he took on a role as one of the club's ambassadors on match days, mixing with other ex-players from his own era such as Eric Caldow, Jimmy Millar, Ralph Brand, Willie Henderson, Alex Willoughby, Davy Wilson and others. It was not a role that would have suited him during his wilder days, but now that he had virtually stopped drinking it was only the 'Dr Jekyll' image that was on public display and a story Jimmy Millar tells reveals that. At one game Millar and Baxter were on duty together in one of the lounges when a supporter came up and began to ask the two ex-players who were the best footballers they had ever seen.

Millar takes up the story: 'This was not too long before Jim died and we were in the Argyle Suite and we talked about great players to the lad. Then I turned it on him and asked him who was the best player he had seen. He pointed to Jim and said: "He was, Jim Baxter was the best I've seen." And I thought I would have a bit of fun.

'I said to him, "How could he be the best player you ever watched? He couldn't kick the ball with his right foot. He couldn't tackle. He couldn't run. He couldn't head the ball. He didn't do any work. What are you talking about here?" Now I had winked to Jim before I started all of this and he was laughing away in the background, but this fellow, he didn't know what to think or what to say before he realised that I was having him on. But, you know, while it was a wind-up there was a lot of truth in what I was saying and Jim knew that. He couldn't do any of the things I had listed – but with the ball at his feet, especially at that left foot, he was magnificent. He had superb vision and was a wonderful passer of the ball, and because we had such a good, well-balanced side back then we could give him the little bit of latitude that he needed.'

While Baxter laughed at Millar's critique, it is difficult to imagine him accepting the remarks even as a joke, a few years earlier, particularly if he had been drinking. It was, by now, a newer Baxter, a mellower Baxter, who had emerged from the illness that had threatened his life and was now moving towards the further menace that would eventually kill him.

14 THE FIRST FIGHT AGAINST ILLNESS

The fall out from Baxter's indiscretion was immense. It was not portrayed as a slip on the way to as full a recovery as possible. Just as football had seen him as a man carrying 'too much baggage' along with him, so the general public viewed him as someone who had been handed a chance and had blown it. The fact that he had not been drinking for more than a year counted for little. Suddenly he found himself being pilloried, and the hospital and the medical staff were criticised for allowing him to have the operation when there were supposed 'needier' cases. It became a cause célèbre across the country. Protest groups voiced their feelings. Newspaper columnists derided him. And the initial sympathy that many had felt for him began to evaporate. Baxter was hurt by the media attention. He was, after all, more used to being lauded than vilified and, to be fair to him, the outcry was hysterically over the top. After that first blowout he retreated to the diet of tea and orange juice which he had reluctantly adopted – albeit unwillingly – in the year or more following the transplant.

During his time at the Paisley Road pub he held court there frequently and once, when I was working with the *Daily Record*, we placed him and Charlie Tully together to talk about an Old Firm game. Tully had been almost as big a legend in Glasgow when he played with Celtic in the 1950s as Baxter had been in the following decade with Rangers.

That day gave another insight to the Fifer's character. Pat Crerand has always maintained that beneath the swaggering style he adopted when he was at the peak of his career there was still a 'shy boy from Fife', though that was a side normally only seen by those close to him. But as the day with Tully progressed, it was interesting to see the younger man defer to the man from Belfast whose antics had captured the imagination of their adopted city ten years before Baxter's arrival on the scene. It was Tully who famously sent the ball into the net from a corner kick twice within minutes in a Scottish Cup game against Falkirk at Brockville. With Celtic trailing 2–0 at half time Tully took a corner kick soon after the game had restarted. The ball flew directly into the net but the referee ordered the kick to be retaken. Tully then sent his second effort past the bewildered Falkirk goalkeeper and this time it counted and the feat inspired Celtic to a 3–2 victory. That was the kind of attitude, the chutzpah, that Baxter admired and, as the tales from Tully's times were retold, he insisted that the one-time Celtic star repair to his pub, where the doors were locked for an afternoon of drinking and reminiscing. The two men, who had a common approach to the game and to life itself, enjoyed each other's company so much that the Irishman almost missed his evening flight home.

That was just one of the long days I spent in Baxter's company working on one feature or another – but for him this was a near-daily occurrence and his years as a publican were seriously to damage his health and alter his life.

Most of his days were spent in the same way, not in the illustrious company of those such as Charles Patrick Tully, but more often with the Damon Runyan-like characters who went to the pub for after-hours drinking and for heavy-duty gambling. Card schools where thousands of pounds would change hands were common. One customer lost a Mercedes in a shoot pontoon session. Pool games where side stakes of several hundred pounds were involved also filled his afternoons when the pub was supposed to be closed and, always, there was the bookie's where he would wager several hundred pounds almost every Saturday afternoon knowing full well that, for the most part, he would be a loser.

It was no surprise that his marriage broke under the strain. He accepted all the blame for that failure, recognising that his wife Jean and his two sons Alan and Steven had suffered because of his errant behaviour. After the divorce he met Norma, his partner for seventeen years, and the woman he always credited with saving his life when he was struck down with liver damage in 1994. He had been in poor health for some time before the full extent of the illness was diagnosed. His weight had ballooned to such an extent that anyone meeting him for the first time would wonder how he could ever have been given the nickname 'Slim Jim'. When he eventually agreed to see a doctor he was, predictably enough, told to stop drinking, but that was never going to be an easy instruction for Jim Baxter to follow. His adult years had been spent drinking in pubs and clubs, and a more sober and sedate lifestyle was not something he could readily embrace.

When telling a friend that he had been told by doctors that he might die if he did not stop drinking, he commented: 'I'll give it a year and see how it goes.' The problem, though, was that he did not give it a year. He thought life should simply go on as before and, when he ignored the warnings, he soon found himself in hospital.

His friends recognised the quandary he faced and Billy McNeill still says: 'What was Jimmy Baxter going to do if he stopped drinking? He couldn't just stop and change his lifestyle very dramatically because he had always lived life in his own way and I know that he thought it was too late to change. He would come into my pub, just off Victoria Road, sometimes to have a few drinks – and remember this is a Celtic pub we are talking about here! Anyhow, he would come in and he would chat away with the regulars and he would joke with me: "Big man, I'll leave before I'm a nuisance" – but I have to say he was never a nuisance. He was never any trouble at all. His pals all knew that he could be a pest at times and that he could be hard going when he had one or two too many. If that happened, as it could do, then you forgave him because of all the other good aspects to his character. Lives can drift apart in all walks of life and to some extent that was the way it was with Jimmy and I, but when we met up it was as if we had never been away from each other. If you were a friend of Jimmy's then that was it forever.'

Alex Willoughby had warmed to the man, when Baxter had ignored pressing business of his own to run the young player to Stobhill Hospital in Springburn to see his mother who was ill, stopping en route to buy her flowers and a fruit basket 'the size of a wee table', according to the highly impressed reserve.

Later in life Willoughby, who keeps in contact with almost all the former Rangers players not only from his era but from others too, became even closer to his flawed hero. He was with him just a couple of days before the collapse that saw Baxter being rushed back into hospital, a collapse that subsequently brought about the liver transplant that was to give him seven extra years of life.

'He had been in hospital a few times and he had always signed himself out,' says Willoughby. 'He would not persevere with the treatment the doctors were trying to give him. You have to say that he brought this collapse on himself because he would not do what he was told to do. He knew that, of course, and he always held on to the fact that he was to blame for the condition he found himself in. Anyhow, we were down at Ayr at a restaurant there, some place out of the road because by this time Jimmy was looking terrible. His skin had gone a bright yellow, almost a canary yellow. My cousin Jim Forrest was there too and we bumped into Bob Reilly who was the commercial manager for Rangers at the time. He had not seen Jimmy for a wee while and he signalled to me that he wanted to have a word. He asked me how Jimmy was and admitted that he had not realised how serious the illness was – this is just looking at him from across the room, remember!

'Apart from his colour, his eyes were sticking out like organ stops, and he had on a collar and tie and they were sitting way down on his neck. He looked terrible, death was looking out of him that night and forty-eight hours later he collapsed and was back in hospital.'

Forrest confirms his cousin's assessment, adding: 'You could see death in his face that night. He was jaundiced, very seriously jaundiced. All the alcohol he had downed over the years had a dreadful effect on his body and so even when he did make an effort and go a few weeks without a drink it did not help his physical condition very much because all the damage had been done. You could see that even before the liver problems flared up. When those symptoms appeared they simply confirmed your worst fears for him.'

Willoughby saw how desperately low in spirit his friend was then. There were occasions when he visited the Victoria Infirmary on Glasgow's south side when Baxter threatened to kill himself if his health deteriorated any further.

'He was in this ward on the top floor one of the times he was admitted,' Willoughby recollects, 'and he had all these pills he had to take and he was very, very low, and that was not like him at all, because throughout his various problems he had managed somehow to present a brave face to the world, never letting people know just how ill he was. Now, though, it hit him and when I went to see him he would ask me to open one of the windows and leave it open because he said that if things got any worse for him he would throw himself out rather than keep on suffering. It is not easy seeing a pal as desperate as he was then but, still, he never looked for any sympathy. He never asked me to tell the other former Rangers players or any of his mates that he was so critically ill. By this stage of the illness he was taking something like 25 to 30 pills every day just to keep himself alive!

'But, despite all the problems he had during his life and all the wrong turns his career took at times, he did carry some luck with him. This time that luck was on his side when he was taken into hospital that Monday following the night out we had had down at Ayr. What happened was that the consultant had been delayed that day and he was doing his rounds in the afternoon, and when he saw Baxter lying there he took a look at his notes. Now, Jimmy, being Jimmy, was asking him why he was bothering to do that when everyone knew what was wrong with him. But this was the man who told him that it would be possible to perform a liver transplant operation. He asked Jimmy if he would take an assessment and added that he would have to go through to Edinburgh Royal Infirmary where the Liver Transplant Unit was based.

'No one had suggested this earlier because the hospital had always hoped that he would respond to the medication they were giving him. This time the specialist decided that more drastic action had to be taken to help him. When he went for the assessment two weeks later he was told that there was no option but to go ahead with the transplant operation. The first one failed and a second operation had to be done forty-eight hours later. People should realise that Jimmy never asked for the transplant. It happened just the way I've told you and if he had been told back then that he could not get the operation then he would have accepted that just as he accepted the illness itself. He never pushed himself forward because he had been a great footballer or anything like that. If that specialist had not come round that afternoon then he would not have had the extra seven years or so he was able to enjoy after the liver replacement.'

There was criticism at the time of the operation as people queried Baxter's right to be given this opportunity when he had, in their eyes, damaged himself. Later, when one of the tabloid newspapers discovered that he had been drinking, there was a public outcry that hurt Baxter deeply. Essentially he had worked hard to stop drinking and his friends had helped as much as they could.

Alfie Conn, who was working in a pub in Great Western Road, had Baxter as a lunchtime regular during that period, and stresses: 'When he came into the pub for his lunch, and this was three or four times a week I would think, he didn't touch a drink. We wouldn't have served him in any case but he was happy enough to sit with a cup of tea or an orange juice and have something to eat. Mind you, while the drink was being given a rest, the gambling was still as serious as ever. He was still punting a couple of hundred pounds a day in doubles and trebles and Yankees. He had started gambling in the pits and that never left him.'

Back to Willoughby, who explains: 'When he came out of hospital in Edinburgh after the transplant operation he didn't have a single drink for maybe a year or fifteen months. Not a drop. I'd meet him and he would sit and have a cup of tea or a soft drink and then he would complain a bit about this and ask me how I could sit around drinking tea all night. It was easy for me because I never did drink and I was happy with that. He knew, of course, that if anyone ever offered him a drink then I would not allow it. I knew that it would be wrong for him and almost everyone realised that and respected it. No one wanted to encourage him to start drinking again. He stuck to that and, unlike previous times when he would sign himself out of the hospital and pay no attention to what the doctors said, he was going back and forward for regular checks. To begin with he was going once a week and then, gradually, as he made progress, that was cut back to once a month as the specialist continued to monitor his condition. And he stuck to the regime he had been given. And then came the day he fell off the wagon.'

Perhaps it had only been a matter of time because Baxter's own logic might have gone something along the lines of – 'I had one liver which lasted me for fifty years when it was getting a lot of abuse and now I have a new one so it should last me all right too, even if I do start to take a drink now and again.'

Joe Public did not see it that way, nor did the teetotal Willoughby when he discovered, as he was making one of his business calls to a pub in Shettleston Road one morning, that Baxter had returned to drinking in a spectacular fashion. Let him take up the story: 'I came out of this pub and bumped straight into a taxi driver I knew. Right away he told me, "I had your mate in the taxi last night, Alex. Jimmy Baxter was poured into the back seat. He was in some state." So, no need to tell you, I flew at the lad because Glasgow is the kind of place where stories go about and they grow arms and legs and I didn't want that to happen because I did not believe the story in the first place. Stanley had been doing so well and I didn't want him being damaged by rumours running round the city. But the taxi driver stuck to his story and then, when he saw how angry I was, he shrugged his shoulders and drove off in his cab.'

All these years later Willoughby remains angry as his memory carries him back to that morning in Shettleston when, despite his instant dismissal of the taxi driver's story, he found himself suddenly riven with doubts, wondering if Baxter had indeed fallen off the wagon after months of abstinence.

'The doubts invaded my mind just as the lad drove off,' he says. 'He had not budged on his story; he did not withdraw one bit of it even though I was arguing with him. I got into my own car and started to drive down the street, and when I saw a phone box I found myself drawing in alongside it and getting out of the car again. Then I was going into the box and dialling Stanley's number. I can still hear the phone ringing and ringing at the other end as I waited for him to answer. It seemed to go on forever before, eventually, he lifted the phone and I asked him how he was and he answered: "I'm OK, or I was until you wakened me up. What time is it anyway?" So I told him that it was now half past eleven in the morning and it was then that he admitted that he couldn't even remember getting back home the night before.

'That's when I knew the taxi driver hadn't been simply spreading silly rumours, that he had been telling me the truth, and there I had been getting ready to fight with him over it while all the time Baxter had been out on the tiles. If I had been angry when I heard the story first, I was even angrier now. I blew up at him. I told him that he was totally out of order and that he was letting down everyone who had stood by him as well as the doctors and the nurses and that he would destroy all the good that had come through that transplant. His reply was that, at his last monthly check-up at the hospital a few days before, the specialist had told him it would be OK if he started having a drink again, that he had improved so much it would not do him any harm.

'I told him that he was talking rubbish and there was no way I was going to believe that story and then I banged down the phone. To me it seemed that he was about to wreck all the good things that had been happening to his health since the operation. Deep down I felt that he would be putting his life in danger again and I could not understand it.

'As all of this was running through my mind I realised that I still had a pile of change in my hand for the phone because I had cut Stanley off so abruptly. It was then that I decided to look up the number of the specialist in Edinburgh and call him to find out what really had been said at their last meeting.

'Within a minute or two I was speaking to his secretary and then I was put through to the man himself – I had got to know him through the time Stanley had spent in hospital – and I asked him if it was true that he had given Jimmy Baxter permission to start drinking again. Then he listened as I explained what had happened the night before and relayed the gist of my conversation with Jimmy. After that he told me his side of the story, which was considerably different from the version I had heard earlier. What he had said was that Jimmy had made really good progress and he wanted to acknowledge that. That's when he said that because the transplant had been such a success, especially after the initial problem, it was now possible for him to enjoy a glass of wine – maybe even a couple of glasses of wine – with a meal. And, even at that, this was only permissible at the weekend as a kind of special treat. He then assured me that he would take care of things from there on in and that he would speak to Jimmy that day and get the message over to him as soon as possible. I went on about the rest of my own business still furious about what had happened but comfortable in the belief now that the specialist would spell things out to his patient.'

It was later that day, when Willoughby was at home having his evening meal, that his telephone rang and he found Baxter on the other end of the line, a Baxter who was far from penitent and who was complaining that his friend should not have interfered in his life by making the phone call to Edinburgh.

Willoughby exploded again. 'When he started talking that way it was too much for me. It had been a long day and I had had enough of all of this and I told him that, adding that, as far as I was concerned, he was a liar. He had told me a pack of lies about what the specialist had told him and he had let down his friends by going back on the bevvy again. What was wrong, of course, was that he knew he had been found out and he was annoyed at me phoning his doctor. The thing was I knew Jimmy Baxter and had known him for close on forty years and I had asked the specialist how long he had known him. His answer was that he had only known him for around eighteen months, so I had explained that expecting Jimmy to accept the expression 'a glass or two of wine' literally, was well off the mark. He would have taken that as a green light to start serious drinking again – and, of course, that's exactly what had happened.'

The fall out from Baxter's indiscretion was immense. It was not portrayed as a slip on the way to as full a recovery as possible. Just as football had seen him as a man carrying 'too much baggage' along with him, so the general public viewed him as someone who had been handed a chance and had blown it. The fact that he had not been drinking for more than a year counted for little. Suddenly he found himself being pilloried, and the hospital and the medical staff were criticised for allowing him to have the operation when there were supposed 'needier' cases. It became a cause célèbre across the country. Protest groups voiced their feelings. Newspaper columnists derided him. And the initial sympathy that many had felt for him began to evaporate. Baxter was hurt by the media attention. He was, after all, more used to being lauded than vilified and, to be fair to him, the outcry was hysterically over the top. After that first blowout he retreated to the diet of tea and orange juice which he had reluctantly adopted – albeit unwillingly – in the year or more following the transplant.

As Billy McNeill has already pointed out, it was difficult to see Baxter turn into a total abstainer but, while there was still the infrequent binge, for the most part he stayed away from any serious drinking. No one who was around him during this period would say other than that he tried his best to stick to the regimen which allowed him the 'one or two glasses of wine' prescribed by his doctor. For months on end he would go down that route and then there would be a day or two when he would lapse, as Willoughby can bear witness to. He admits: 'We patched things up after that first drinking session and he accepted that I had been trying to help him when I phoned the specialist. The bad publicity hurt him and he knew that he had let down a lot of people who were close to him and who were offering him support. So he did make a serious effort to stay away from the booze. Sure, over the years there were one or two blow-outs, but he never did go back to drinking as heavily as he had done in the years before the operation.

'Really he was pretty successful even though he never learned how to enjoy tea or mineral water or even fruit juice! Of course, physically, he wasn't up to carousing any more. He had done himself a lot of damage over the years no matter how tough he was. And he was tough, not in a fighting sense, and not in a football playing sense either, because he would never cut you in half with a tackle but, believe me, he was one tough cookie in other ways. After the operation the surgeon spent some time speaking to Ralph Brand and myself and telling us that Jim's metabolism was extraordinary, that his heart and lungs were in superb condition. Our answer was that they had had to be because of the way he had burned the candle at both ends all through his life.

'After the operation, though, he would tire very easily. You have to remember that no matter how strong he was, that body of his had lived a few lifetimes. Of course, the operation gave him an initial boost physically, which is what we all expected. In fact it was better than many of us had thought, and it did give him those extra years of life after that collapse when there were doubts if he was ever going to recover. But he was not going to get back to where he was and, while he had an odd drink or two, he was taking care for the most part. It would be wrong to suggest that he went back to his old ways, because that was not true. He tried very hard to stick to the doctor's orders and, while he had some heavy sessions, they would come and then they would vanish again, and for months he would not have a drink at all. Any time he thought he had been overdoing things he just went back on the wagon. He didn't take many chances.'

It became obvious to his friends that even though he had cut down on his drinking severely, the years of excess were catching up with him. Even if he had wanted to do so, Jim Baxter was not physically able to cut a swathe through Glasgow's nightlife as he had done so often in his younger, wilder days. He would still frequent the pubs where he was known and where his friends would look out for him, but those times when he stepped out of line grew fewer and fewer.

Once he asked Alfie Conn to join him on a trip to Inverness where he was to be a speaker at the local Rangers Supporters' Club. An official invitation for the younger man was forthcoming and they travelled north together, but Conn tells you now: 'We were sharing a room and, by this time, he was ill and he knew it and I knew it. He was taking all kinds of pills as well as a drink that he told me he had to take just to stay alive. All these various medicines were laid out in the room. It was quite worrying. Yet he went into the dinner and spoke, and he was magnificent, and the fans gave him a standing ovation. You know what, he took just two drinks before the meal and that was it. He didn't have another for the rest of the night. People wanted to buy him a drink but he kept refusing. You could see that he was trying to look after himself. When we went upstairs to bed I was frightened to sleep because his breathing was so laboured I was sure that something was going to happen to him. It was typical of Jim Baxter, though, that no matter how ill he was he knew he had promised to speak at that dinner for the Rangers fans and he went through with it. He knew things were bad but he didn't want anyone to feel sorry for him. And, naturally, the last thing he wanted to do was disappoint these people up there in Inverness. He just did not want to let them down no matter the cost to himself although the journey, and the dinner, and the speech, did take a lot out of him. His health was deteriorating by that time.'

Over a period of almost four decades Billy McNeill watched Baxter move from centre stage in Glasgow to a place in the wings, though in the memories of everyone who saw him play for either Rangers or Scotland he would always be in the spotlight. As a rival in Old Firm games, as a team-mate for their country, and as a friend, he had a sense of what Baxter was about both on and of the field, both in and out of the glare of publicity.

Now he comments: 'I thought the criticism he had directed at him, when people found out that he had been out drinking more than a year after the transplant operation, was over the top. He didn't deserve to have all of that thrown at him. They should have seen him in hospital where he was always trying to make light of his illness, and they should have seen the efforts he made to stay away from the drink when there were always people ready to buy him one. The times I was with him socially, after the operation, he would usually take only one or two glasses of red wine and then call a halt.

'It could not have been easy for him because Jimmy liked nothing better than to be in good company when he was having a drink. In my personal view he was not an alcoholic. He certainly drank too much, far too much for most of his life, but drink was never a crutch for him. He just liked to be in company, and having a drink with friends, and he would sing a few songs and revel in the attention he would get, and that was him.'

McNeill is not alone in refuting suggestions that Baxter suffered from alcoholism. Willie Henderson, Ralph Brand, Alex Willoughby and others were swift to point out in interviews that there was no real evidence of any dependence on alcohol. No one attempted to describe his drinking as anything other than excessive. But excess is not enough to produce 'chronic alcoholic dependence syndrome', to use the medical term.

Indeed, one or two binges apart, he was obviously able to limit himself to the 'one or two glasses' of wine with a meal that the specialist had allowed him. Those friends who saw him frequently during his last months commented on how he was able to handle life without the kind of alcoholic intake that had brought his career to an early end and had severely damaged his health. He was a product of the 'drinking culture' of his times as Sir Alex Ferguson has pointed out. Perhaps even a victim of the prevailing attitudes, although you would have to say that he was never less than a willing victim when anyone in his company in his playing days suggested going for a drink!

McNeill adds: 'You have to understand that Jimmy was happy when he was enjoying life and whenever you speak about Jimmy Baxter you get back to that – this immense love of life that he had and that he shared with those of us who were lucky enough to be his friends.'

But all those good times among friends were coming to an end. He was still being lauded for his talents. A huge assembly at Hampden rose to honour him when he was named as one of the players in a best-ever Scotland team that had Denis Law and John Greig from the 1967 game chosen and, sadly, an empty seat for Billy Bremner who had died some years earlier. Although Law edged in front to take the award as Scotland's best player, the reception afforded Baxter told its own story.

The people who were there stood to applaud realising, perhaps, that this might be one of their last opportunities to salute one of the greatest players ever to wear a Scotland jersey. It was, indeed, the last major function he was to attend where the memories of his unique skills would be toasted. There were many there who had never seen him, except for those moments captured by television and transferred to video to allow another generation to sit and watch in wonder at what he was able to do when that ball was sitting there so comfortable and so secure at his unrivalled left foot.

He might not have been the Slim Jim of those filmed images, but there was still a hint of arrogance about him as he stepped forward to take his award and join the other players from both his and other generations for a photograph. Jim Baxter still had a sense of his own worth and of his own place in the folklore of Scottish football. And you could sense the respect flowing from the younger men who stood on the platform with him as Jimmy Johnstone and Kenny Dalglish and Graeme Souness and Andy Goram and others, who had earned the right to be there with him, deferred to the shy Fifer who had twice made Wembley, the home of English football, his very own fiefdom.

There were players there with more caps, players who had

most definitely scored more goals than the three that Baxter had managed for his country, but few who had the aura that surrounded him or the stardust that still lingered even then more than thirty years after he had stopped playing. And still fewer had the ability to inspire the legends which surrounded him down through the years of that all too brief career. He believed himself that his real club career had lasted no longer than eight years – his apprenticeship at Kirkcaldy where Willie McNaught and the other seasoned professionals there had taught him so much and those five glittering, trophy-filled seasons with Rangers. The times in England brought him the money he sought at the time but didn't leave him a solitary memory worth cherishing. That was the eternal tragedy that stalked him down through the years and, doubtless, haunted him as he surveyed the squandering of his skills after he left Ibrox.

15 GRACE UNDER PRESSURE

When the final diagnosis was made at the end of January the news soon spread that one of the greatest footballers the nation had ever known was left with months to live. He returned to hospital for a spell but no miracle cure was available. All the staff could do was try to keep him as comfortable as possible. Those who visited him then all speak of the courage he displayed in the last few months and the almost casual manner in which he faced up to death. Throughout his life, on and off the field, Baxter had style and he held to that until the end. If ever anyone demonstrated that quality defined by Ernest Hemingway as 'grace under pressure', then it was the man who had left the pits behind him forty years earlier and gone on to carve out a worldwide reputation as a footballer of sublime skill. It was not only in Hill o'Beath that his imminent death was being mourned, it was all across Scotland and England, Ireland and Wales and in all the countries of Europe wherever football people gathered to reminisce about the great ones.

That gala night at Hampden was the last major public appearance Jim Baxter made. No one knew at the time but, while the cancer that was to kill him had still to be diagnosed, its deadly work had begun and there are indications that he sensed that something was seriously wrong with him before the doctors confirmed the news that no one wanted to believe.

The honour accorded Baxter and those other Scotland greats took place on 3 December 2000 – but less than two months later the specialists had discovered that he had cancer of the pancreas and told him that he had only a few months left to live.

Earlier, however, he had spoken to close friends in a more intimate way than normal, letting slip the mask he employed to cover any problems that beset him. He had been invited back to Ibrox – the prodigal's return indeed – by John Greig to work in the sponsored lounges along with some of his contemporaries, and before one match he sent a message to Willie Henderson that he wanted to see him for a chat.

Henderson says: 'It was just a few months before his final illness that he sent this message to me. I was working in one of the lounges and he was in another. Anyhow, when I got to Argyle House this day one of the waitresses told me that Jim Baxter had been looking for me. Now that was unusual in itself because that was not Jimmy's way. He never went looking for anyone. People had to go to him!

'He left word where he would be and I went to that area to look for him and he suggested that we go into one of the boxes – the supporters had not started to come into the ground yet and we were on our own – to have a wee cup of tea. We did that and when we sat down I asked him straight out what was wrong. I'd known him long enough to realise that this was out of character and I suspected that he had maybe had bad news about his health again. He told me that he had been to the doctor for one of his regular check-ups and that he had been given three of the belt because his cholesterol count had shot up. The doctors had been monitoring his health carefully since he had the liver transplant and this time they had found his cholesterol was at 9.3, which was far too high, of course, and he had been told to get it back under control.

'I just said to him that he had never done things by half as long as I had known him and here he was acting in the same old way, not doing what he was told he had to do. I went on to say that there was no alternative for him but to listen to what he was being told, and then the answer, when it came, was just pure Baxter! "Look," he told me, "I like a scone and I like butter on it. I like a roll with an egg on it and I like another roll with bacon on it every morning and I like butter on these rolls as well. So that's it," and he meant it. My advice to him was to change his diet, make the alterations to his lifestyle the doctors suggested and he would be OK, but he replied, "If I start listening to them too much then I cannae have anything that I like."

'After that he closed the subject, he didn't want to talk about his health worries any more. Instead for the next half hour or so he went down memory lane, he was off telling stories about all the things we had done in the past and the scrapes we had got into and it was really sentimental stuff, which wasn't the way Jim normally was. I wondered at the time why he had come looking for me and, in the light of what happened later, I believe that while nothing had been discovered, he knew that time was running out for him. I think he knew that he did not have an enormous amount of time left on this earth, that his life was going to end sooner than any of us realised.

'That was about the only time I ever saw him being as emotional and as sentimental as he was that day. The mask dropped away, the confidence he always showed to the public had slipped, and I could see how badly he was suffering. But that was a rare moment and even then he never once looked to blame anyone else for what had happened to him during his lifetime. Jimmy Baxter knew he had only himself to blame and he accepted that right to the very end. Funnily enough, around the same time as he talked to me he also spoke in the same vein to Billy McNeill. Big Billy told me about his own experience later and we both thought it was strange that he should unburden himself to the two of us when he normally kept his real feelings hidden.'

McNeill suspected that his friend knew that illness was about to consume him once more just as Henderson had and for the same reasons. It was out of character for Jim Baxter to parade his troubles in public even when he was speaking to his closest and oldest friends. Neither man had experienced that before. McNeill has never forgotten that night, and he emphasises: 'When I look back at that conversation I am sure that he had an inkling that there was something seriously wrong with him. That was the one time I saw this level of remorse and self-regret and I was taken aback by it.

'We had been at a function at Bothwell and I had picked Jim up and taken him there and was driving him home again. He had had a few glasses of red wine but he was taking care then that he was not drinking too much but, when we got back to Glasgow, he didn't want to get out of the car. He wanted to sit there and talk, and that's what we did. I was with him for two hours and he did most of the talking and he told me things that he wouldn't normally have discussed. Now the fact that he had cancer wasn't known at this time but I am fairly sure that he suspected something because he began to go through all the mistakes he had made in his life. I had never heard Jimmy talk that way before. It was unnerving because it was so unexpected.

'He was saying things to me like, "I've been an eejit the way I've lived my life", and that was scarcely something you could disagree with. He was talking about all the opportunities he had wasted, the chances he had been given and then had messed up in one way or another. Then he was back talking about Jean and how her father had offered to buy them a house when they got married. It was to be a wedding present. Now he was very, very fond of Jean's father and had told me that before. This time he told me just how much he had liked and respected the man but there was always that devil in him wasn't there? And he admitted that and he told me, "I was my usual daft, cheeky self when he made this offer to buy us a house when we were getting married. I don't know why I said these things at times, but I always did, and I asked him if he thought that I couldn't buy his daughter a decent house or wasn't going to be able to look after her, and I turned down the offer. It was stupid but I did it and I wish I hadn't."

'It was almost as if he was totting things up in his mind and keeping score of all the mistakes he had made in his life. And as he was doing this the enormity of all that he had squandered was hitting him. But, typically, he never blamed anyone else. He knew he had made the errors and even that last time with just the two of us sitting in the car it was all self-recrimination. He never once pointed the finger at anybody else for whatever had happened to him over the years. And you know he had great respect for the two women in his life – he accepted that he was at fault for the break-up of his marriage, and after that happened he had a long and strong relationship with Norma, who was very good for him. Also he never lost touch with his sons. They're good laddies and I think if Jim had been as sensible as his boys then things might have been different for him. But he was never ever going to be sensible or careful. That wasn't in his nature and you didn't expect that from him no matter what was going on in his life. It was strange for me when he did get out of the car that night because I had that awful feeling that things were going to go badly for him even though he never said that to me. And then I spoke to wee Willie and he had a similar experience around the same time and it was almost as if we both had a premonition that Jimmy was not going to live for too long.'

When the final diagnosis was made at the end of January the

news soon spread that one of the greatest footballers the nation had ever known was left with months to live. He returned to hospital for a spell but no miracle cure was available. All the staff could do was try to keep him as comfortable as possible. Those who visited him then all speak of the courage he displayed in the last few months and the almost casual manner in which he faced up to death. Throughout his life, on and off the field, Baxter had style and he held to that until the end. If ever anyone demonstrated that quality defined by Ernest Hemingway as 'grace under pressure', then it was the man who had left the pits behind him forty years earlier and gone on to carve out a worldwide reputation as a footballer of sublime skill. It was not only in Hill o'Beath that his imminent death was being mourned, it was all across Scotland and England, Ireland and Wales and in all the countries of Europe wherever football people gathered to reminisce about the great ones. As so many of his contemporaries, team-mates and rivals have insisted, Jim Baxter was always more than able to hold his own in the most exalted company. On several occasions he did just that as he appeared in World or European selects and never looked out of place for a second. These soccer showpieces, after all, carried him on to the game's greatest stages, and that is where he always believed he should be parading his talents.

The lost years in England were ignored, and his displays for Rangers and Scotland celebrated. That was as it should have been, after all. Baxter's contributions to his country's national game had been, at times, unforgettable. As well as doing so much to shape historic victories, he had given many of us, who were fortunate to watch him in his prime, memories that will never fade, and he handed us as his legacy a deeply held belief in how the game of football should be played. With style. With verve. With arrogance. With extravagance. With boundless imagination. And always with a smile on its face.

While thousands of Scots looked back and saluted him as he fought once more against illness, Baxter was behaving with great courage – and demonstrating a fortitude which surprised all who saw him or spoke to him in those final weeks after he had been told that death was inevitable.

His old friend from the earliest days in Glasgow, Pat Crerand, saw him at Hamilton a couple of months before his death and spoke to him on the telephone while he was in hospital. The two men had a strong and lasting bond which went back to the time they had crossed that great Old Firm divide in the city of Glasgow to initiate a comradeship which lasted for four decades, but even Crerand was moved by the strength his old mate showed at the end.

'When I met him up at Hamilton a couple of months before he died,' says Crerand, 'he told me that he was seriously ill again and he also told me what the doctors expected to happen. Then he went back into hospital and I spoke to him on the phone and by this time he had been given the news that he was going to die. Even knowing that he was still able to joke with me, saying, "But there's some good news too, the wee nurse here came up to speak to me after the doctor had gone away and told me it would be OK for me to have a drink now," and I just didn't know what to say. You just felt that this should not be happening to him. If the truth were told he was taking the news far better than I was! It really got to me and I didn't want him to realise that at the other end because he was showing such tremendous courage. Sometimes when I think about it all and my mind drifts back to the early days when we were running about the town together, I do believe the big city helped destroy him and, you know, if he had gone to London, say, instead of Sunderland, after leaving Rangers, it might have been even worse for him.'

Willie Henderson, too, his old comrade in arms with Rangers and Scotland, went to see him in hospital and discovered the same strength that had impressed Crerand. When he arrived to visit him he did so believing that there was a possibility of recovery from this latest bout of ill health. Henderson explains: 'When I heard that he was ill again I went to the hospital in Edinburgh to see him and it was there in the ward that he told me that he was very seriously ill. But the way he led up to telling me was strange and I wasn't prepared for it at all. It was as if he didn't want to make any fuss about the illness even though, by this time he knew how bad his health was and that he was, in all probability, dying. While we were sitting talking he suddenly said, "I had to go for some tests with the doctor a few days ago and the liver was fine. There were no problems with that at all. But here, during the same examination, they found a wee bit of cancer the size of a twenty pence piece on my pancreas."

'Well, that hit me hard because I had not been expecting things to be as bad as that. That must have shown because he then added, "I'm not going to get myself too worried about this because there's nothing that the doctors can do about it." Then he changed the subject entirely and began to ask where Ralphie Brand was. He told me that he had sent Ralphie out for a pudding supper with extra chips and he was taking too long, as far as Jimmy was concerned, to get back. He switched from talking about his own death to this pudding supper without a pause. I didn't know what to do then. I just said to him, "I see you're still taking care of yourself then, looking after your diet." And his justification was that these were the best pudding suppers you could get and that was that.

'Anyhow, ten minutes later Ralphie came in and, sure enough, he had this parcel that looked about the size of a suitcase and he handed that to Jimmy. He opened up the brown paper and there was a mountain of chips with this black pudding and, you know something, he never gave us a single one of his chips. He polished off the lot himself. After that first time I went to visit him regularly and I would come out after sitting with him and would wonder whether it was cancer or the toothache he had. That's how he treated the whole thing; as if it was something minor that was wrong with him. He just refused to allow the thought of death to intrude too much into the last weeks of a life he had enjoyed to the full. Somehow he was able to retain the same cavalier attitude facing death as he had held to right through his life. He was very, very brave in the way he handled things and faced up to his death in the last few months. Not many people would have behaved with that kind of courage, but Jimmy Baxter was always a special person and he always seemed able to do everything with a bit of style, he still had that style right to the end.'

Ralph Brand, who had been a team-mate at Ibrox and at Roker Park, too, now drives a taxi in Edinburgh, and so he would go in at all kinds of hours to sit with Baxter, who was often finding it difficult to sleep as his health deteriorated.

'Wee Willie's right,' he points out. 'Stanley used to send me out to this chip shop not too far from Edinburgh Royal Infirmary because he thought they made the best pudding suppers in Scotland. But I cleared all of that with the nurses, who knew that there was nothing that could be done for him and allowed him to have some of the food he most enjoyed. It was too late to make any difference to him as regards his health.

'Because I have the taxi I often work all kinds of odd hours and, as he wasn't sleeping too well, if things were quiet I would go up to see him and sit and talk with him whenever I could. The nurses would let me in and we'd sit there blethering away about things until he would be tired enough to get some rest. He said to me once, "I'm not being brave about all of this, you know. I don't want to die but there is nothing that I can do about this illness I have and there is nothing that the doctors can do either. It's all over for me and I have to come to terms with that and accept it."

'And that's what he did. He always did go his own way and he was always able to surprise you, but never more so than when he was desperately ill. He might have tried to tell me that he wasn't being particularly brave but I saw how much strength he showed in those last weeks. It still hurts when I think about those nights I spent with him because he deserved so much more out of his life. His attitude to things at the end was magnificent. I will never forget the way he was and the way he behaved when it must have been very, very difficult for him. Everyone wanted to do something for him, and all those nurses loved him and had a lot of respect for him too.

'There are times even now that I still pop in and speak to some of them and remember Stanley and how fearless he seemed to be even when he knew that he was facing death. It was a lesson to us all, the way that he came to terms with everything, and the calm way he accepted the news when it was broken to him that the doctors had diagnosed cancer in his pancreas. He had come through the liver transplant and that had given him seven years of life and then this came up to snatch that away from him again. Yet he took it all on board and he scarcely ever allowed people to see how seriously it must have affected him. He had always been a class act and here he was still being a class act right to the very end. It was amazing.'

Dave Mackay was another who went to visit him, travelling up from his home near Derby after Willie Henderson had alerted him to the extent of that last illness. Like all the others who saw Baxter then, Mackay was impressed by the dignity with which he had accepted his fate. He admits his surprise, saying: 'After wee Willie had called me I made arrangements to travel up and meet him and then go with him to visit Jim. The three of us spent three or four hours chatting and talking about our playing days. It was hard to believe that this man was dying because he was laughing the whole time and was just taking it all so well. It was astonishing how he seemed to accept what was going to happen to him and, for me, he showed a lot of courage at that time. I think that everyone who saw him then will tell you the same thing. It was all very sad the way it ended but, when Jim looked back on his life, he still saw it as having been lived the way he wanted to live it. You couldn't argue with that!'

His old Rangers captain Bobby Shearer echoes Mackay's story, telling how, when he went to see him, Baxter spent the time telling jokes and recounting stories from the past as if there was nothing wrong with him.

Others could not face the thought of seeing him so ill. Neither Davy Wilson nor Willie Johnston visited, with Wilson calling him to explain: 'I want to remember you the way you were.' He adds now: 'He had been carrying a lot of weight near the end, kind of bloated, and we were both working at Ibrox. There was all that talk about him drinking again but I never saw that. A glass of red wine now and again and that was the extent of his drinking as far as I could see. He faced up to that last illness very well and I spoke to him and I know he appreciated the call and understood the sentiments. He told me that, and I still have my memories of him, and they are treasured memories. There will never be anyone else like him. He was a unique character, someone you meet only once in a lifetime.'

Johnston, who followed Wilson into the Rangers first team, shared his predecessor's feelings about the man who had taken him under his wing when he had arrived at Ibrox as a teenager – and a fellow Fifer! Johnston recalls: 'When it was obvious that he was ill again I saw him a few times at Ibrox when I was through for games. He didn't look good but he still had his sense of humour and, if there had not been these signs of physical deterioration by then, you wouldn't have known, from his attitude, that there was anything wrong with him. A few of the lads have told me that he was exactly the same when he was in hospital near the end. I didn't go there, and maybe that was because I just wanted to remember him as he had been when I first met him and he kind of took care of me. He was a one-off, and I'm sure everyone who knew him would say the same.'

The 'physical deterioration' mentioned by Johnston and Wilson also struck Alfie Conn, and once when he came into the Great Western Road pub, where Conn worked, for lunch, the one-time Rangers, Spurs and Celtic player had to move quickly into the back room to regain some composure after the shock of seeing Baxter in such decline.

Conn admits: 'I was shocked when he walked in. People had told me that he was ill and that he was not looking too good, but nothing prepared me for how he was when he came in for his lunch one day. When I saw him come through the door I couldn't believe it. I found myself in tears just looking at him and I went into the back shop to recover a bit before he could see how upset I was. There was no way I wanted to hurt him, after all. He was a terrible colour, his skin had gone yellowy brown, and he could hardly walk. His movements were laboured, he was like an old man, and it took him several minutes just to walk across from the door to the bar – it was awful to see him in that condition. Honestly, I felt so sad for him and so sad, too, that there was nothing that any of us could do for him. It had been some time since I had seen him and his health had deteriorated badly. I was shocked to say the least. He was so frail and weak that getting up off the seat was a struggle. It seemed to be an effort for him just to move. We all knew in the pub that day that the end had to be near.'

As the months and the weeks and eventually the days began to pass, Baxter began to make arrangements for his own funeral. The man who had carried a laissez-faire attitude throughout his life, who had lived only for the day, was now making plans for his death.

His aide-de-camp as the funeral details were being organised was the ever-loyal Alex Willoughby, who still points out: 'Jim Baxter would stroll into Ibrox without a care in the world even when he had the worst of all hangovers, and that was how he went through life. Carefree on the surface especially to the outside world – even if he did have problems that he was keeping to himself. When it came to the end he was exactly the same. I can remember him three months or so before he died. He had just been told what was going to happen to him and he told me about it and he looked neither up nor down. He just took it all on board and didn't allow people to see him look upset at the thought of death. When Rangers came in and offered to help make the funeral arrangements he asked me if it was possible to get a piper there. "I'd like to have a piper," he said. "Do you think that could be arranged?"

'I told him that it shouldn't be a problem and I did get on the phone to the right people and I did get a piper organised to play at the funeral, and then he said, "I don't want any old piper. This has to be the best piper, I want to have the top man there." And I just asked him what difference that was going to make as far as he was concerned because he wouldn't be hearing him. And his answer to that was, "Aye, OK, but I want everybody who's going to be there to hear a good piper so just you make sure of that."

'That was him, almost at the end, and yet keeping himself busy by organising his own funeral and not showing the slightest trace of fear even though he knew that he had only a very short time to live. It was extraordinary to see him then and you know what, he didn't ever offer up any regrets about his lifestyle. He had done things his way and that was the only way, in his book, that he could have taken. Even knowing he was going to die very soon didn't change Stanley too much! His courage was unbelievable.'

Even as his life ebbed away he refused to let down his friends. He had only a few weeks left to live when he was invited to a function at Gleddoch House Hotel near Glasgow. It was a dinner he attended each year and Alex Willoughby would always accompany him there. This time, of course, Willoughby knew it would be the last time they would go there. And so, quite naturally, he wondered if Baxter would be fit enough to attend but confesses now: 'I should have known better than to doubt that he would want to go as usual,' he says. 'We had been going along together for quite a few years by this time and the organiser was a friend who told me that he would quite understand if Jimmy didn't want to go. He knew the circumstances and I don't think he expected him to be able to turn up. But Stanley insisted that he was going, mainly because he knew as well as we did that this would be his final appearance. That's just the way he was – he didn't want to let anyone down even when he was very seriously ill. He was very weak by this time and we arranged that he would stay overnight. When he became overtired towards the end of the dinner, I drove him round to the hotel area which was a wee bit away from the function suite. He really struggled to get out of the car, everything was an effort for him by this stage, and then I gave him a helping hand to get into the reception area.

'Now, there were two couples sitting there having a drink, this was maybe around the back of midnight, and people are not expecting to see this man Baxter, who has just been told he has only months to live, walking about a hotel at that time of night. I can recall he had on a mustard jacket that night – which was just about the same colour as he was by the way – and you could see the four people turning round to take a better look at him. He saw that, of course, he never did miss too much, and that imp he had in him that was never too far away took over and he started to act as if he was drunk. Now they had seen me helping him out of the car and into the hotel so they were maybe looking for some scandal, so Jim started to stagger a bit and he was saying things to me like, "That was some night we had, wee man. That was great," and they were looking at this, and then we went in behind a pillar on the way to his room, and we heard one of them saying how disgraceful this was. "Just look at the state he's in and he's not meant to be drinking at all any more." Well, of course, he hadn't had a drop to drink. It was just Stanley winding them up and they fell for it.

'When I came back downstairs the four of them were still sitting there and I said to them, "You all thought he had been drinking, didn't you?" and they denied that, but I knew what they had been thinking. I had heard them when they thought we were out of earshot. I told them he had had nothing to drink at all that night but whether they believed me or not I don't know. As for Baxter, he didn't care, even at death's door he still had that capacity to laugh at life. He was incorrigible and he remained that way right to the end. It was as if he was saying to the world that nothing was going to change him. And nothing did. He would not allow that. It was always as if he was determined to go out still enjoying life as much as he could, even though that became more and more difficult as time ran out on him. Even the fact that he went to that function at Gleddoch was his way of telling everyone that he might be down but he was still not defeated.'

Defeat did come, of course, and it arrived on 15 April, less than eleven weeks after the doctors had told him that nothing more could be done for him. He was at his home when he died and the news soon swept around the city. The reaction was one of universal sadness from all football supporters and even from those who did not follow the game. Baxter's feats with Rangers and Scotland had been brought to the fore once again after the news of his fatal illness had been made public. Fresh generations realised the magic he had created in his short spell at the peak of his profession. Those who had not followed football as avidly as others recognised the human tragedy that had been played out over his lifetime in the years that brought him glory, and in the years that he had wasted, and in the sad final years when his excesses caught up with him and Jim Baxter, that weaver of dreams, that icon of Scottish soccer, that legendary Wembley hero, had been brought low and had proved to be as human as the rest of us.

Except, that is not quite how all of those who had been privileged to see him on a regular basis looked at things. For many of them James Curran Baxter was someone very special, someone who had emerged from the dark and grim Fife coalfields, who would never really die as long as memories last and as long as those old and grainy black and white videos of his Wembley games survive. Someone who held aloft the standard for the style of football that was fashioned in his country and that he believed in more than anything else in the world.

INDEX